To Geri

With thanks for your leadership
& encouragement of my research

Don MacLeod

24 May 2007

This book is made possible in part
by generous grants from the
Tyndale House Foundation
and the John Bolten Charitable Foundation.

C. Stacey Woods

and the Evangelical Rediscovery
of the University

A. Donald MacLeod

IVP Academic

An imprint of InterVarsity Press
Downers Grove, Illinois

InterVarsity Press
P.O. Box 1400, Downers Grove, IL 60515-1426
World Wide Web: www.ivpress.com
E-mail: email@ivpress.com

InterVarsity Press® *is the book-publishing division of InterVarsity Christian Fellowship/USA*®*, a student movement active on campus at hundreds of universities, colleges and schools of nursing in the United States of America, and a member movement of the International Fellowship of Evangelical Students. For information about local and regional activities, write Public Relations Dept., InterVarsity Christian Fellowship/USA, 6400 Schroeder Rd., P.O. Box 7895, Madison, WI 53707-7895, or visit the IVCF website at <www.intervarsity.org>.*

Design: Cindy Kiple

Images: University of Washington: Altrendo Travel/Getty Images
      C. Stacey Woods: InterVarsity Press

ISBN 978-0-8308-3432-7

Printed in the United States of America ∞

Library of Congress Cataloging-in-Publication Data

MacLeod, A. Donald (Alister Donald)
  C. Stacey Woods and the evangelical rediscovery of the university/
  A. Donald MacLeod.
    p. cm.
  Includes bibliographical references and indexes.
  ISBN 978-0-8308-3432-7 (pbk.: alk. paper)
  1. Woods, C. Stacey, 1909- 2. Evangelists—Biography. 3. Church
work with students. 4. College students—Religious life. 5.
Evangelistic work. 6. Inter-Varsity Christian Fellowship—History.
I. Title.
BV3785.W66M33 2007
267'.61092—dc22
  [B]

                              2007011186

P	17	16	15	14	13	12	11	10	9	8	7	6	5	4	3	2	1
Y	21	20	192	18	17	16	15	14	13	12	11	10	09	08	07			

For Judy

carissima mea

Love's not time's fool

Contents

Abbreviations

AFES	Australian Fellowship of Evangelical Students
BGC	Billy Graham Center and Archives, Wheaton College
CB	Christian (i.e., Plymouth) Brethren
CC	Cedar Campus
CCC	Campus Crusade for Christ
CHT	Charles H. Troutman
CICCU	Cambridge Intercollegiate Christian Union (IVF at Cambridge University)
CIM	China Inland Mission, a.k.a. Overseas Missionary Fellowship
CIW	Campus-in-the-Woods
CTS	Calvin Theological Seminary
CRC	Christian Reformed Church
CSSM	Children's Special Service Mission
CSW	C. Stacey Woods
CWH	Chua Wee Hian
DJ	Douglas Johnson
DTS	Dallas Theological Seminary
FMF	Foreign Missions Fellowship
GBU	Groupes Bibliques Universitaires (Francophone IVCF)
GCTS	Gordon-Conwell Theological Seminary (formerly Gordon Divinity School)
GF	Graduates Fellowship
HJO	Harold John Ockenga
HJT	Herbert J. Taylor

HK(FES)	Hong Kong Fellowship of Evangelical Students
HWS	H. Wilber Sutherland
IFES	International Fellowship of Evangelical Students
ICCC	International Council of Christian Churches (Carl McIntire)
ISCF	Inter-School Christian Fellowship
IVCF (C)	Inter-Varsity Christian Fellowship (Canada)
IVCF-USA	InterVarsity Christian Fellowship (United States)
IVF	Inter-Varsity Fellowship (U.K.)
IVP (UK)	Inter-Varsity Press U.K.
IVP (US)	InterVarsity Press U.S.
JB	Joe Bayly
JBSr.	John Bolten Senior
JBJr.	John Bolten Junior
JRWS	John R. W. Stott
KGK	Japanese Inter-Varsity
LCWE	Lausanne Congress on World Evangelization
LES	League of Evangelical Students
ML-J	Martyn Lloyd-Jones ("the Doctor")
NAE	National Association of Evangelicals
OICCU	Oxford Intercollegiate Christian Union (IVF at Oxford University)
ORB	Oliver R. Barclay (A. N. Triton)
OMF	Overseas Missionary Fellowship
PCC	Presbyterian Church in Canada
PTS	Princeton Theological Seminary
SCM	Student Christian Movement
SFMF	Student Foreign Mission Fellowship
SM	Schloss Mittersill
SMD	German Inter-Varsity
SU	Scripture Union
SVM	Student Volunteer Movement
TCF	Teachers' Christian Fellowship
UESI	Union of Evangelical Students of India
WCC	World Council of Churches

WEF	World Evangelical Fellowship
WSCF	World Student Christian Fellowship
WTS	Westminster Theological Seminary
YKW	Yvonne Woods

Preface

AS I ARRIVED AT MANCHESTER AIRPORT TWO WEEKS AGO I caught the front page headline in *The Times* of London: "Students sue over Christian rights at colleges." The article described how university Christian unions are being discriminated against "by student associations because they refused to allow non-Christians to address their meetings or sit on ruling committees." Christian unions, according to the Universities and Colleges Christian Fellowship (UCCF), "faced a struggle 'unprecedented' in their 83-year history." Learning something of that eighty-three-year history never seemed more urgent. InterVarsity started as a group committed to evangelize the university.[1] In a postmodern, politically correct era the biography of someone who was first and foremost InterVarsity's "evangelist to the campus" provides useful background information to a contemporary struggle.

Learning about C. Stacey Woods has been a preoccupation of mine since Laurel Gasque suggested to me that his biography needed to be written, and that there was no better occasion than to have it in time for the sixtieth anniversary of the International Fellowship of Evangelical Students (IFES) when the IFES World Assembly meets in Ancaster, Ontario, July 11-20 of 2007. In this yearlong journey of discovery I have been aided by Yvonne Woods, whose indefatigable spirit, unfailing prayer support and gracious willingness to share her life with Stacey Woods with me, have been a daily source of strength. I am also grateful to Stacey's three children, Stephen, Geoffrey and Jonathan, who have been true sons to their remarkable mother.

In Australia I found many individuals anxious to provide background for Stacey Woods's heritage. I single out my friend Stuart Braga of Sydney, who has been a veritable research assistant. How it never occurred to us fifty-six years ago—as we sat in adjacent desks in Form 2A of King George V School, Hong Kong—that we would be lifelong associates and our lives would run on parallel tracks. Stuart opened many doors for me: to Rev. Dr. Bruce Kaye, Rev. Dr. John McIntosh, Sir Marcus Loane, Archbishop Donald Robinson, Professor Stuart Piggin of Macquarie University, and Professor Hutchinson of South Cross College. In Ocean Grove I spent time with Stacey's cousin and look-alike, Charles Stilwell. In Bendigo, I met with the folks at the Bendigo Regional Genealogical Society, where they spent an afternoon digging up more material about the Stilwells than I could possibly use. I also met with the Right Reverend Andrew Curnow, bishop of Bendigo, and with Rev. Dr. Ken Cole and Ian Smith of St. Andrew's Cathedral. In Geelong Tanya Assender was most helpful. In Auckland I appreciated time given me by Professor Peter Lineham, head of the School of Social and Cultural Studies, Massey University. Since returning from "down under" I have had help from Dr. Kenneth John Newton, Brisbane; John Prince of Perth; and Garry Warren, St. George Christian Church, Hurstville.

Archives have been my most useful source. The largest cache of material about Stacey is in the Billy Graham Center, and after four visits there I record my gratitude to David Malone and his staff. Professor Tim Larsen of Wheaton was able to track down copies of the *Christian Beacon*. In the Canadian Inter-Varsity Christian Fellowship (IVCF) office there is a rich lode of priceless (and uncensored) archival material that, alas, is in precarious condition. I thank Geri Rodman, CEO, for permission to use it. The Bouma archives at Calvin Seminary were useful, and I thank Richard Harms. At Dallas Theological Seminary, Lolana Thompson has been exemplary in her diligence. At Gordon-Conwell Theological Seminary my former parishioner Garth Rosell opened the Ockenga papers for my inspection. At Westminster Theological Seminary, Grace Mullin was, as always, helpful in piloting me through the Machen and Stonehouse archives. John H. Lutman of the University of Western Ontario archives provided access to the Rowland Hill diaries, again a useful tool. Surprisingly it was at Bible Society of Australia that I first encountered Charles Troutman's diaries through Stuart Piggin, and they gave me free access to a photocopier. And at the John Rylands University Library, of the University of Manchester, the Christian Brethren archives provided insights into Fred Woods's career. The National Library of Ireland in Dublin helped illustrate J. N. Darby. Rose Carleton of the CIM/OMF (China Inland Mission/Overseas Missionary Fellowship) archives in Mississauga, Ontario, was most thorough in her research. Hugh Rendle of the Horsey Library, Tyndale University College and Seminary, where I am research professor, has delved into our archives for me. His staff have been most cooperative and patient.

My administrative assistant at Tyndale, Dahlia Fraser, has kept the ship on course when I was preoccupied. I thank my colleagues at the seminary for their patience, and I'm grateful for the support of our dean, Dr. Janet Clark, as well as President Brian Stiller. A generous research grant from the John Bolten Sr. Foundation has funded this project and was disbursed by the Tyndale Foundation. I acknowledge with thanks the support of John Bolten Jr., Osorno, Chile.

In Canada there still are many who knew and loved Stacey Woods. In Vancouver I interviewed Ruth Oliver Cummings and her brother Fred Rich, as well as Fred Lang and Rev. Dr. Ian Rennie. In Ontario, the A. J. Stewart siblings—Muriel Beatty, Pat McCarthy and particularly their brother David Stewart—assisted with memories and photos. My near neighbor Robert O. Stephens had many anecdotes. I visited former IVCF-USA staff along the Eastern seaboard, including Barbara Boyd, Peter Haile, Anne Childs Hummel and Ruth McKinney. Keith and Gladys ("Rusty") Hunt put me up at their beautiful cottage close to Cedar Campus. I spent time with Jim and Ruth Nyquist in Downers Grove, Illinois. Bob Fryling and Andy Le Peau of InterVarsity Press (IVP) reminisced, and Andy shared the first chapter of his IVP story. I also contacted Ned Hale, Pete Hammond and Peter Northrup. Helen Hammond Baldwin, Hollis, New Hampshire, was a fund of information about her mother and her grandmother, Mrs. F. Cliffe Johnston. Tim Bayly represented his family and that of the Taylors, his in-laws. Bob Baylis and Neil Rendall also sent me material from their years on staff. Gina Lamb of Toronto provided information about her father, E. G. Baker.

In England I had the full cooperation of the IFES office and the outgoing general secretary Lindsay Brown. Kirsty Thornburn in the office I single out for her cheerful helpfulness. Oliver Barclay, Elizabeth Catherwood, Michael Griffiths, Iain Murray and John Stott all responded to my queries. Reverend Peter Guinness of Lancaster took me through photo albums of his father Paul. Felicity Houghton Bentley-Taylor helped as did Myfanwy Bentley-Taylor of Toronto. On the continent I had a pleasant weekend in Lausanne with Frank and Anne Horton, as well as at the church Stacey pastored. Jennifer Johnston Favré was delightful in reminiscing about the IFES office. Intimate family correspondence from her predecessor, Phil Van Seters, was generously shared with me by her brother Arthur of Toronto. At Mittersill all the files were open to me thanks to Carl Armerding's preparation, and I am grateful to Isabell Wagner in the office and Hans Brennsteiner in the kitchen. Alex Williams was also available for questioning.

I am greatly indebted to Samuel Escobar, my immediate predecessor as General Director of IVCF-Canada, on IFES staff for twenty-seven years. I spent a day with him at his son's home in suburban Washington, D.C., and he has shared letters and invaluable memories.

I thank InterVarsity Press and my copyeditor, Drew Blankman, for many courtesies. My own editor, Colin Duriez, formerly of IVP-UK, moved recently from Leicester and, fortuitously, is now in Keswick. I am thankful to him for many insights and for his helpfulness in preparing the manuscript.

In a work covering so much detail there will inevitably be slips and omissions. If there are errors, I would be grateful if these were drawn to my attention. Due to size concerns, I was unable to use all the material I was given, nor could I include even a fraction of the memories shared. There is a whole canon of Stacey lore. As an academic historian by profession and instinct, I set out to chronicle not only the man but his huge legacy. I did so in the hopes that his accomplishments and vision will be retained for generations yet unborn. Stacey was very human, very fallible and very broken, but he was also a man whom God used mightily. I loved him personally and without qualification. But I write with objectivity since he asked that his biographer paint his portrait "warts and all."

Finally, thanks to my family. My son Alex has followed in his father's footsteps as Presbyterian minister and campus worker. My other son, Kenneth, provided technical help, which was essential. I hope that the dedication of this book to my wife will indicate some of the debt I owe her. It is almost forty years since, on the eve of Ascension Day 1967, I crossed the threshold of 39 Bedford Square, the IVF (Inter-Varsity Fellowship) headquarters in London, and was ushered into a whole new world of marvels and adventure. She has been, as Yvonne was to Stacey, my tower of strength over these years, particularly during the five when I was IVCF general director in Canada.

God, whom Stacey Woods loved and served, still reigns. *Sola gloria deo.*

A. Donald MacLeod
The Ghyll, Applethwaite
Keswick, Cumbria, England
St. Andrew's Day, 2006

Conference for the Advancement of Evangelical Scholarship, Plymouth Rock, 18 August 1944: (L to R) Carl Henry, Harold Ockenga, Leonard Lewis, P. B. Fitzwater, Wm. Emmett Powers, Clarence Bouma, John Bolten, Stacey Woods, Terelle Crum, Allen McRae, Cornelius Van Til, Henry Thiessen, Everett Harrison and Merrill Tenney (Courtesy of Gordon-Conwell Theological Seminary archives)

Introduction

MUSLIMS HAVE THEIR DOME OF THE ROCK, Scots the Stone of Scone and Americans claim Plymouth Rock. Plymouth Rock is uniquely American. The rock under the dome in Jerusalem may or may not be the one on which Abraham was to sacrifice Isaac, the Stone of Scone is unlikely to be Jacob's pillow, but Plymouth Rock is supposedly grounded in history. When the Pilgrim Fathers set anchor in Plymouth harbor, so legend has it, they stepped onto shore on a small stone that is now an American icon. "The Rock has become an object of veneration in the United States," early tourist Alexis de Tocqueville reported to Europeans on his return home. Plymouth Rock, with the date 1620 carved into it, is a symbol of everything America represents. The Pilgrim Fathers arrived in the New World committed to a society based on liberty and equality.

And faith. These Puritans were deeply religious. On their ship, the *Mayflower*, before they made landfall, they had compacted "to plant the first colony in the northern parts of Virginia" "for the Glory of God, and Advancement of the Christian Faith, and the Honour of our King and Country." Plymouth Rock epitomized America's deep religious roots: several of the original thirteen colonies were established by rigid Calvinists, pious Quakers, runaway Baptists, evangelicals all.

As the Second World War was in its final year, thirteen men gathered at Plymouth Rock to reclaim the heritage which it represented.[1] On 18 August 1944 they signed their own compact, *An Evangelical Manifesto*. Two world wars in the past thirty years had signaled "the failure of modern philosophy, both idealistic and naturalistic, to save western culture from disintegration and collapse." There was a "general ethical irresponsibility" growing inevitably out of "a man-centered philosophy of life and growing moral decadence." The group described itself as the Plymouth Conference for the Advancement of Evangelical Scholarship. For the next generation the signatories would signal a renascence of American evangelicalism.

They covered the gamut of contemporary evangelical academic leadership. Three of them were from the Bible school tradition, two came from Wheaton College, billed the Harvard of fundamentalism. Another represented a conservative ethnic tradition that had preserved the faith through linguistic and cultural isolation. Five came from breakaway institutions founded to protest the rise of liberalism in the historic theological seminaries. Their leader was minister of a historic church founded in 1809 to rise above the flood of Unitarianism that swept away the Puritan and Pilgrim heritage of New England. Harold John Ockenga would champion a new evangelicalism, a new seminary, just as he founded a new National Association of Evangelicals two years previously. His name was at the forefront of evangelical hopes for a new and brighter future after their cataclysmic isolation, decline and division in the 1930s.

And the remaining two, neither of them American, might have felt like intruders to a sacred mystery as they stood by Plymouth Rock as the other eleven made their vows. Both were immigrants, both raised Christian Brethren, both came to the United States to pursue a dream. John Bolten arrived from pre-Nazi Germany because he had confronted Hitler, a guest in his home, after making an indecent gesture to his wife. With an uncanny knack for anticipating the future, he found safety in exile and reestablished his fortune in a deserted mill town in Massachusetts' Merrimac valley. He was the host for the event, picked up the tab at the Mayflower hotel, and made himself indispensable.

He would be a self-styled godfather of evangelicalism in the postwar period, his anonymous charities funding a variety of significant advances, including that of Billy Graham. At the time he had forged a close bond with his pastor, Harold John Ockenga, and enabled Ockenga's enterprises. But it was with Stacey Woods that he bonded, and the story of Stacey Woods for the next thirty-five years is inextricably interconnected with John Bolten Sr.

The other outsider was a short bantamlike Australian. C. Stacey Woods was definitely the odd man out: he had neither money nor academic distinction. He did not share the fundamentalist legacy that energized the other men. His was a wider vision. His burning passion was to reclaim the Moody heritage of student evangelism and missionary recruitment that had been abandoned as the Student Volunteer

Movement, birthed at Northfield at the western end of Massachusetts in 1886, lost its vision and sank into a liberal morass. Stacey was the only one invited to speak on a nonacademic subject, evangelism. After only five years in America his organization was gaining a reputation for effective outreach. His was a fresh voice—enthusiastic, visionary, nontraditional.

Evangelism and the university simply did not connect in the thinking of most evangelicals in 1944. Historically they had watched each of their institutions slip out of their control. From Harvard to Yale and now Princeton, these schools who had taken their patrimony were no longer friends but enemies of orthodox Christianity, bastions of liberalism where no evangelical would venture without certain apostasy and abandonment of everything he or she had learned in the fortresslike churches they had been raised in. Christian young people went to Christian postsecondary schools: Bible institutes, missionary training schools or a college such as Wheaton or Taylor that would protect the faith of impressionable young people.

Such isolationism usually meant that evangelicalism was ill-equipped to engage the culture. There was an atmosphere of defeatism as intellectual pursuits were regarded as unspiritual. Few evangelical educators had graduate degrees from reputable institutions, let alone earned doctorates. The signatories to the Plymouth manifesto were a new breed. Three of them had Harvard Ph.D.s, Harold Ockenga received his from the University of Pittsburgh five years earlier, and others had (or were working on) similarly impeccable credentials. There was an atmosphere of renewed confidence, of optimism even.

Still there were those heathen universities. What was to be done about them? At the undergraduate level, it was thought, very little. Impressionable young people could easily be swayed by "the assured results of modern science." They might be mocked by professors who brought up the 1926 Scopes "Monkey" Trial. A whole procession of children of evangelicals had gone out into what, to their parents, was a spiritual wilderness as a result of challenges to their faith while at secular schools. The pressure was too much, the resources they could muster to counterattack too few, and the protective fears on the part of the Christian community too great.

And then there was this young Australian saying that not only could evangelical young people survive in a hostile university environment, they could evangelize their peers, challenge them to faith, go from defense to counterattack. It seemed that postwar America might be hospitable to just such a Christian engagement with the university. Reports were coming back from the military overseas about the need for religious belief, given the barbarity and evil of the war. From the Pacific, where islanders converted through missionaries rescued stranded Allied invaders, to heroic Christian resistance to Nazi tyranny in occupied Europe, faith gained new credibility. These were the men who would overcrowd the universities under the U.S. GI Bill and Canadian government educational subsidies. A new seriousness marked the postwar undergraduate, often older and seasoned by war. No longer were there goldfish swallowing contests, finding how many could squeeze into a telephone booth or so many wild drinking binges. The reality of the Holocaust, the rise of Soviet Communist imperialism and the mushroom cloud of an atomic bomb contributed to an earnest new generation of university students.

The meteoric rise of Stacey's organization, the InterVarsity Christian Fellowship, in the immediate postwar period can only be explained by this sea of change in the collegiate culture. In 1946 the organization hosted its first missionary conference. The Urbana Student Missions Convention (or simply Urbana), as it was later known, made InterVarsity a major player in the evangelical world as the missionary movement shifted from the historic denominations to faith missions. Missionary recruitment, shrunk by the depression and religious liberalism, regained momentum as a result of InterVarsity's emphasis on crosscultural evangelism. Seminaries, particularly but not exclusively the ones whose beliefs meshed with the movement, increased their enrollment thanks to IVCF alumni/ae. InterVarsity Press, founded in the United States by Stacey, gave evangelical scholarship new credibility.

Although he had both a quick mind and verbal fluency, Stacey Woods never regarded himself as an intellectual. He was too much a man of action and a pioneer to be engaged in head trips. He left a detailed philosophy of the university to his longtime colleague and successor Charles Troutman. He did, however, spot trends and was always thinking ahead. His shrewd insight into human nature meant that he could connect quickly with people across intellectual, cultural and linguistic divides. He had a prodigious memory for names, places and events, though his ability as a raconteur could obscure the accuracy of his verbal recall. His energy was unbelievable; his impatience with inefficiency and hypocrisy legendary. Only a man with his extraordinary gifts could have accomplished what he did.

Stacey Woods was a man of paradoxes and contrasts. He still remains to many of those who knew him best an enigma. His concern for the glory of God meant that he could never be a self-promoter. Essentially humble, even shy (though few would have said that of him) and very private, he was voluble, occasionally talked too much, and could deeply antagonize individuals, even those once closest to him. He refused to accept numerous honorary doctoral degrees, not out of false modesty but rather the concern that such recognition obscured the sacrificial contribution of others to the movement to which he had given his life.

C. Stacey Woods has been dead for almost a quarter century. His contribution to evangelicalism, particularly in mid-twentieth century America but also to worldwide Christianity, has never been recognized or acknowledged except in his immediate circles. To follow his life in this book the reader will suddenly see the interconnectedness of so much of evangelical life in that era, the incredible networking that went on as well as the far-ranging interests of a man who started with a vision and went on to change the face of contemporary evangelicalism. It is time that his story is told. He helped American fundamentalism to come out of its self-imposed exile and engage the university, be responsible in addressing the culture, and raise evangelicals to new levels of intellectual and academic accountability. And his warm, spiritual passion inspired a movement and a generation.

I

Bendigo Brethren Boyhood

LIKE NO OTHER EVENT, FUNERALS AND WEDDINGS are rites of passage that reveal otherwise hidden intergenerational dynamics. For Charles Wilfred Stacey Woods that revelation came at the funeral of his mother's father, Charles Robert Stilwell. By Stacey's own account, "Grandfather stood almost in the place of God in my young life." On 24 September 1928, Charles Robert Stilwell died, active right to the end of his eighty-nine years. The next day the mining community of Bendigo, northern Victoria, Australia, marked his passing with what almost amounted to a state funeral.

Charles Robert Stilwell was the last of a generation of pioneers who opened up Australia at the time of the Gold Rush. He had arrived in Melbourne on his thirteenth birthday, 20 December 1851. His mother, a Stacey, is a shadowy figure, unlike the father. Charles Stilwell, physician and surgeon, was ship's doctor for a boatload of dispossessed Gaelic-speakers from Skye, immigrating to Australia, a voyage that took three months. He hailed from Elwell, Surrey, south of London, where he had received his medical training.

On arrival the father headed immediately north to Eaglehead Flat near what is now Bendigo (then Sandhurst) with his children, eager not to miss out on anything. Eighteen-year-old daughter Catharine Margaret kept house. For the rest of the

1850s Charles's medical skills were in constant demand throughout the goldfields. Stories abound about the heroics of doctors in that wild and dangerous time. At one point, since he had performed an autopsy on a victim, he was a witness in a murder trial. Charles died in his eighties after an exciting life. Longevity seemed to be hereditary. Charles Robert, as heir, pursued a quieter career in business. He became the city patriarch, full of years, outliving his contemporaries and able to remember an earlier time. Now one of the city's last links with its past was gone.

"The large and representative assemblage which attended the funeral of the late Mr. C. R. Stilwell was testimony to the honourable place he had filled as a citizen," the *Bendigo Advertiser* reported in breathless prose that filled an entire column.

> The deceased was valued by all as a gentlemanly associate in business and a man of sound religious principles who did a lot for the community in which he lived. His business associations, extending over a long period of years had made for him many valued colleagues, who recognised that in his death the business circles of this district had suffered a severe loss.

The mayor, the municipal council, representatives of the Farmers and Citizens Trustees Company, which the deceased chaired, the Bendigo Fruitgrowers Cooperative, the Bendigo Benevolent Asylum, and the children's court, where he sat as justice of the peace, all gathered at the family homes at Williamson and Hopper streets. The allotment had been granted half a century earlier by the crown. Following prayers by two elders of the Gospel Hall, founded by the deceased, the coffin was carried to the hearse by six of his grandsons. The cortege started down Williamson Street, passing over railway tracks and turning onto Meyers Street. The corner was the site of Albert Bush's grocery store. Charles Robert had started working there at the age of seventeen, became manager, and retired after forty years to pursue other business interests.

As the cortege turned onto Hopper Street it passed St. Paul's Anglican Church, standing on property given by Albert Bush. Both Charles Stilwells, father and son, were members of the 1868 building committee. As the procession moved past the church the bells of St. Paul's pealed out a favorite hymn, "Rock of Ages." It was an extraordinary tribute. Charles Robert Stilwell resigned from the vestry committee four years after the erection of the building. But good will seemed to have prevailed. As he left, his departure was recorded with "united thanks for the action had so long taken in the general interests of this Church."[1]

His resignation said something about the fierce independence of the Stilwells. St. Paul's was a protest against All Saint's across town. The incumbent there had introduced high-church liturgy, regarded as papist by many Anglicans of the day. The founders of St. Paul's had learned from that experience: they set up a governing leadership committee independent of any clerical involvement. The minister was not even allowed to attend, which is probably the reason why the first minister at St. Paul's only lasted two years. The second, John Christian MacCullagh, defied all

Charles Robert and Mary Ann Faul Stilwell on the fiftieth anniversary of their wedding, 15 October 1912 (Courtesy of Charles Stilwell)

odds, patiently consolidated his power and lasted for forty-seven. Charles Robert, unable to keep the clergy at bay, established a Christian assembly where there would be no clerical interference. Simple biblical worship would be led by unpaid lay leaders. There would be a weekly breaking of bread in which only the presumed regenerate could participate.

"Rock of Ages" receding into the distance, the cortege turned left down Carpenter Street. Two blocks to the right on Hargreaves Street, where two of Charles

Robert's sons—twenty-four-year-old Fred and twenty-year-old Ernest—started a furniture business in 1893. They were joined later by brother Roy. It became a thriving business that continues to this day. The funeral procession made its way out of town along Carpenter Street to the Bendigo cemetery. Not far inside the gate the procession stopped at the grave site. A eulogy was delivered by a business colleague, since moved to Melbourne, reported verbatim in the newspaper:

> [Charles Robert Stilwell] had found his Saviour in his young life in his digging days. It had made all the difference in his life, and he had told many times of what it had meant to him. He had found not only a Saviour, but a Father. He had often said that all things work together for good to those who loved God. He took as a tribute to the deceased the assemblage, representing as it did the commercial, civic, and religious life of the community.

The committal service concluded with a prayer by an assembly elder. The pallbearers lowered the "massive oak casket" into the ground. Standing nearby were surviving sons Fred and Roy, and daughters Violet Rose Baker and Alice Chambers. Today in Bendigo cemetery a small white marble stone with name and dates, alongside that of a stillborn child, mark the final resting place of Charles Robert Stilwell.

FAMILY CONFLICT

Nineteen-year-old Stacey Woods was not at his grandfather's funeral. His mother, the only absent surviving child, was in Sydney, a journey of four or five days. Daisy May and her husband Fred Woods moved from Bendigo seven years earlier to suburban Hurstville. The family circle had already been broken, not by distance but by schism. Eight years earlier the Bendigo Gospel Hall was split over a matter of doctrine. Fred and Ernest, partners in Sitwell's furniture store since 1893, no longer fellowshiped together. Ernest (who died in 1926 at the age of fifty-three) and Roy remained with their father in the assembly. Fred went off with an ex-Anglican remembered today by the family as "Ferguson." Ferguson taught what to them was the heresy of soul sleep.

"The sleep of the soul, or as it more accurately be named, its nonexistence after death, is a most insidious and plausible error, especially when bolstered up, as it usually is, by perverted Scripture," a 1921 article in the *Believers Magazine*, an authoritative Christian Brethren periodical.

We believe it to be a false charity that fails to openly and definitely warn fellow-believers of the evil effects of listening to the teaching of one who has apostasised from the faith, and equally so of the danger of reading his writings. And to set the bad example to others unable to judge for themselves in going to hear, or fraternising with such persons, is worthy of the very strongest condemnation.[2]

Stacey Woods experienced firsthand the cost of schism. For the rest of his life he maintained that Christians, especially students and the young, need to know orthodox Christian doctrine and be taught biblical truth. In that small Christian Brethren Assembly he learned that ignorance has a price. Theology mattered to Stacey Woods. He insisted on sound teaching that stuck to the Bible, avoided speculation and refused to go off on tangents. No one knew better than he what tragedy and suffering religious controversy could cause. He had seen it in his own family.

Ironically it was the strong bonds of Stilwell family unity that first attracted Fred Woods. As an only child in a dysfunctional family, when he visited the Bendigo assembly in the early 1900s with his ministry colleague Tom Baker, there was immediate rapport with the clan. The two of them had been on the road, without a base, traveling around New South Wales and Victoria as colporteurs, driving a wagon through all the small towns of the Australian frontier. There was a rhythm to their church planting: advertise meetings in a community center or school, hold services, sell Bible portions and other books (particularly providing keys to biblical prophecy), and invite people to accept Christ as personal Savior. Depending on the response, they organized an assembly,[3] built a modest worship hall and then moved on to the next town. "God used him to found quite a number of churches in Queensland, New South Wales and Victoria," the son remembered.[4] The father had a passion for evangelism.

Fred Woods was born on 1 September 1873 in Glossop, in the Peak district of Derbyshire, England, fourteen miles from the urban center of Manchester. When he was nine, his family emigrated to Queensland, Australia, settling in Brisbane. This was the end of his formal education. His father, an alcoholic, died driving a horse through water while in an intoxicated state. Fred, apprenticed as a carpenter, became the sole support of his mother. Converted under the ministry of Brethren tent evangelist George Grove on one of his annual trips to Brisbane, Fred Woods received a call to ministry at the age of nineteen.[5] In 1896 he was commissioned by his assembly in South Brisbane, known for being effective for discipling and calling young men to Christian service. Fred began as a colporteur evangelist with an older man named Fleishman. Apprenticeship complete, he teamed with Fred Baker, a young man with similar background.

Their travels took them to Bendigo. At the assembly they noticed the two younger daughters of Charles Robert Stilwell. Fred Baker began seeing Violet Rose. Fred Woods had his eye on her sister, two years younger, again with a floral name, Daisy May (born 4 March 1877). Love was the incentive they needed to be more settled, and Baker and Woods opened an electrical supply business. On 20 January 1906 at "Ewell," the home of Mary and Charles Robert Stilwell, the couple were married. A Methodist minister (the Christian Brethren were not licensed at the time to officiate at weddings) named Blackwell, later to die as a missionary in a remote part of South America, tied the knot. There is no reference in the newspaper write-up to any member of the Woods family being present, citing only the mother of the groom as "the late Mary Woods." There is no mention at all of the father.

Fred and Daisy Woods had striking contrasts in personality but also shared many common interests and values. Married later than was usual at the time—Fred was thirty-two, Daisy twenty-eight—the two were both committed to Christian ministry. In the best Christian Brethren tradition they traveled as a team: Fred preached and Daisy played a little pump organ and sang solos. "Mother stood 100 per cent with Father," their son observed, something that made "a deep impression on me."[6] "My parents did not preach one thing and live another. The reverse was almost true. They lived this life of faith in God but did not talk about it." Fred was quieter, disciplined, aware of the sensitivities of others, had penetrating insights into human character and personality, and made great demands on himself. Impeccably groomed at all times, he had a horror of disorder, indiscipline and chaos, a legacy from his past. Largely self-educated, he taught himself to write (and speak) fluent prose based on his intimate knowledge of the authorized King James Bible, and had excellent penmanship. Daisy, whose home life had been secure and who had enjoyed status as the youngest daughter of a prominent citizen in Bendigo, was confident, outspoken, possessed of definite opinions she was not afraid to share, and could easily ruffle feathers, which Fred would then attempt to smooth. Their personalities complemented and supplemented each other. In the best tradition of the Christian Brethren, Fred managed the ministry and Daisy the home. One can see strands of each in their son.

Charles Wilfred Stacey Woods was born 10 September 1909 at the home provided for his parents by Charles Robert on the family compound, 105 Williamson

St., Bendigo. For the first five years of his life he was an only child, with adoring aunts and uncles, playing with his cousins and surrounded by love. The official photograph of his grandparents' fiftieth wedding anniversary, 15 October 1912, has Stacey on his grandfather's knee, surrounded by aunts, uncles and cousins along with doting parents and grandparents.

By that time Bendigo was a city in serious economic decline, its glorious mining days over. The economy of the town had been dominated by two men, generous philanthropists called quartz kings.[7] Their death at this time marked the end of an era of prosperity and enterprise. The gold mines went deeper and deeper into the

Stacey Woods, age 3, sits on his grandfather's lap at the family celebration of his grandparents' fiftieth wedding anniversary, 15 October 1912 (Courtesy of Charles Stilwell)

ground. Seventy million gallons of water had to be pumped each year. On the night of 14 June 1910, water broke through into one of the largest mines, Victoria Quartz, and the world's deepest goldmine was rendered unworkable. Though there was a new discovery at 311 feet at the Central Red, White and Blue Mine, the reprieve was short-lived. By 1918 not a single mine in Bendigo provided a dividend. Fourteen years earlier £322,915 had been paid out, the equivalent in today's currency of eighty-two million dollars.

Stacey Woods called Bendigo "a dreadful place of drunkenness and violence" that he was inclined to connect with the early Australian convicts.[8] Though as a mining town it had its roughnecks and violence there was considerable culture in the city. Bendigo remained a strong and prosperous community of 30,000 with a respectable art gallery and many cultural interests. In 1913 the New Lyric Theatre opened on Bendigo's own Charing Cross at a cost of £15,000 (today's equivalent of three million dollars). Residents filled the facility for *Les Miserables* and *Quo Vadis?*

There was also a downside. Respiratory disease, miner's tuberculosis caused by the inhalation of silica dust, was a major cause of death. There were labor troubles, with a strike in 1912 when management charged miners with gold theft. Tensions surfaced between the different ethnic and religious cultures that constituted Bendigo society, particularly rivalries between Irish and Germans, Roman Catholics both, and the Protestant majority. In 1898 the Roman Catholic community in Bendigo started a building project, one of the larger churches in Australia, that would only be completed years later. Even today the impressive gothic Roman Catholic cathedral dominates the Bendigo skyline.

Stacey Woods's earliest days reflected some of this ambivalence. He gained a respect for culture and beauty. But Bendigo had its rough and rowdy side. He was a part of denominational rivalries, boyish wars of Protestant lads attacking Roman Catholics with catapults. On at least one occasion he snuck into their cathedral and put black ink in the holy water fonts. He appears to have been high-spirited and mischievous. One time he was caught by the local police in a misdemeanor, charged and made to appear before a judge, who unbeknown to the policeman, turned out to be his grandfather. The date of the hearing arrived and Stacey was quaking as he appeared before Charles Robert Stilwell. He was sternly lectured without a trace of familiarity, found guilty, given a suspended sentence and then taken out for an ice cream.

WORLD WAR I

Days of innocence would too soon be over. On Sunday 2 August 1914 editor George Mackay of the *Bendigo Advertiser* received a telegram from the Melbourne office announcing that Germany had declared war on Russia. By the end of the day large crowds gathered outside the newspaper office watching as further bulletins were posted. Twelve days later the first Bendigo recruits left to join the Australian Expeditionary Force. Meanwhile Sir Ernest Rutherford, part of a visiting delegation of scientists and academics, provided a lecture on "Radium" and "the enormous possibilities of this substance in times of war."[9] The day of modern warfare had arrived, even in remote Bendigo. By the next year, 25 April, "one of those typical autumn days for which Bendigo is famous,"[10] the finest young men of Australia and New Zealand landed on a peninsula named Gallipoli. That military fiasco birthed the modern state of Australia, creating the fierce and feisty nationalism that Stacey Woods shared.

Important as the tumultuous events that 1914 initiated were, the year is best known in the Woods family for the birth on 16 August of sister Rosemary. Shortly after, Stacey Woods's father, the peripatetic evangelist, went off to Camp Seymour, a few miles to the north and west of Melbourne. Here the Australian Expeditionary Force was trained and sent off for the trenches of France, the shores of Gallipoli, and the sands of Egypt and Palestine. Only five when his father left home, Stacey remembered his absent dad by a picture: Fred Woods is surrounded by "a sea of hundreds of men in uniform." He stands at the center tent pole. The picture is inscribed: "To my dear wife whose sacrifice made these meetings possible." Fred was officially described as an "evangelistic chaplain." His ecclesiastical affiliation set him apart from the military chaplains of recognized denominations. Like highly respected Salvation Army staff, he was in a special category. Fred Woods spoke seven days a week in a designated tent and did extensive counseling with the boys who were leaving home and country, and setting off to a foreign war.

Australian chaplains went with the troops into a brutal and hellish war sublimely optimistic and confident about their struggle, out of touch with reality. Australian churches in the nineteenth century had been marginalized in a new and self-sufficient society that had few roots and little connectedness with organized and mainstream Christianity. Military chaplains in the First World War found themselves relating to a whole generation of young men with whom they had no previous contact. As the war wore on, as casualties affected many Australian homes, as patriotism's demands became both shriller and less plausible, the whole of the country went through a dark and terrible phase.

Fred Woods served in this context. Daily confronted with men who had little contact with Christian faith, let alone the evangelical variety that he espoused, he developed a depth to his ministry, an ability to identify with those outside his own limited circles, that stood him well in postwar ministry with a broader constituency. After the war, bereaved families tried to connect with their dead through spiritualism. Communicating with the departed was one way of dealing with the inconsolable pain that parents and loved ones felt. Soul sleep was an understandable if mistaken interest of some that made comprehensible the emotions that divided the Bendigo Gospel Hall. The 1920s in Australia were a time of deep spiritual hunger and a period when, to quote one recent commentator on the Australian Broadcasting Corporation, "the churches lost their way."[11]

Fred Woods saw the spiritual vacuum of the hour. The year before the war he had written of the need for

> impassioned earnestness to rescue the perishing. In this cold critical age there are cold icebound souls trying to extinguish this inflammatory note in preaching, by turning on the hose of higher criticism. With such the head is everything, the heart is nothing but if we wish to be soul winners, we shall need to remember that people have hearts to be kindled as well as head to be enlightened, and we shall need hearts as well as head if we are to woo them to Christ and win them for Him.[12]

The war and his experiences at Camp Seymour simply reinforced that passion and rekindled his zeal to reach a society looking for answers.

Growing up in Australia during the First World War affected a whole generation, Stacey's generation. His single-minded commitment to evangelism, his vision of reaching individuals with the good news, his uncompromising gospel that dealt with realities of sin and death and his refusal to temporize came from the lessons of that terrible time when Australia established its identity and the churches were not there. In the next major conflict, a generation later, he would demonstrate that he had learned these lessons well.

2

Australian Adolescence

THE IDYLLIC CHILDHOOD OF A BOY IN SMALL-TOWN AUSTRALIA came to an abrupt end in 1921. Fred Woods returned from meetings in Tasmania to announce that the family was moving to Sydney. The largest city in Australia would provide him with greater opportunities for ministry. It would also represent a quantum leap in culture at an impressionable age for young Stacey Woods. He was no longer a part of the now-fragmenting family circle of Stilwells that up until now had defined his life. On the threshold of adolescence he was to have a whole new horizon open for him. His father would be traveling greater distances, absent for longer periods of time, and Stacey's grandfather would not be there either as a backup. Gone were his cousins and familiar playmates and schoolmates. Growing up as teenager in comparatively cosmopolitan Sydney exposed him to many new opportunities but also confronted him with many life-changing challenges. It made him as an adult remarkably adaptable to ministry moves and frequent relocations.

The family settled at 12 Alma Street, Hurstville, a lower-middle-class suburb of Sydney. They chose Hurstville for two reasons: religious and educational. When they settled in the suburb there was only one Christian Brethren assembly, in South Hurstville. Whether it was this one that Stacey later described as "a meaningless barren wasteland" is not known. If it was, it is understandable why in 1925 Fred

Woods and several others founded Hurstville Central Assembly. The reason given at the time was that they were "desiring a wider ministry to the main town." One of the other church planters was Wilfred E. Porter, an outstanding classicist and educationalist. Porter was one of the few secondary school teachers who had an academic degree. He also modeled for young Stacey Woods thorough scholarship integrated with a broad-minded faith. Wilfred Porter took a prominent part in the Katoomba convention, which brought together evangelicals across the denominational spectrum.[1]

The expository ministry of Fred Woods as "a godly, able speaker and teacher" is still revered by older members of the present assembly.[2] As a young man one of them went to downtown Hurstville on a Friday night wearing a sandwich board with Scripture verses front and back and handed out gospel tracts. He remembers "his trepidation and his great encouragement, when walking through a throng of shoppers Stacey stepped out and walked with him helping to give tracts to the passers by."[3] Stacey was not always forthright in his witness: he recalled in one sermon late in life[4] how in high school he turned up at a religious gathering to discover a classmate he had known for three years was also in attendance. "What are you doing here?" he was asked. "I didn't know you were religious." Stacey had to admit that in three years of friendship the boys had never shared their faith with each other.

STACEY'S EDUCATION

A good education for his son also mattered to Fred Woods. An autodidact himself, having left school at nine on immigration to Australia and compelled subsequently to provide for his widowed mother, he wanted the very best for his boy. Fred Woods was fiercely ambitious and highly protective of his only son, hoping to provide for him advantages he had never known. The Hurstville Public School, where Stacey was enrolled in 1921, was described as a *superior* public school not because of its scholars or their parents being superior in intellect or social class, but because it provided instruction beyond the six years of primary schooling. At that time in Australia education beyond age fourteen was for a small, privileged minority. Hurstville Public School, as a regional superior school, was assigned some of the best teachers in the city.

Urban Sydney provided new evangelistic ministry opportunities for Fred Woods.[5] In 1922 he launched the "People's Gospel Mission" whose goal was to reach the masses, using picture theaters as a venue for Sunday evening services. Films, soon to become talkies, provided both novelty and escapism after the trauma of the World War I. Australians attended the movies in droves. In the 1920s, out of a population of six million, on any given weekend two and a quarter million would attend a local motion picture theater.[6] For those in the Assemblies, attendance at the theater was highly dubious if you were living "the separated life." Going to movie theaters, even for an evangelistic rally, would surely (it was argued) break down a Christian's inhibitions. Undeterred by such concerns, Fred Woods saw only potential, fearlessly seeking by any means to win some. For two years crowds attended his rallies, and there were many conversions. The lesson stayed with the son as his father said to him: "Stacey, the great thing is to understand the movement of the Holy Spirit in your day and then pray that God will catch you up in His purposes and that you will be carried on in the way that the Holy Spirit is working in your particular moment of life."[7]

In 1923 Stacey went on to the Canterbury Boys' High School. Instead of apprenticing to a trade as was the custom for most in Hurstville, he was given a privileged opportunity in a neighboring suburb to pursue education beyond the age of fourteen. Canterbury Boys' High School is now celebrated for its most famous alumnus, John Howard, present prime minister of Australia. In Stacey's time it was a school with growing numbers and confidence under the strong leadership of a headmaster named Rourke. Just after Stacey left it was reclassified as a "First Class High School." Initially Stacey was in a class of over forty, with little personal attention. He passed the Intermediate set of examinations (when most left school) in 1925 and then he joined the elite in a small class of eighteen.

Stacey was the only one in his class, 4B, who contributed essays to the school magazine *Canterbury Tales* the following year. They show a gift for expression and observation. One, titled "The Surf," describes the exhilarating pleasure of a robust surf. The second, "Our Japanese Visitors," speaks of the visit of the Japanese fleet to Sydney with acute observations. The final one, titled "Drought," is sensitive about an important aspect of the Australian national consciousness. Unsurprisingly, Stacey Woods received the merit certificate in English in 1927. That year he went to Fort Street School Hall in Petersham (the oldest government school in Australia) and took his leaving certificate exams. It was an anxious moment that would determine his academic future.

The results were credible but did not qualify him for entrance to Sydney University. He failed Latin (as he had previously) as well as French and chemistry. Mathematics II he rewrote, bringing up an F to a B-. The only subject in which he excelled was modern history, gaining him second class honors. He received a leaving certificate but did not matriculate. Stacey was awarded a (Sydney) Teacher's College Certificate with an allowance of £50 (present value: $13,000). If he accepted it and became a teacher, he was bonded to spend four years in the Australian outback, often in primitive conditions.[8]

There was irony here: a person later known as an advocate for evangelical engagement with secular higher education was never to enter university. Stacey went to work in the office of a steel manufacturer and is said to have taken night courses in bookkeeping. This is questionable because later he would claim never to have been able to read a balance sheet! Fred Woods later quoted his son's boss to the effect that, had he continued there, he could eventually have run the company.

One life-time friend Stacey made during those years was Vincent Craven, better known by his nickname Cobber. At the age of fourteen, a year after Stacey, Craven moved to Sydney with his family and never returned to complete his secondary school education. There are various stories about how he came to faith, the most colorful is that he was dragged out of bed one evening to attend a service where "he found the Lord."[9] Stacey came to a clear faith at a beach mission at Broken Bay in 1924.

EDMUND CLARK

Both boys had been helped by an Englishman and children's worker named Edmund Clark. Clark was on his second journey to Australia from England. He came first in 1912 as an accidental tourist, following the death of his young wife. In England he had served as a staff member of the Children's Special Service Mission (connected with Scripture Union), an organization committed to children's evangelism, summer beach missions and Scripture reading with helpful daily notes. When Clark returned to England in 1915 he was not rehired by CSSM, a fact whose significance only became apparent later.[10] He resurfaced in Australia in 1922, saying that he had to start over again since the three whom he had most affected were all killed in World War I. He remained in Australia for six more years.

Clark had strong financial backing from a remarkable Christian Brethren industrialist named James Beath Nicholson. JB, as he was known, was the managing director of the electric elevator company Standard-Waygood. For many years he hosted a prayer gathering in his home, known humorously as "the exclusive brethren," which drew a dozen evangelical leaders from across the ecclesiastical spectrum. The Nicholsons had a profound commitment to Bible-based ministries, particularly to youth. Described as "abrupt, gruff and unapproachable," once, while escorting Craven to his front door after a ministry briefing session, he put his arms around him. Looking him straight in the eye Nicholson said with great feeling: "Vincent, I'd give anything I possess if I could lead a boy to Christ."[11]

Former archbishop of Sydney Donald Robinson credits Edmund Clark with an influence out of all proportion to the time he actually spent in Australia. He should know; his father, archdeacon R. B., chaired Australian Scripture Union and his mother was Clark's pianist. In spite of being the archetypical "pom,"[12] by his passionate and persuasive faith and his unique gifts for children's ministry, Clark left an indelible impression. For instance in a 1926 mission Clark brought future archbishop Sir Marcus Loane to faith.[13] Among the Clark "trophies" none were more loyal than Vincent Craven and Stacey Woods.

"This man became almost a second father to me during my difficult teens," Stacey later reminisced.[14] One way in which Stacey identified with him was height. Clark was only 5' 4". Stacey never went beyond 5' 5".

> What an unlikely leader of teenage boys he was—a fussy English widower without any ability at games or athletics. To the horror of an Australian boy he could not even swim. However, many were led to Christ through his ministry and dozens went out into various avenues of the Christian ministry because of him.

At Broken Bay, at the age of thirteen, "Pa" Clark taught Stacey how to live under canvas in virgin bushland, cut poles and ridgepoles for tents, and dig trenches around them. Water had to be carried in, and food was provided by fishing. "Work, preparing meals, cooking, hauling water, cleaning up, was part of camp life. We had no paid cook. In it all, dapper Pa Clark, only occasionally seen without coat and tie, was everywhere supervising every detail of the camp. Woe to the boy who was a slacker and did not pull his weight." Clark was given to caning campers who had been guilty of some misdemeanor. For four years on Saturdays five to eight boys would gather in the Scripture Union office. While doing simple office chores Clark would provide "a nonstop stream of counsel, criticism, admonition, encouragement and Christian teaching." He would take them out to a restaurant for lunch, and afternoons they would surf and lie in the sun. "Girls and any form of dating was absolutely forbidden. One sad result of this type of influence was that quite a number of Pa's boys never married, not unlike the story of so many 'Bash' campers of the Scripture Union in Great Britain."[15]

Then, as Stacey recalled it, sometime in 1927, "suddenly our little world crashed around us. Pa Clark had seriously failed and the Scripture Union in Australia unfeelingly and with no place for forgiveness, returned him to England in disgrace." Fred Woods was the only one who stood by "in spite of the fact that he had every reason to turn against him." Whatever this meant it appears some sort of impropriety was implied, though it was never spelled out. A group met with Clark and heard the accusations. Stacey and Vincent Craven must have been present because Stacey reported that during the proceedings Clark turned to one person "who owed everything to this man but had turned on him to rend him" and quoted the verse "He that thinketh he standeth, take heed lest he fall." "I can still hear his words to this day," Stacey said fifty years later. Stacey and Vincent Craven were two of the handful that waved goodbye at the pier in Sydney as Clark left for England. They went on by train to Melbourne to catch the boat again and "give our broken farewell." He concluded, "But this changed the two of us from boys to men and compelled us to take over the work that Edmund Clark had been forced to leave behind him."

It was soon apparent that both young men had unique gifts in youth work. Vincent was asked to join the Scripture Union committee. Unlike Woods, who was struggling with schoolwork and whose studies suffered with all these distractions, Craven had a job where his employer, Sir Arthur Cox, president of the Australian YMCA, gave him time off at company expense and actively encouraged his ministry. Together the young men developed the work in three or four orphanages and ran a weekly meeting for boys that grew into the hundreds. When the health of Mary Nicholson, honorary Scripture Union secretary and JB's daughter, gave way in 1930, the twenty-two-year-old Vincent Craven was called back from a course funded by Mary's father at Melbourne Bible Institute. In 1945, following over a decade with Australian Scripture Union and wartime service in New Guinea, Stacey Woods brought "Cobber" (as he was known to two generations of Pioneer campers) to Canada, where he served on IVCF staff for twenty-eight years.

Years later Paul White, famed for his "jungle doctor" books and an InterVarsity staffer, was asked about Stacey, his youth in Australia and his reasons for leaving for North America. "It's one of those things we just don't talk about," he allegedly told Charles Troutman.[16] In those days Clark's departure, and the reason for it, were not open for discussion, let alone counseling. Both Stacey and Cobber were left for the rest of their lives with a deep, unaddressed pain, psychic scars that were never opened to the air for healing and health, and could never be shared. Only as his end approached could Stacey set out his unspoken hurt in a written memoir as he attempted to sort out his latent anger.

HOWARD GUINNESS

In 1929 J. B. Nicholson wired to Howard Guinness in Canada a Macedonian call: "Come under and help us."[17] Guinness was a member of the Grattan branch of the Dublin brewing family prominent through their patriarch Harry in every aspect of ministry at the turn of the century, a veritable evangelical dynasty. Guinness's trip to Canada, where he founded the Inter-Varsity Christian Fellowship, remains an integral part of its collective mythology. A dashing and handsome rugby player who was completing a medical course at St. Thomas' Hospital London, Guinness was sent by students who (so legend has it) sold their tennis rackets to fund a one-way ticket to Canada. Actually most of the money was provided by surgeon Arthur Rendle Short, later professor of surgery at Bristol University, an IVF vice president and senior treasurer.

From Montreal to Toronto and out to Vancouver and back on the prairies, east again and then west once more, Howard Guinness found a ready response everywhere, though not always positive. "Impetuous, untidy, stubborn, dramatic, and over optimistic," was his frank and personal self-analysis. He left behind in Canada a mélange of camps, university chapters and high school ministry that evidenced little clear strategic thinking. Exhausted by these initiatives, after a week at a hotel in Seattle studying the biblical book of Romans, he returned to Vancouver and set sail for Australia. Here again there was a bizarre twist. The cable from Douglas Johnson of the British IVF sending funds had a typo: forty pounds became four hundred. Guinness bumped himself up to first class before the mistake was discovered. His aunt, Mrs. Howard Taylor (daughter-in-law and biographer of Hudson Taylor, founder of the China Inland Mission), once again came to his rescue and made up the difference. It paid to have connections.

Meeting Howard Guinness at the Sydney dock was brother Harry and the ubiquitous J. B. Nicholson. J. B. took him out to his Burwood estate. Shortly thereafter Howard Guinness made his way west to the Blue Mountains and the home of another Christian Brethren scion, Margaret Young. At the Katoomba convention then in progress Guinness was introduced to the entire transdenominational evangelical community in New South Wales. At the conclusion of this convention, patterned after that of Keswick in England,[18] he journeyed to Bayview on Pittwater, north of Sydney, where Stacey Woods and Vincent Craven were leading a beach mission. It was their first encounter with a man whose family name and breeding and personality opened doors that neither young man would ever be able to, given the class system of their day. Guinness went on to enlist "Crusaders," a name he gave chapters in the public schools (exclusive private schools), as he nurtured them in faith.

Stacey Woods became ambivalent about Howard Guinness. Fifty years later, when Guinness's reminiscences appeared, he commented that "Howard was a visionary. Undoubtedly God used him in many individual lives. We all owe him a debt. One regret is that there is no sense of teamwork in his story. Simply the exploits of one individual."[19] Stacey felt Guinness's exuberant and charismatic personality got in the way of having a God-centered rather than a personality-centered ministry, always a concern of his.

Fred Woods's work was increasingly outside Australia. In 1924 he traveled to New Zealand and, in spite of ill health, had taken gospel meetings on Sunday evenings at assemblies in Invercargill and Wellington.[20] The next year he was in Queensland. Shortly after Christmas 1927 he set out from Sydney on an extensive round-the-world journey that would take eighteen months.[21] Disembarking from his boat at Port Said, Egypt, he crossed Sinai to tour Palestine. One of the features of his ministry had been a large (and portable) reproduction of the Old Testament tabernacle that Stacey remembered helping him carry to meetings. From now on he would be able to provide eyewitness accounts of biblical scenes in his preaching.

From Jerusalem Fred Woods went on to continental Europe and Great Britain, and then to North America. While in Canada he spoke at a week of meetings in Bethany Gospel Hall in the steel city of Hamilton, Ontario. "Real blessing to saint and sinner resulted. Quite a number professed. Four have been baptised lately," the *Believers' Magazine* reported.[22] One of the elders in this assembly in the gritty east end stood out. Horace Lockett was principal of the Normal School, the local teacher's college.[23] Five years later Dr. Lockett, as chair of the executive of the Inter-Varsity and Inter-School Christian Fellowship of Canada, issued the invitation for Fred's son to become general secretary.

When Fred returned to Sydney, he received a warm welcome. On 31 July 1929 in the downtown Chapter House seven hundred people from eighteen urban assemblies attended a missionary conference at which Fred Woods was featured as speaker. He inspired the gathering by providing an encomium of the worldwide Christian Brethren movement. He had found it "a spiritual force in the earth." He noted its fundamental orthodoxy: "we remain as sound as an uncracked bell." There was also a healthy variety, "slight shades of difference in assembly polity . . . uniting to captivate and capture the young as never before." And there was unprecedented opportunity: modernism was "breaking to pieces Protestantism" and "Ritualism is pulling toward Rome." He concluded with a challenge: "our communion must be as big as the heart of God, as broad as the activities of God, as warm as the sympathies of God, and as true as the Word of God."[24]

During his travels, while in New York City (according to Stacey's account), Fred Woods met George E. Guille, a visiting faculty member at the Evangelical Theological College in Dallas, Texas.[25] Guille had pastored Presbyterian churches in the south before developing an itinerant ministry out of Athens, Tennessee.[26] As a visiting professor at the Texas institution he was responsible for month-long courses in English Bible. He was a significant booster of the new school and a persuasive advocate of the training that it offered, particularly in English Bible. Fred Woods was impressed.

The Evangelical Theological College was founded in 1924 by three leading evangelicals. Lewis Sperry Chafer who had inherited the mantle of C. I. Scofield; Englishman Griffith Thomas, dismissed in 1918 as principal of Wycliffe College (the low-church Anglican theological faculty at the University of Toronto); and A. B. Winchester, minister *extra muros* at Toronto's Knox Presbyterian Church. The first prospectus of the new school announced that it was established to provide "the usual courses of proved value together with that comprehensive and intensive training in the Scriptures which is an essential requirement for spiritual power and the faithful presentation of God's revelation."

On hearing from Fred about his son Stacey, Guille arranged to have a catalog sent to Australia. When it came in the mail, apparently Stacey was incredulous. The only training in Texas he could imagine was to be a cowpoke, so he dismissed the idea of going there out of hand. Six months later the registrar wrote to inquire whether he was coming that autumn. His father, now back in Australia, was away on ministry. His mother was visiting family in Bendigo. Separately they came to the same conclusion after prayer that Stacey should attend. His friend Vincent Craven was increasingly drawn to full-time ministry with the financial support of J. B. Nicholson. Freed to respond to what he now considered an unmistakable call of God, Stacey Woods set off for Dallas. A new chapter in his life had begun.

3

Dallas Dynamic

ON THE PIER OF THE CANADIAN AUSTRALASIAN LINE in mid-August 1930, the uncompleted Sydney Harbor bridge was clearly in view the day that Stacey Woods family came to say goodbye. The two ends of the bridge had met in an engineering spectacular the week before. As he mounted the gangplank of the SS *Aorangi*, Stacey looked down at Vincent Craven, who was there with his family, turned back, ran over to him and with dramatic flair said, "Pray that I will have grace to love the unlovable."[1] There was still residual anger from the Clark affair. From the deck he threw down streamers to his waving family. As the boat left the pier the paper became taut and eventually snapped. Foghorns blasted out as the luxury steam ship, only six years old and the pride of Glasgow's Fairfield shipyards, passed out into the Pacific.

TRAVELING BRETHREN

Stacey went down to steerage to inspect his berth. Then, as Australia disappeared on the horizon, Stacey went up on deck and hid behind one of the vessel's two masts so as not to be seen and wept. It was at that moment he had a premonition: he would never return to his homeland again. Indeed, in all his travels around the globe, visiting many countries, he returned to Australia only three times: twice in the 1930s and finally in late 1961 for six weeks. As with both his grandfathers, moving from one continent to another was a fresh start, a new beginning. Behind him were his growing up years in a home where there was a strong female presence and an absent father. But particularly, he could shut out emotions that focused on Edmund Clark: Edmund's disgrace, the angry confrontation at which Stacey had been present, and his subsequent dismissal. Any feelings of betrayal and abandonment were left behind.

When the *Aorangi* docked in Auckland harbor 25 August 1930, the rest of his life would be represented by names on the passenger list.[2] Paul Guinness would be his traveling companion and close best friend for the next three years as they set off for theological studies in Dallas, Texas. Another family boarding the boat became lifetime partners in ministry. Rowland Hill, a friend of his father, was a successful shoe store operator and an elder in the Christian Brethren assembly in London, Ontario. With Rowland was his wife, Mollie, and their seventeen-year-old daughter Dorothy Mae, returning after a six-week journey to Australia and New Zealand. Rowland wrote that day in the diary he meticulously kept for sixty years: "A fine young Englishman started out on our good ship this morning joining young Stacey Wood (*sic*) on his way to Dallas (Texas) Bible Training School. His name is Paul Guinness, a younger son of Grattan Guinness and uncle of Dr. Howard Guinness who visited us in Canada last year."[3]

Paul Guinness's father (and Howard's grandfather), Grattan Guinness, scandalized Victorian evangelicals in England when at age sixty-eight, with seven children and numerous grandchildren, he married Grace Hurditch, forty-one years younger. He fathered two more before he died seven years later. Grattan Guinness, grandson of brewery founder Arthur, was an early member of the Christian Brethren, a flaming evangelist, an educationalist who founded Bible and missionary training schools, and friend and colleague to many leading evangelicals of his day, such as Dwight L. Moody, Charles Haddon Spurgeon and Hudson Taylor. He was also absorbed in millennial and prophetic speculation in which the Jews, in whom he had a great interest, figured prominently. Paul, although he never knew his father, was molded by his widowed mother into the Guinness tradition, being a part of the formidable Guinness network of friends, colleagues and supporters. Geraldine, Grattan's daughter, married Howard Taylor, son of Hudson Taylor, the founder of the China Inland Mission, thus linking two evangelical dynasties. She appears to be the person responsible for encouraging Paul to leave New Zealand to attend a school just founded in which she had a vital interest. Paul had originally gone to New Zealand to build up his strength by working on a sheep ranch. Subsequently he attended the Auckland Bible Institute. His nephew Howard had met up with him earlier that year on a yacht in Auckland harbor. Paul's friendship with Stacey cut across social barriers. Stacey was his best man when he married a Canadian in Montreal five years later.[4]

The five Christian Brethren travelers met for Bible study each day in Dorothy Hill's large stateroom. The boat arrived in Suva, Fiji, four days later. There the Hills received a letter from son Arthur "telling us of much blessing on the camp work in Muskoka where all the boys of the first hut who were not saved confessed faith in Christ."[5] They did not join in the frivolities of crossing the equator and ignored King Neptune's dunkings. Attendance for their studies grew. Sunday the captain gave permission for a song service to supplement the 11:00 a.m. formal reading of the liturgy. "Paul Guinness gave a splendid gospel message," Rowland reported. The Hills parted company at Honolulu, while Stacey in steerage and Paul in first class continued on to Vancouver. Just before the boat reached Vancouver harbor, Stacey celebrated his twenty-first birthday.

The trip to Dallas became an adventure that both caught with their brownie cameras. First a biplane, courtesy of Air Ferries Limited, brought them down the Pacific coast. They stopped over in Oakland, visited Stanford University and the observatory at Mount Wilson. At Los Angeles they acquired a secondhand automobile, which required constant changes of oil as they traveled east. They drove to Phoenix, Arizona, on to the Grand Canyon, and finally coming to El Paso on the Mexican border where they stayed overnight. They arrived in Dallas for the term opening on 27 September 1930. Quite an adventure for two expats.

The Evangelical Theological College[6] was located on a large lot on Swiss Avenue, with two recently constructed buildings on campus. One, completed December 1927, provided offices, a chapel on the first floor, classrooms on the second and a library on the third. The other, a dormitory built the following year, provided rent-free rooms for students during the term. Other than a small charge for laundry and a dollar a day for meals and textbooks ("twenty-five dollars the first year"), there were no costs—tuition was free. The student body numbered between sixty-one and eighty-two students during the years Stacey was in residence. Needless to say, the school had continuing financial crises during those years. Faculty salaries were a low priority and were only paid out when all bills had been met. Morale among staff often suffered.

"I learned," Stacey said, "that Texas was not so much a state in the American Union in those days as a state of mind, a distinct way of life, a unique civilization, an empire in and of itself."[7] The first faculty reception was a shock to the Australian: several students from the southern states came in puffing big black cigars. Within several weeks, without draconian methods, tobacco was no longer used by any of the students. Indeed the whole atmosphere at the seminary was voluntary. If the president, Lewis Sperry Chafer, had his way there would have been no exams and classroom, and chapel attendance was completely voluntary.

DISPENSATIONAL THEOLOGY

Lewis Sperry Chafer had, and continued to have after his graduation, a big influence on the young Stacey Woods. "The door to the president's office was always open. Dr. Chafer loved his students as a father did his own children," Stacey recalled. Chafer provided a direct link with the revivalism of the nineteenth century that had shaped American evangelicalism. After three semesters at Oberlin Conservatory (he never took the college course nor did theology there), Chafer went on the road singing and preaching in revival meetings throughout small rural Midwest churches. In 1901 he came to Northfield, Massachusetts, the summer conference grounds Moody had founded, as music director. Mount Hermon School for boys, where he taught during the winter, had been the site of the great Student Volunteer Movement rallies of the 1880s. In Northfield Chafer attended the Trinitarian Congregational Church, where Moody's pastor, C. I. Scofield, held forth. Chafer fell under Scofield's spell from the time he attended Scofield's first Bible school class. "I am free to confess that it seemed to me at the close that I had seen more vital truth in that one hour than I had seen in all my life before."[8]

For the rest of Scofield's life, Chafer followed close behind. With the appearance of the bestselling Scofield Bible in 1909, Chafer helped set up schools in New York and Philadelphia to popularize the dispensationalism it espoused. Soon almost all American Bible and missionary training schools adopted the same hermeneutic and theology, one of the few exceptions being Toronto Bible College, which would later be a significant factor in the theological and eschatological neutrality of Stacey's Toronto-based ministry. Dispensationalism had wide popular appeal at the time,

with charts and graphics that appeared to simplify biblical interpretation and sat-
isfy curiosity about world events and the future.

In 1922 Chafer moved to Dallas to become Scofield's successor at First Congregational Church (subsequently renamed Scofield Memorial Church). In March
he met with Griffith Thomas and A. B. Winchester in the Piedmont Hotel in Atlanta to plan a postgraduate training school for pastors. They "spent the entire day
and well into the night in conference and prayer."[9] What subsequently emerged was
a curriculum that would perpetuate a summer conference-type Bible ministry for a
new generation of pastors skilled in making the Bible plain to laity and employing
a dispensational hermeneutic.

"Rightly dividing the word of truth" (2 Tim 2:15 KJV) was the key to how the
Bible was interpreted and taught. Following J. N. Darby, a founder of the Christian
Brethren movement, the methodology was familiar to Stacey from childhood. Biblical history was divided into seven dispensations: "These periods are clearly separated and the recognition of their divisions with their divine purposes constitutes
one of the most important factors in true interpretation of the Scriptures." Chafer
went on to state emphatically, "Man's relation to God is not the same in every
age."[10] In keeping with this method, Chafer maintained that the church and Israel
have a radical discontinuity. Prophecies in the Old Testament are to be literally fulfilled and do not refer to Christians today because the new covenant community
cannot appropriate promises made under the old covenant for God's people: "The
outcalling of a heavenly people from Jews and Gentiles is divergent with respect to
the divine purpose toward Israel." There was a complex eschatology (or the doctrine of the end times). The church will be snatched from the world in a "rapture,"
no believer will be "left behind." A terrible tribulation follows, though there was
debate as to whether Christians would be present. Israel will finally be saved. The
nations come up against Jerusalem and the battle of Armageddon commences. As
the battle rages, Christ will be seen by all combatants returning to earth with his
own.

This theology shaped much of evangelicalism during the 1930s as it did Stacey.
Indeed much of what he became can be understood only as an interaction with and
reaction to it in creative tension. Dispensational premillennialism, with its focus on
the end times, easily becomes escapist. A popular fundamentalist hymn said it all:
"This world is not my home." Believers need not respond to the culture or become
engaged in pursuits of social justice and political activity, except to ensure that so-

cial restraints such as Prohibition would be maintained. If the church is a parenthesis, as dispensationalists taught, then ecclesiology didn't matter. The struggle to maintain doctrinal purity in compromised denominations was immaterial because Jesus' return was what mattered, not the health of the bride who awaited him.

Seen in this context the achievement of Stacey Woods is all the more remarkable. His influence helped many Christians engage the university and respond to the culture. He founded a movement that was increasingly committed to issues of social justice and broad political action. He said an emphatic no to an individual who offered a generous amount of money if IVCF in the United States would include a premillennial statement in its doctrinal basis, something at the time that was almost a condition of orthodoxy among many American evangelicals. And many in the organization took the church very seriously. IVCF trained a generation of women and men who were in the vanguard of church leadership and renewal. Stacey was an independent and free thinker, bound only by the Scriptures and unafraid to think outside the mold he had been cast in.

When Stacey was a student there, Dallas Theological Seminary was not rigid about some extreme positions of dispensationalism that for a time, fairly or unfairly, it later became identified with. "In those days," Stacey maintained later, "the Seminary was not characterized by an insistent dispensationalism." He also stated—though some might argue the point—that some professors "were anything but pretribulation dispensational rapturists. We were all a happy family and the freedom and integrity of the individual was always respected."[11] There was also a strong representation of mainline clergy among its leadership. Chafer continued throughout his long life to be a minister in good standing in the Orange Presbytery of the southern Presbyterian church (PCUS). William Madison Anderson, minister at First Presbyterian Church of Dallas, the largest southern congregation at the time, was a founder of Dallas Theological Seminary along with Griffith Thomas and A. B. Winchester. Several of the faculty such as Wick Broomall in Old Testament, Everett Harrison in New Testament, and Fred Leach in church history, had trained at Princeton Seminary before the disruption of 1929. And there was a close tie between the seminary and Wheaton College, which continues to the present.

It is significant that three of the leaders in interdenominational youth ministry were trained at Dallas Theological Seminary in the 1930s. J. Irwin Overholtzer, a graduate, founded Child Evangelism Fellowship in 1937; Jim Rayburn started Young Life at the Gainsville, Texas, high school the following year while still a student; and Stacey Woods, who led InterVarsity. A 1944 editorial in the seminary's journal *Bibliotheca Sacra* reflected on this phenomenon: "The effective work of these directors serves to indicate the emphasis which this school of the prophets places on soul-winning work and indicates the devotion and energy which is assigned to evangelism by the faculty and alumni of this institution."[12]

SUMMER MINISTRY IN CANADA

One student at the seminary in 1930 was Canadian Anglican cleric Fred Glover who was doing doctoral studies and received a Th.D. at convocation the next year.[13] A 1920 graduate of Wycliffe College, University of Toronto, where he had studied under Griffith Thomas, two years later he came to St. Margaret's Church of Winnipeg, a low-church evangelical congregation. English by birth, he knew all about the Children's Special Service Mission (CSSM). Canon Glover summered at Victoria Beach, a community of cottages in which Winnipegers found relief from their humid summers. When Fred Glover heard Stacey was familiar with CSSM, Fred invited Stacey, on behalf of an interdenominational committee, to come and lead beach missions during the summer of 1931.

So while Paul Guinness went off to Canadian Keswick in the Muskoka region north of Toronto and fraternized with the evangelical elite of Canada, Stacey found

Stacey at the Children's Special Service Mission at Victoria Beach, Manitoba, 1931 (Courtesy of Ruth Oliver Cumming)

himself in children's summer beach ministry. But Stacey was glad to return to a familiar ministry and culture. The local paper, announcing a service in the golf clubhouse, spoke of Mr. C. Stacey Woods as "a fluent and interesting speaker" who

The Children's Special Service Mission at Victoria Beach, Manitoba, 1931: (L to R) Fred Lang, P. J. Rich, Archie Lockhart, Stacey Woods (Courtesy of Ruth Oliver Cumming)

"has a special message for the resident of Victoria Beach to hear." Stacey's photo album of that summer is filled with pictures of tanned youths, burly young men, adoring women, and Stacey perched high on a bank of sand with "Thou shalt be like a watered garden" or "Christ died for our sins" spelled out in big letters with a CSSM banner stretched between poles. Stacey, tanned, with jacket and tie, had a team of young people whose school blazers betray a private school education.

Friendships made that summer lasted a lifetime. As always, Stacey's Christian Brethren connections stood him in good stead. The Rich family from St. James Brethren assembly with their three children, Percy, Ruth and Grace, cottaged at

Victoria Beach. Ruth Rich became a lifelong confidant of Stacey's and with her first husband, Jack Oliver, a promoter of his many causes.[14] Another he got to know was Sidney Smith. Smith came to Winnipeg in 1902 (from London where he was part of the Brethren assembly Rowland Hill attended) and, as president of the Reliance Grain Company, became a multimillionaire. In 1927 he bought his very own church building which he called Elim Chapel. The Elim pulpit brought dispensational notables from across North America, including Lewis Sperry Chafer, Smith having been a major financial backer of the Dallas seminary. Stacey Woods soon came to Smith's attention, and three years later Smith would offer Stacey a job as a youth worker in Winnipeg. Fred Lang, a member of Elim Chapel, was another connection Stacey made at Victoria Beach. He likewise was successful in business, moving to Vancouver after the World War II, and a booster of Stacey's ministries.

Stacey returned to Victoria Beach for two further summers: 1932 and 1933. A clip from a local paper in 1932 says:

> The keen interest shown by parents and children and the success of the previous year's effort would auger well of the coming season's operations. Sports, hikes, camp fires, competitions and evening services will also be included in the programme. Work among the 'teen age young people, under the auspices of the Inter-School Christian Fellowship of Canada, an associated and kindred organization of the CSSM should provide for those no longer classed as children.[15]

His final summer there was even more response: "Mr Stacey Woods drew to the club house last Sunday morning one of the largest gatherings of the season, and his simple but fervent discourse was very effective. Mr Woods has an easy delivery, a fine and attractive personality and holds his hearers to the end of his sermon." At the end of the summer the Victoria Beach newspaper stated, "It was the feeling that this has been the most successful and satisfying of the three."

FROM DALLAS TO WHEATON

Stacey developed at Dallas a coterie of friends, many of whom would be significant leaders in evangelical circles. In 1933 Stacey brought future missionary statesman Kenneth Strachan to Victoria Beach.[16] On 6 June 1933, en route to Winnipeg, Strachan and Woods, along with Paul Guinness, stayed at Rowland Hill's home. They had a meeting that evening at London's Central Collegiate Institute (i.e., high school) under the auspices of Inter-School Christian Fellowship (ISCF). Paul left for Toronto the next morning, returned four days later with Willard Aldrich and traveled on to Detroit.[17] Aldrich was later longtime president of the Multnomah School of the Bible in Portland, Oregon. The Hill home at 49 Gerrard St., London, became Stacey's Canadian address.[18]

"Stacey has done very hard and faithful work and has won a reputation for himself in this vicinity and also at Winnipeg as a gospel preacher of unusual clearness and power. We anticipate that he will take a very large place in the plan and purpose of God."[19] Lewis Chafer's assessment of his promising student came toward the end of his final year. Stacey recalls how his father, on receiving this correspondence (or a similar one), wrote back "Well, Stacey, I don't quite understand it, there has either been a most extraordinary change in you or Dr. Chafer must be blind to some of your shortcomings."[20]

Indeed Stacey had made a dramatic academic turnaround. Chafer, who, as he

Foreign students at Evangelical Theological Seminary, Dallas, 1931: (L to R) Juan Delmendo, Philippine Islands; Lorne H. Belden, Elmer H. Henderson, Canada; Fritz Schwartz, Germany; C. Stacey Woods, Australia; Paul G. Guinness, England; Tom Van Puffelen, Holland; Stuart Law, Angus M. Ross, Scotland (Courtesy of Don Regier, Dallas Theological Seminary, Dallas Seminary Archives)

admitted, "regarded all his students through rose-coloured glasses" had given him A+ in all three years of systematics. His biblical studies, Old and New Testament, showed similar ability. In public speaking and homiletics along with evangelism (100 percent), as well as spiritual life, he scored high. Other more substantial courses were not quite as impressive, and Hebrew proved his nemesis. In the first year he was in the first group, with a grade point average of 1.297 (the grades going from 1, an A, on to 4, a D). The following years he slipped, being dragged down by a D+ in Hebrew the second year (grade point average 1.59) but pulled his average up to 1.36 in his final year. It was an impressive showing, given (as Chafer said in his letter), "he did not have all of the academic background when pursuing this course."

On 9 May 1933 in First Presbyterian Church, Dallas, "Charles Wilfred Stacey Woods of Hurstville, New South Wales, Australia," received the diploma of the Evangelical Theological College, along with seven others. Six were granted the Bachelor of Theology degree, including two from Manitoba, their choice of Dallas encouraged by Sidney Smith. There was one among the four who got a master's degree and one received a doctorate. Honorary degrees were conferred on four individuals including a later IVCF supporter Donald Grey Barnhouse, well-known dispensationalist preacher at Philadelphia's Tenth Presbyterian Church. "The days in Dallas were God's great gift," Stacey said. "I was given a love for expository preaching, an understanding and love of the Gospel of the grace of God and above all an appreciation of the truth of God's grace."[21]

Chafer wanted Stacey to go on to doctoral studies, clearing up his undergraduate work with a year at Wheaton College. His father had written a painful letter to Chafer soliciting assistance, noting that they had, thanks to the exchange rate of the Australian pound, little to help Stacey pursue this goal. Chafer wrote to Wheaton on 27 April 1933, stating, "It is not often that I would recommend a young man so entirely without reservation as I recommend Stacey Woods to you. I believe he will be one of the great men of the next generation if our Lord tarries, and it will be an honor to us all to have had any share in his preparation."[22]

Stacey did somehow muster the funds to go to Wheaton College to complete his B.A. with credits from Dallas. Wheaton students in that era often lived in homes on streets adjacent to campus. Stacey's residence was Bartlett Hall, a basic white-clapboard, two story house at Center and Main, which was purchased by Wheaton College in 1922 and housed the campus YMCA as well. Considering his lack of academic background in the arts, Stacey did well, graduating forty-sixth in a class of 133. His courses were history, philosophy and English, with two electives, one in "rhetoric: newspaper writing" and the other in mental hygiene. During the summer of 1934, to complete his degree requirements, he took child psychology and Shakespeare. His work at Wheaton was completed 13 July 1934.

One friend he made at Wheaton was Charles Troutman, premed class of 1936. Troutman came from Butler, Pennsylvania, where his father was a successful manufacturer and served on the board of the college. Troutman later reminisced that Stacey made frequent visits to the registrar's office, juggling credits so that he could get his B.A. and then qualify for his B.Th. at Dallas. Eventually his importunity won out, and he was listed with the Wheaton class of 1934 and received his Dallas degree *in absentia* in 1935.

With his work at Wheaton College almost completed, he wrote Lewis Chafer again, requesting a letter of introduction to the archbishop of Sydney. Howard Mowll's recent consecration had filled Anglican evangelicals with hope for the future. "He is new to Sydney and is an outstanding evangelical," Stacey explained. "I expect to return to Sydney for a time at least next spring." In preparation for holy orders in the diocese of Sydney, he had been confirmed on 12 November 1933 in Trinity Episcopal Church, Wheaton.[23] He noted that his new permanent address was now 149 Gerrard Street, London, Ontario. But he seemed curiously reticent to describe a new development in his life that would, it turned out, keep him permanently away from Australia.

4

Canadian Challenge

"STACEY WOODS LEFT THIS A.M. WITH the boys for Pioneer Camp Muskoka. He is a nice young chap (an Australian) and expects to take up the work of the 'Inter-Varsity Christian Fellowship' during the coming autumn & winter visiting universities & collegiates." Rowland Hill's journal entry for Saturday 21 July 1934 was the first intimation of a new era about to begin. After a year as interim general secretary, Hill's son Arthur had returned to medicine as a surgical intern at Toronto's Grace Hospital. "It became abundantly clear to me by the end of that year that the Lord had not called me into full time service and that I should go back to the study and practice of medicine," Arthur later recalled.[1]

A year earlier the Fellowship had reached an impasse. "Tiny" Palmer, 6' 8" in height, with his towering wife, cogeneral director Josephine, granddaughter of the founder of the Salvation Army, resigned, having been reduced to half-time the year before. The generous support of stockbroker A. J. Nesbitt, which initially bankrolled the Fellowship, had collapsed under the weight of the great economic depression. Howard Guinness, briefly in Canada en route to Australia, appealed to all his friends in Canada: "Until now the cost of the work has been carried largely by one or two people to whom we are eternally grateful. But we thank God that they have now had to drop out for financial reasons, because it puts the responsibility where it ought always to have been and that is on us."[2]

General Secretary of IVCF Canada

Arthur Hill, serving without salary, was at best a stopgap measure providing immediate financial relief. When on 2 May 1934 Horace Lockett invited Stacey to be general secretary at a salary of fifty dollars a month (half what Sidney Smith promised him if he would go to Winnipeg), he replied, "I am happy about the financial arrangements and with the committee who look to God to supply all things spiritual will trust God to meet the spiritual need." The ministry itself was not strong: the most vigorous work was in secondary schools, with fifty Inter-School Christian Fellowship groups in Ontario and thirty-five in the west. University chapters existed only at Toronto, Western, and British Columbia. There were seven or eight members at Queens. "When I became General Secretary in 1934," Stacey wrote, "there were no functioning groups in the Maritime Provinces. There was no group in Winnipeg, Saskatoon, Regina or Edmonton."[3]

But he was not discouraged. His response to the executive committee's invitation was robust. "It is with the sense of the great responsibility and wonderful privilege being accorded me that I look forward to the coming fall and winter." He was guarded in his commitment beyond the year but confident that the way would be clear when the time came. "I know the mind of the Lord for this year but more I know nothing."[4] In *Some Ways of God* Stacey recounts how such certainty came to him, but the details are a bit confusing.[5] Howard Guinness (whom Stacey says asked Stacey to join him) went that summer to India, only returning as scheduled to England in time for the IVF Swanwick conference the following April.[6] Stacey stated he had already booked a ticket as far as England, planning to travel that far with Paul Guinness. He was uneasy, wondering if Canada was "my Nineveh," alluding to the prophet Jonah's disobedience. Separate letters came from each parent, helping him discover God's will and enabling him to make his final decision. One year's commitment to IVCF in Canada turned into eighteen.

He plunged into the work. His staff report lists eighteen services taken during September, and visits to Guelph, Peterborough, Toronto and London. By October he was covering even more territory, conducting thirty-one services, starting groups at the Toronto and Stratford teacher's colleges or normal schools and McMaster University as well as three high schools. He visited Waterloo College and seventeen other high schools, emphasizing as he went the daily prayer meeting. He immediately discovered that the principle of student leadership, basic to the InterVarsity approach, did not apply to high schools and that because of inadequate leadership and "in many instances work that has been commenced has not prospered but has seriously declined." On the other hand, "The university work is limited in its scope and effectiveness, from the human standpoint to the amount of time etc. the interested university students can give to it. It would seem that advance might be made were there a person concentrating on the university field, should God so guide."[7] He had within weeks spotted the challenge of bringing high school and university work together in a single organization, an ongoing issue for Canadian InterVarsity, which wrestled with either having two completely separate entities and approaches or either dumbing down university work or ministering over the heads of the average high-schooler. When he brought InterVarsity into the United States, it is significant that, aside from Hawaii, he left high school ministry to his friend Jim Rayburn.

By November he was featuring rallies in Hamilton and Toronto, and providing leader training on "the value and method of Bible study." At the start of the new year it was apparent that his whirlwind travels were influencing fellow staffer Cathie Nicoll.[8] The only staffer when Stacey arrived, Cathie had been initially been hired, just out of business school, to be office secretary in 1930. A graduate of Chefoo schools, the CIM educational institution for missionary children, on her return to Canada she went to secretarial school. It is significant that in spite of never having been beyond high school and with no formal theological training, she proved to be the most effective staff worker InterVarsity ever had: high schoolers, university students and campers found that her teaching of the Bible communicated in a way that was magnetic. Known as "Nikki," she served for fifty years and grew to iconic status when she received the Order of Canada in 1987. Cathie always said she owed a great deal to Stacey, whose energy and enthusiasm enabled her to develop to the full her gifts. She continued to be loyal to Stacey to the end. She was the first of many women that Stacey freed for ministry. By the end of November, Stacey and Cathie were raising enough funds to pay Inter-Varsity's total monthly salary commitments of $135.

When he came to Toronto, Stacey found accommodation at the China Inland Mission home at 150 St. George Street, south of Bloor. This large Victorian house was surrounded by other evangelical causes. In a six block radius there were six faith-missionary organizations,[9] Toronto Bible College and two strongly evangelical churches: Knox Presbyterian and Walmer Road Baptist, whose pastors (A. B. Winchester and Elmore Harris) had been consultant and editor of the Scofield

Bible. There was also Bloor St. United Church, which attracted some evangelicals to the preaching of George Pidgeon. Until the World War I, the fundamentalist-evangelical communities in Toronto were interconnected, cohesive, socially power-ful and influential. That was starting to break down when Stacey came on the scene. He used to say that Canada was small enough so that everyone in evangelical circles knew everyone else. In the United States one was much more anonymous.

Throughout Stacey's years of leadership in North America he would continu-ally stress his indebtedness to the China Inland Mission and the vision of its founder, Hudson Taylor. The statement of faith that Inter-Varsity Christian Fel-lowship adopted before he came to Canada was almost directly cloned from theirs. The culture or "feel" of Inter-Varsity was borrowed from that organization: its in-ternational blending of widely divergent backgrounds, its days of waiting on God, its dependence on divine aid for every need, its low-key methods of promotion, and its understated refusal to self-advertise were all a part of it. Many of Inter-Varsity's early personnel, such as Cathie Nicoll and Muriel Clark (who joined the office part time in 1935, full time the year after),[10] and later Margaret Fish Stinton,[11] Ruth Bell Nyquist, Marie Little,[12] and Doris Leonard Weller[13] either had been born into the Mission or served it as adults. The China Inland Mission exercised a lasting influence on Stacey and on the Fellowship.

The Canadian director of the China Inland Mission, E. A. Brownlee, and his wife Edith[14] soon became surrogate parents for Stacey Woods. E. A. (never known by his first name) had gone out to China in 1909, returning eight years later to become secretary of the Mission, a position he occupied for thirty years. A quiet, self-effacing man, he was known for the warmth of his friendship to missionaries and particularly to their children, whom he counseled with wisdom and grace on their return from the field. With only one child of his own, "Mr. Brownlee," Stacey recalled, "became my father adviser. . . . It was with him that we prayed through to a conviction that for Inter-Varsity we should not ask for money, we should make our needs known and ask them to pray and this was the policy and practice during the years of my leadership in Canada and the USA."[15]

KEY PEOPLE IN STACEY'S EARLY MINISTRY

The venue for a weekly gathering for prayer that Stacey described as "one of the spiritual foundations of the Inter-Varsity of Canada" was 150 St. George Street.

Three women—Edith Brownlee, Eva McCarthy and Joyce Ritchie—met with him at 3:30 one afternoon a week. It became his spiritual anchor.

Eva's grandfather John McCarthy sailed to China in 1866, the year CIM was founded. Her father, Frank, John's son, was for thirty-four years headmaster of Chefoo schools.[16] Eva returned to Chefoo to teach mathematics in 1920, only settling in Canada a decade later when her parents retired to Northern Ireland. For several years she maintained a Bible teaching ministry among women of means. As Margaret Clarkson recalled, "she had entrance into the fanciest homes in Rosedale where she could conduct Bible classes. She was welcome in places like that. She had breeding and an innate sense of affair."[17] In 1934, with little formal academic training,[18] she started to teach at the Toronto Bible College, where she was a favorite among the students.[19]

"She was not an easy woman, but she was a saint," Stacey Woods was once quoted as saying. In *Men Who Have Helped Me Go with God*, he commented, "in my estimation she was one of the great women of God of our generation. Her influence on individual lives has been incalculable, and yet she lived and died unknown so far as the world of evangelical constellations was concerned." Stacey made no major decision in life without first consulting her, including the move to the United States, his going with IFES, his purchase of Schloss Mittersill, to name but three.[20]

The third to influence the young Stacey was Marjorie Joyce Ritchie, the widow of a prominent Toronto lawyer and granddaughter of a father of the Canadian confederation, the Hon. William McDougall.[21] Joyce Ritchie's husband died in 1920 in the worldwide influenza pandemic. She raised three children—Yvonne, Charles and Joce-

Eva McCarthy (Courtesy of Tyndale UC and Seminary archives)

lyn—without a father and on slender financial means. One way of adding income was to accept boarders at their home at 130 Spadina Road, Toronto, among them was Cathie Nicoll, just back from China. The Ritchies attended the Anglican Church of the Redeemer, along Bloor Street at Avenue Road. The children were also part of a separate Sunday school for privileged children of the parish, hosted in a mansion further up Avenue Road, not far from the Ritchie's family home. Eva McCarthy taught at the school on Sunday afternoons.

His first Sunday in Toronto, Stacey attended the Olivet Christian Brethren assembly near Ossington and Bloor. Eva McCarthy worshiped there, as did a number of leaders of Christian causes in Toronto. After the service, true to Christian Brethren tradition, he was asked by Charles W. Stephens to join the family for a meal. It didn't take long for Stacey to enlist Charles, who was general manager of the Dominion Paper Box Co., as his treasurer. Thus began one of the features of Stacey's lifetime, an ability to size individuals up on the spot, assess their potential, share his vision and receive their often lifelong commitment to his ministry.

Another early Stacey contact was Edwin George Baker, director, president and later chairman of the Moore Corporation and also the Canada Life Assurance Co. "First and foremost," his obituary stated, "Mr. Baker was a Christian in the finest meaning of the term: quiet and unassuming, devoted to Christ, a lover of the Bible and of the people who needed to know Him. This spirit of dedication penetrated his business life as he rose to prominence in Canadian business, and to positions of responsibility that few others have attained."[22] Baker was a member of Deer Park United Church. "His door was always open to me," Stacey recalled, and his "wise, discreet, ethical counsel was of inestimable value."[23]

The Bakers lived on Toronto's most prestigious street, at 135 Dunvegan Road in Forest Hill. Further along was the home of Victor Smith, manufacturers' distributor, who wrote to Stacey in 1936, "Don't forget that there is a standing invitation open for you at 211 Dunvegan Rd., and I should love to see you some time, even if it is only at dinner time for a quick meal, if you have to leave afterwards for an appointment."[24] Stacey also enlisted Dr. John Howitt, head of the Ontario [Psychiatric] Hospital in Hamilton, Ontario, later at Queen Street Psychiatric Hospital in Toronto and an elder at Knox Church.[25] Board member Willis Naylor was also an elder at Knox Church.[26] Stacey was an inveterate networker.

Early in 1935 George Elliott, of the YMCA in Toronto, held a luncheon at the exclusive National Club in the heart of Toronto's financial district so that Stacey Woods could "declare the purpose of his coming to Canada and the work that he set before him through the InterVarsity Christian Fellowship."[27] The guest list included E. G. Baker, John Howitt, Willis Naylor, Charles Stephens and twenty-eight-year-old Donald Methuen Fleming of the law firm of Saunders, Kingsmill, Mills and Price, and a member of Bloor Street United Church. Fleming went on to a notable political and business career, becoming Minister of Finance in the government of John Diefenbaker from 1957 to 1962, and subsequently chairman of the Bank of Nova Scotia.[28] In 1983, at Stacey's memorial service, Donald Fleming recalled that occasion: Stacey "made a profound impression upon those business and professional men present."

Donald Fleming was first enlisted, following the luncheon and his expression of willingness to help, in drafting a constitution for Inter-Varsity. The work took a year, and on 20 January 1936, it was adopted by the executive committee. They were now to be replaced by a board of directors comprised of "not less than nine non-student members and the President and Vice President of the Dominion Student Executive." This was a substantial difference from British Inter-Varsity, which is "a representative movement composed of delegates from independent unions. The Canadian IVF has no such representative character. Effective control is in the hands of the General Secretary and the Board of Directors."[29]

Supporting the board was a council of reference who would vouch for the fledgling organization and provide reassurance for the wider Christian community. The council comprised individuals across the evangelical spectrum of Canadian Protestant churches. The executive committee adopted, along with the constitution, a new statement of faith. Although an initial creedal statement had been approved the year before Stacey had come to Canada, based primarily on that of the CIM, this new statement added "historic fact" to the statement of the bodily resurrection. It was now expected that all those on the council of reference, the board of directors, the president of each local fellowship, the leader of each study group, and every officer appointed by the Fellowship, shall, in order to qualify for office, "subscribe *ex animo* to his belief in . . . the Basis of Faith."[30]

The new board consisted of two women, Eva McCarthy and Joyce Ritchie, along with E. G. Baker, Arthur Brown, George N. Elliott, Donald Fleming, Cliff Harstone, John Howitt, Professor Isherwood of Wycliffe College, Professor Lockett, Victor Smith and Charles Stephens. With the exception of Professor Isherwood, there were no clergy on the board so as not to exacerbate rivalries and cause friction. Powerful and articulate women were also featured. Stacey appeared comfortable with their leadership in spite of being Christian Brethren. Involving women became a pattern for Stacey, as did choosing business persons rather than academics to serve on boards. He would attribute many of the later difficulties of InterVarsity Christian Fellowship, both in Canada and the United States, to an increasing preponderance of academia over business on IVCF boards.

Having established a strong base of operation and provided administrative cohesion, Stacey started to travel more widely, his first two years having been basically confined to the London-Montreal axis. April 11-13, 1935, he ventured into evangelistic ministry at the University of Western Ontario, the first mission ever held there. Almost immediately after this venture he journeyed to Australia and New Zealand. He returned to welcome his first staff appointment since taking office, 6' 4" Toronto graduate Maurice Murphy, who only stayed a year before going to Wycliffe College to prepare for the Anglican ministry.[31] He was replaced by Charles Troutman. By the autumn of 1935, with sufficient staff support on the field and in the office, he felt free to venture further afield, covering the prairie provinces and British Columbia. The work in the prairies was not encouraging. With the exception of two chapters each in Calgary and Edmonton, there was no high school work. The Inter-Varsity chapter at the University of Alberta in Edmonton was holding its own. What he discovered on the Pacific Coast was more encouraging. A trip west, and after 1938 a trip east, became a part of Stacey's annual routine.

Stacey was beginning to redefine the responsibility of a general secretary. He was now to

> devote himself to the general supervision of the work throughout Canada, speaking of the work at such meetings as local committees may arrange; and call on friends and donors of the Fellowship, acquainting them with the progress and development of the work, that he gradually work in other secretaries to take over the direction of the annual summer Camp activity.[32]

INTER-VARSITY CAMPS

The place of Pioneer Camp in Ontario in the total ministry of Inter-Varsity had finally stabilized after several years of uncertainty and conflict. Unlike the rest of the organization, which had been floundering when he arrived, the camps were thriving. Stacey went to the camp in the summer of 1935 and was put in charge of the docks and boats and asked only to assist Cliff Harstone[33] who had been camp director since 1930. Harstone was a high school teacher and, as a member of Knox Church, headed up that congregation's inner-city ministry called Evangel Hall. There was a strong commitment to making the camp accessible to all, charging everyone ten dollars a week. Harstone had been very successful in operating the camp, located since 1931 on Doe Lake. He was the legal trustee for the camp. The lease for the Doe Lake property was to expire in 1937. The first meeting of the new camp committee, responsible for management, dates, general policy and finance, was held at the Ritchie home on 5 February 1936, and three weeks later "the lease, equipment, name and goodwill of Pioneer Camp" were now turned over to Inter-Varsity. Initially scheduled to be a codirector with Stacey Woods the following summer, that night Cliff Harstone resigned, ostensibly over the charging of fees that would preclude the poor attending. His resignation was accepted "with re-gret." Stacey would now be free to shape the camp as he wished. Pioneer never looked back from that moment.

With the indispensable help of Donald Fleming as chair of the camp commit-tee, Stacey had finessed his way through a difficult situation that called for consid-erable skills of diplomacy. He had shown a certain toughness, being willing to withstand the criticism of those whose loyalties were with Harstone, and yet a clear sense of vision as to where the camp should go. During the summer of 1936 Stacey showed creativity in programming, organizational skills and an uncanny knack of putting the right people in the right place: Maurice Murphy was in charge of Junior camp, Marshall Bier at the waterfront, and Stacey's father, Fred Woods, over from Australia on a visit, as chaplain.

On 29 January the following year Stacey was authorized, with Joyce Ritchie, to find a new location for the summer of 1938; again, Donald Fleming proved indis-pensable. A friend of his, Cyrus Dolph,[34] was approached about making available some property he owned on Lake Clearwater near his summer home in Port Sydney. After Stacey, Joyce Ritchie and Donald Fleming had reconnoitered the property and convinced Cyrus Dolph about the ministry, in the summer of 1937 Mr. Dolph do-nated 250 acres, soon to be supplemented on his death shortly thereafter by acreage in the same amount sold for a nominal amount by his widow. That was the final sea-son at Doe Lake, with Stacey directing along with Charles Troutman. By a camp com-mittee meeting on 15 December 1937 Stacey reported that the road to the new boys camp had been completed, and operations were about to commence at Lake Clear-water. During the month of August, eighteen boys had built a road through the bush twenty feet wide and a mile and half long. Charles Troutman says in his diary that he spent eighteen hours a day on the project. One of those involved would later state that "Stacey was the one man I know who could get kids working their heads off un-der those rather rough circumstances and convince them that it was a privilege!"[35]

Charles Troutman carries fellow surveyor Stacey Woods at Pioneer Camp, 1937 (Courtesy of Yvonne Woods)

Other than being on the camp committee and directing the girls camp, Joyce Ritchie had another claim on Stacey's attention; she was about to become his mother-in-law. Yvonne Ritchie had attended Havergal College, a private girls' school in north Toronto, on a scholarship provided because her mother was a graduate. She had declined the opportunity to "come out" as a debutante, having made a religious commitment at the age of eleven.[36] She was an all-round woman: athletic, playing on the university's basketball team and a swimmer. She would be a gold medalist when she graduated.

At the 1934 annual meeting three weeks after Stacey arrived in Canada, he heard Yvonne's report on behalf of the Toronto chapter that "the year's prayer meetings were continued regularly throughout exams." One participant who was shortly to write an exam was asked, "Why are you so beastly calm?" Yvonne replied, "Come up to the Tower tomorrow noon and see!"[37] Throughout her life with Stacey there would be many calls for that calmness, but she always exuded a warm, some say classy, ability to rise above every circumstance and challenge.

The family's financial situation improved with a legacy her grandfather left.

Joyce Ritchie was determined to go to Europe that summer of 1937, but Yvonne's engagement to Stacey had just been announced and she didn't want to leave him. But Yvonne did travel with her mother and sister Jocelyn. She attended the Budapest conference of the fledgling IFES,[38] little realizing that her husband, a decade later, would become its general secretary. Nor was Joyce Ritchie correct when she urged Yvonne to travel saying she might never get to Europe again: she was destined to live in Switzerland for forty-two years. In the mean time Stacey, as director of the last boy's camp at Doe Lake, was being razzed with "My bonnie lies over the ocean, Bring back my bonnie to me." The three women were away for six months.

On 30 April 1938 in the Church of the Redeemer, Yvonne Katherine Ritchie was married to Charles Stacey Woods. Rowland Hill noted in his diary for the day: "Mollie and I were in Toronto (by train) to see the wedding of Stacey Wood [he still hadn't got it right] and Yvonne Ritchie in an Anglican church then were at the reception. It was a very happy affair."[39] Stacey's proud parents were there to witness the event. Yvonne's uncle Eric McDougall gave her away. Her sister Jocelyn was her maid of honor. James Cowee, a classmate of Stacey's at Dallas, was his best man, and the ushers were Roger Deck, from Australia, in training in Canada to be a dentist ("a quiet, gentle, most conscientious man, dedicated to his profession and to supporting the Lord's work in every way that he could");[40] a cousin of Yvonne's,

Yvonne and Stacey on their wedding day, 30 April 1938, leaving the Anglican Church of the Redeemer, Toronto (Courtesy of Yvonne Woods)

Harry Dawson, and staffer Maurice Murphy. Stacey's later comment on his choice of a bride was, "I did one thing right. I prayed for the wife I needed and God gave me the wife He knew I needed."[41]

With Stacey's bachelor days now over, he could look back on the past four years in Canada with a sense of accomplishment. For a young man only twenty-eight, he had achieved a great deal and laid the foundation for a lifetime of ministry. He had resurrected a ministry that was about to go under, created an organization with a base of loyal supporters, many of whom were young and able, and had reined in a chaotic administrative structure as well as brought under control a camp that was going off on its own. It was a remarkable achievement in a time of economic depression and political stalemate. A year later Canada would be at war. But Stacey's horizons were broader; having established a base in one country, he was about to branch out into another. The mark of a successful Canadian has always been to make it big in the United States. Stacey Woods was about to do just that.

5

A League Beleaguered

HAVING SUCCESSFULLY LAUNCHED THE Inter-Varsity Christian Fellowship and shown considerable skill in bringing together the disparate evangelical and fundamentalist communities in Canada, it was inevitable that Stacey Woods would look south. There is a magnetic pull that draws Canadians with ambition to the United States. Particularly in the 1930s, Canada was a bit of a backwater, though very much in the center of the evangelical axis between Philadelphia (the CIM headquarters) and Chicago (Wheaton College and Moody Bible Institute).

In the United States at that time and within that network, polarities were developing. The breakup of that bastion of conservatism, Princeton Seminary, in 1929, with a new school, Westminster Theological Seminary, being established in Philadelphia; the fragmentation of the missionary effort with the 1934 formation of an Independent Board for Presbyterian Foreign Missions, headquartered in Philadelphia; the growth of Wheaton College under its new president, Presbyterian James Oliver Buswell, destined to become a player in the conflicts; and the rise of the Bible school movement with its related faith missionary organizations were all a feature of the time. In a way the United States was where the action was, and Stacey wanted to be part of it.

At the center of several of these developments was the towering figure of

J. Gresham Machen. A Southern patrician bachelor from Baltimore (his mother was from Georgia), he was a man that you either followed unquestioningly wherever his current cause might take you or you developed an intense dislike of him. Machen and Princeton Seminary had parted, starting a chain reaction of divisions arguably inevitable by what some saw as a courageous stand for principle and others an abrasive need for self-assertion. Either way, one had to admire Machen's tenacity, his singleminded pursuit of ecclesiastical purity, his intellectual brilliance and his self-deprecating and eccentric personality. He mesmerized a whole generation of students, both at Princeton and then Westminster.

LEAGUE OF EVANGELICAL STUDENTS

Machen was behind the formation of an organization called the League of Evangelical Students, founded in 1925 as a breakaway from an interseminary student movement that had just decided to include a Unitarian school. Initially the League drew membership from twenty postgraduate theological schools, but subsequently it branched out, allowing colleges and Bible schools to join. At its peak in the early 1930s under general secretary William Jones there were fifty chapters, with the balance increasingly tilting toward undergraduate institutions. The emphases of the League were on "the importance of doctrine to life, the place of apologetics in student witness, and the exclusiveness of supernatural Christianity."[1]

The formation of the League in 1925 was the first of a series of separations that took place among Presbyterians: the reorganization of Princeton Seminary, the formation of an Independent Board of Foreign Missions, and the establishment of a new Presbyterian denomination (only to split the following year into two fragments). The League was drawn into the conflict though it was supposed to be strictly interdenominational and not even specifically Reformed. Of the seven general secretaries during its eighteen-year life, the first four were graduates of what became known as "the old Princeton," and the last three were from Westminster Seminary. "It is giving away no secret to say that there has been a certain amount of tension within the League between the adherents of a Reformed world and life view and others," Robert E. Nicholas, the last functioning general secretary admitted. J. Gresham Machen's shadow towered over the League, and when he died tragically on New Year's Day 1937 it became part of his legacy, one to be preserved at all costs. In the view of some in the League, to allow it to collapse would be an act of betrayal to the memory of Machen. Its preservation was deeply emotional to some of its leadership. The League was part of a chain reaction that led to the loss of Princeton Seminary in 1929 and having been bought with that blood its continuance was a sacred obligation to ensure all the suffering was not in vain.

Stacey Woods had come to know of Machen while at Dallas Seminary, which had several Machen devotees on its faculty. At Wheaton he knew the strong biases of President Buswell, who later lost his job for being too emotionally involved in a denominational conflict. In late 1936 Buswell wrote Machen critiquing Westminster's emphasis on apologetics, what he saw as deemphasising evangelism, and its attitude toward the "separated life."[2] There was talk of a Wheaton College versus Dutch Calvinist polarity at Westminster, with the strict Calvinists led by Dutch-born Cornelius Van Til, professor of a new apologetic quite different from that of the "old Princeton" (and it might be added of the original Machen). When Charles Troutman and a car full of students came to the tenth annual convention of the League, held in Philadelphia's Tenth Presbyterian Church 21-24 February 1935, they were already primed. Troutman was not pleased. But looking over the program, it is not clear what brought down his ire. "There wasn't a single address I could understand," the pre-med student complained. The only member of the Westminster faculty on the program was systematic theologian John Murray, who spoke on the Friday afternoon of the conference. Murray, with his thick Scots brogue and uncompromising Calvinism, could be pretty obscure for the uninitiated.

The League's eleventh convention was held the next year in Chicago's Moody Bible Institute, hardly a bastion of Reformed theology. The story of that meeting is almost legendary in InterVarsity circles; Stacey came down from Toronto. Troutman stood up at one point and asked for help in reaching students for Christ: "I spoke for more than five minutes. I wasn't exactly coherent," he recalled later. He claimed that Cornelius Van Til "tore up to the rostrum and said he demanded an investigation of liberalism among the members. And then he said evangelism was the curse of the church."[3] Troutman started to apologize, as he remembered it, and that led to another round. As the time for adjournment came, Machen strode up to Troutman—this much sounds authentic—and said, "Now look, you keep trying to get help for evangelism. The League needs it."

Troutman and Woods drove back together to Wheaton, and Charles asked, "Stacey, what did I say tonight?" He continued, "And he sort of chuckled and then he explained to me in Australian English, and that was sort of the end as far as the League was concerned. The opposition to evangelism and devotional rites and help for undergraduates was so blatant, that was the last of the large annual conventions." Troutman's explanation for the demise of the League is somewhat simplistic. Two months later Stacey wrote Machen, "We feel that it would be a great contribution and blessing to our student work in Canada if you are able to help us at our Eighth Annual University Conference,"[4] requesting him to be a speaker at the eighth university conference in the autumn. In his letter he contrasts the approach of the League with that of Inter-Varsity: in the United States delegates to the annual meeting made their own arrangements for accommodation while in Canada the seventy students were in residence. Machen was being asked to speak on the resurrection "from its practical and doctrinal aspects at our four morning sessions." The previous year, he notes, the theme was the atonement. It was heavy doctrinal fare.

Machen, as he always did, replied immediately, requesting more information and indicating that he was off to the General Assembly. Four days, he explained, was "an extensive commitment and the calls upon me are very burdensome." In response, urging him to seriously consider the invitation, Woods wrote:

> Our situation in Canada is rather different from that in the United States. Our students are not as alert to the theological issues of the moment. With many their Church association is such that while they are not being confronted with definite denial and unbelief, yet there are serious omissions. This produces a condition of apathy which results in acquiescence of Modernism, or failure to appreciate its true significance when presented.[5]

He then added most significantly that he hoped that Calvin Knox Cummings, general secretary of the League at the time, would come with Machen. "I hope that there may be some opportunity for the discussion on the subject of apologetics in the programme of the Inter-Varsity Christian Fellowship. Up to the present this has not been our forte." So much for the impression that the break with the League claiming the issue was apologetics versus evangelism. It was certainly not seen as a dividing point in the 1936 Woods-Machen correspondence.

On 11 June 1936 the General Assembly that Machen referred to elected him first moderator of the newly constituted Presbyterian Church in America. The day before, he had written Stacey declining his invitation, "I am very glad to know that your Inter-Varsity Christian Fellowship is increasingly aware of the necessity of

Christian apologetics. I should do anything I could to stimulate such interest." But there were "multitudinous duties" that were weighing him down in "an extremely trying and overcrowded time." Westminster faculty had written intemperate articles describing premillennialism and dispensationalism as heresies. Machen, crushed by the weight of impending division and being unceremoniously dumped as head of the Independent Board the month before, went off exhausted to South Dakota during the Christmas holidays and died there of pneumonia on New Year's Day at the age of 55. With his death many of the causes he championed were threatened. Westminster almost went under, and the days of the League were clearly numbered. Most seriously, an atmosphere of vitriol prevailed among erstwhile allies. As Chafer wrote Woods in 1940 about the four specifically evangelical seminaries (Westminster, Faith, Grace and Dallas), "we are poison one to the other."[6]

Exploring a Vision

On the ride back from his famous encounter with Van Til, Troutman was asked by Stacey to join Inter-Varsity staff on graduation that spring from Wheaton College. As an American—Charles was the son of a prosperous manufacturer in Butler, Pennsylvania—the likelihood of Charles moving to the United States, after he had served in Canada for a while, was apparently mooted. By January of 1938 Woods was approaching Lewis Chafer as to "the possibility and wisdom of an attempt to extend our Canadian student work into the United States of America."[7]

Chafer was vice president of the League, but in his reply he reflected that it had "never made any progress" and was dominated by Westminster Seminary, which is "now in a great slump and decline." He did not intend to continue with the League and assured Stacey, "If you could come into this country and take over the universities and colleges, of which we have about a thousand, and let our League return to its original purpose of serving seminary students, I should think that we had accomplished very much indeed." Chafer encouraged him to come to the next annual meeting, to be held the following month. Instead, Stacey in his response declined the invitation because, as he admitted, the dates conflicted with an extensive foray he was making to the United States, visiting Detroit, Washington, Baltimore, Philadelphia, New York, Albany and Schenectady. "During this trip," he added, "I hope to discover what possibilities there may be for our carrying on work in American universities."[8]

The chronology of Stacey's several journeys to the United States at that period is unclear, but it would appear the first trip included a visit to Ann Arbor, Michigan, where he dropped "in on a group of students meeting for prayer."[9] Then he went on to Baltimore, where he visited Howard Kelly, the outstanding gynecological surgeon at Johns Hopkins Hospital and a professional colleague of Sir William Osler.[10] Kelly was known for his outspoken Christian testimony at the hospital, delegating surgery in the middle of an operation in order to prepare for a Bible class. When Kelly was commended to the author Sinclair Lewis as a scientist of faith he asked, "What does an obstetrician know about the Virgin Birth?" One of his students commented that "the only interest he manifested in my classmates whether they were saved."[11]

Stacey described his first visit to Kelly's mansion on Eutaw Place in Baltimore's Reservoir Hill neighborhood, at the time an exclusive enclave of Victorian houses overlooking Druid Park. Osler maintained that "he had the highest income of any surgeon in America."[12] Kelly was not home, having gone to see Sonja Heine, whom he explained to Woods when he got home "is my favourite actress." Woods was introduced to Kelly's collection of snakes while taking a bath, the viper being in a box at the end of the tub. "I quickly beat an ignominious retreat to my room leaving the wretched serpent fully in charge."

In 1927 Howard Kelly had bankrolled America's Keswick in Whiting's, New Jersey, where he was a frequent speaker, subsequently a venue for InterVarsity conferences. He was on many boards, including that of CIM, and wrote regularly for Sunday School Times and Moody Monthly. His generosity and self-sacrifice was legendary, not that he ever wanted to draw attention to himself. It is estimated that in the final decade of his life he gave away three quarters of a million dollars, a considerable sum in those days. Kelly had approached Howard Guinness when he came to Canada, promising him a salary and a secretary if he would start a ministry in the United States. From his 1938 visit to Kelly's death in 1943, Stacey noted that Kelly "became one of our first great financial supporters in the United States." Again, Stacey had made a conquest.

From Baltimore Stacey went on to Philadelphia, where he was booked to speak at a weekday afternoon meeting at George Palmer's auditorium, a gathering place for the large fundamentalist-evangelical community in the area. In the audience that afternoon was Margaret Haines, who came up afterward to speak to him. The Haines family was the nearest thing to aristocracy that Americans could admit:

their ancestral home in Germantown, "Wyck," is now a national historic site. The Haines family had over eight generations amassed a considerable fortune. They had been Quakers, but Miss Haines attended the Reformed Episcopal Church of the Atonement, not far from the home that she and her mother now occupied, just down the street from the China Inland Mission's American headquarters.

The lifelong passion of Margaret Haines was student ministry.[13] As a teenager she had attended Northfield summer conferences, went to the 1919 Des Moines quadrennial of the Student Volunteer Movement shortly before leaving for India as a missionary. That meeting marked, as she said, "a drift away from the original standards." Student Volunteer Movement pioneer Robert Wilder, a family intimate, prayed in 1935 at the Haines family worship, "Oh Lord, turn the Volunteer Movements, the Student YMCA's and the World Student Christian Movement back to the old gospel, or, if that is not to be, raise up another movement to take their place founded on the Biblical gospel." On a 1932 furlough, while attending classes at Westminster Seminary (then downtown), she became a "regional staff member" of the League, and traveled south to contact college chapters. Three years later she became convinced that "the League was not moving forward. It needed more emphasis upon prayer and personal evangelism. Moreover, it appeared too defensive." She left Stacey's presentation impressed "that here at last was something that is going to move." "I told Stacey that I felt there was a tremendous need and that I would do what I could to back the movement if he felt led of the Lord to come."[14] Her involvement would be absolutely crucial for the future of the American movement.

Stacey's final stopover en route home to Toronto was Schenectady in upper New York state. The year before a thirty-four-year-old minister was called from Canada to historic First Presbyterian Church there. Herbert S. Mekeel, a lifelong bachelor, had been known to Stacey during his Canadian sojourn as one who had immediate rapport with youth.[15] Schenectady's chief employer was General Electric, and Mekeel sent over 230 men, either young G.E. engineers or members of the local Union College IVCF chapter, into the ministry, on the dubious basis that a call could be assumed unless the Almighty had clearly been negative about the idea. The result could be disastrous. As an early player in the National Association of Evangelicals Mekeel had wide influence and enlisted many into supporting InterVarsity and providing reassurance that the organization was not antichurch. Beginning with Charles Troutman, Mekeel was a confidant of staff, many of whom he recruited.

Union College IVCF chapter was one of the earlier and larger groups, and was dominated by Mekeel and his church.

On 9 March, following his return to Toronto, Stacey wrote Lewis Chafer:

> I have just retuned from a four weeks' trip into the United States, during which time I met a number of Christian leaders, and talked with them concerning the advisability of extending our student work into the United States. Without an exception, those upon whom I called welcomed the idea and promised their support wherever possible. It would seem as though God is leading in this direction.[16]

He received an encouraging response. When at the League's annual convention in Grand Rapids, Michigan, Chafer had spoken of "the possibility of extending [Stacey's] work into the United States. As I anticipated, there was a feeling that this would somewhat confuse their own activities." Instructions had been given Arthur Olson to be in touch "and find out on what ground a more cordial cooperation between the two lines of work might be set up." Then he added the clincher: "As a matter of fact, the League of Evangelical Students of the United States is doing next to nothing."[17]

Stacey reported to the executive committee on "his visit to the United States, stating that there had been requests both from students and Christian friends that the work of Inter-Varsity be extended into that country," and in late March the board approved "the extension of the work into the Maritimes and into the United States." Charles Troutman was the first to take up this opening, visiting, over the Easter weekend (17 April), Schenectady and establishing a close relationship with Herbert Mekeel, and then traveling on to Ithaca. In November he made a further sortie, writing in his diary: "Had an hour chat with Mr Mekeel about the US situation showing him what we have done and have planned. He agrees with me on many lines as opposed to Stacey." Stacey's approach was more cautious. Encouraged by the visionary and impulsive Mekeel, Troutman went on to visit some of the Ivy League schools: Yale, Harvard and Dartmouth.

The meeting between Stacey and Arthur Olson duly took place in June 1938 at a student conference at America's Keswick. Although originally thinking of a comity arrangement, Margaret Haines, having seen that such agreements did not work on the mission field, discouraged it and told him to strike out on his own. "It needs to be emphasized," Stacey reflected forty years later "that we had no master plan to pioneer the American movement, nor was there any thought of empire building, only a growing conviction that God was calling Inter-Varsity in Canada to pioneer evangelical student witness in that great nation south of its border."[18] Certainly the British movement was appalled. Douglas Johnson wrote, "Dear Stacey—I'm *sure* that the Americans don't need our help, the League of Evangelical Students is more orthodox than we—look at those articles by Machen!"[19]

MAKING THE MOVE

Through the academic year 1938-1939, steady progress was made in infiltrating the United States. In the autumn Stacey and Yvonne were invited to visit some students at the University of Michigan in Ann Arbor, the result being the formation of an evangelical union. By February there were three other groups: one in Ypsilanti and two in Wayne State in Detroit and Michigan State in Lansing. These schools drew students from the heartland of the Christian Reformed Church (four League of Evangelical Students annual meetings were held in Michigan, three in Grand Rapids one in Holland) and there was clear conflict with the League, though no staff had visited League chapters in the state since Cummings went there following his appointment as secretary in 1934. There was also a contact at Philadelphia's Swarthmore College, where the novelist Grace Livingston Hill and her factotum, Bob Cressy, were sympathetic. On 19 March 1939, following a visit in Montreal from Stacey en route to Halifax, Troutman wrote in his diary, "I may be in Ann Arbor next year." By 16 July the die was cast. "This afternoon," again to quote Troutman's diary, "Stacey spoke to prospective secretaries on the basic principals (*sic*) of the Fellowship. The more I hear and study our work, the more I feel that for the next few years God is calling us as a mission and as missionaries to bring a new type of evangelism to universities in America." That autumn Troutman went to Michigan, Grace Koch, who had started an embryonic chapter while a student at Swarthmore, was sent to Philadelphia, and Herb Butt, a graduate of the University of Washington, was to include working in the American Pacific Northwest in addition to his responsibilities in Vancouver. In October a bank account was opened in Detroit.

That momentous summer of 1939 the fourth International Conference of Evangelical Students met in Cambridge, England. Stacey was to represent the Canadian Inter-Varsity but pled that the expansion of the work now made that impossible. Professor Clarence Bouma of Calvin Seminary spoke for the League as a member of their advisory board. Douglas Johnson, as secretary, "reported that there were several University Christian Unions in the Northern States bordering on Canada that had entered into friendly relationship with the Inter-Varsity Christian Fellowship of Canada."[20] It was hoped that on Bouma's return to America there could be "friendly consultation" between the two organizations. Clearly the international body was unhappy with the implicit competition between two evangelical student groups.

The final break was not a happy one. "The League faces a crisis," wrote Olsen's successor as secretary, Robert Nicholas, in an undated letter some time in late 1939. Its magazine stopped publication; its funds were exhausted. In 1943 it merged with the fundamentalist (and non-Reformed) Intercollegiate Gospel Fellowship of New York City. There was a sense of betrayal by its leadership, which all of the rationalization by InterVarsity could not erase. Troutman revisited the history a dozen years later; perhaps the date was no coincidence as a bullish young Campus Crusade for Christ was making the same criticisms (lack of zeal in evangelism and staff neglect) that InterVarsity had once aimed at the League. Cummings, providing his take, told Troutman that the rise of InterVarsity (and the destruction of the League) was due to "an attitude of indifference or compromise toward the modernism that was capturing the visible church."[21] Paul Woolley, another secretary, in an extraordinary response accused InterVarsity Christian Fellowship of having "very little interest in Christian doctrine and fundamental Christian ethical principles," and closed by saying, "if you ever rediscover the moral law it will be an excellent additional asset."[22] Woolley, as a custodian of the Machen legacy, felt it had been squandered.

Toward the end of his life Troutman made a striking observation: "We reacted and we never did have the theological emphasis that we should have had, and most Inter-Varsities around the world have. Because after all, Westminster was the conservative seminary, and we turned against them and they turned against us."[23] Certainly if some sort of accommodation could have been reached between the two, perhaps defining their territory as the League's being theological seminaries and that of IVCF's being universities and colleges, there would have been less acrimony and both institutions would have been strengthened. But such was not to be.

6

Expansion South

FRED WOODS WAS DYING. He was only sixty-six years old and had planned a major evangelistic itinerary through Great Britain on his way home to Australia. The day before the elder Woods's were to leave Toronto, after living with the newlyweds for eleven months, Daisy Woods had an emergency appendectomy. As she was recovering from surgery, Fred slipped on the ice, was hospitalized, operated on and after a month succumbed to an infection. On his deathbed in Toronto's West General Hospital he turned to Stacey and said, "For me to live is Christ, and to die is gain."

Fred Woods's death was a devastating blow to Stacey, who was numbed by its suddenness. Charles Troutman, driving in from Montreal, got the news by telegram west of Cobourg, two hours east of Toronto, and hurried to the office, to be told by Stacey when he arrived that there was nothing for him to do. "We talked over camps and the US situation for the rest of the morning."[1] Stacey appeared completely disoriented and found relief in talking about ministry. It would be a different future without his father.

Stacey did not invite confidences, nor did he have close friendships. For a while it seemed that Charles Troutman would fill that void, but their relationship unraveled after the war. There were others to whom he was close, men and women he admired, individuals that influenced him, staff with whom he shared ministry. Friendship with Stacey was a high-risk venture, and few got below the surface as his guard was always up. He was better at giving than receiving advice and help. Fred Woods's death left a gigantic hole in his life. It was fortuitous that Fred died a year and a day after Stacey married. Yvonne was the closest thing he had as a confidant, and his sons in retrospect were not sure that even she got beneath his protective armor.

Fred Woods's funeral was a remarkable tribute both to the cohesion of the Christian Brethren community in Toronto and the impact that his son had already made. Led by E. A. Brownlee, a capacity crowd in the large downtown Central Assembly of the Christian Brethren attended. "It was a wonderful service—a triumphant one," was Troutman's comment. Fred Woods was interred alongside the mother of Cathie Nicoll in Toronto's Mount Pleasant Cemetery in a donated plot. Toronto Christian Brethren had paid all his (and Daisy's) medical expenses, and also bought Daisy's ticket home. Australia mourned Fred Woods: "His bright and attractive way of presenting the gospel always drew large congregations and many can testify to the blessing he brought to their lives" was the tribute in the *Australian Missionary Tidings.*[2] Daisy stayed on until autumn, when Yvonne and Stacey accompanied her to the west coast. He never saw his mother again. It would be twenty-three years before he returned to the land of his birth.

The Fellowship and War

The summer of 1939 was an ominous time. Stacey, as business manager at Pioneer, and Yvonne, as hostess, may have been far away from events in Europe. But at the last prewar meeting of the International Fellowship of Evangelical Students, held in Cambridge, England, 27 June to 2 July 1939, the minutes say:

> In the absence of other matters voted urgent, the Chairman referred to one final matter which he felt was of no small concern to all of those present the imminent threat of another world war. There were many signs indicating that only a divine miracle could avert what seemed to be an inevitable outbreak of war between the European powers probably in the early Autumn of 1939. No one could foresee the results through the world of further tragic happenings such as those which took place in 1914-1918.

It then added a poignant reminder that the "only means of communication (and a *safe* means of communication with each other) might be via God's 'throne of grace.' "[3]

Christmas 1938, Daisy and Fred Woods (left) with Stacey and Yvonne in their
first apartment in Toronto (Courtesy of Yvonne Woods)

Within a week after the outbreak of hostilities on 1 September, Stacey signed a
statement endorsing the conflict. "As an organization we are in full sympathy with
the action of the British Governments and wholeheartedly desire to support this
righteous war in every way the constitution of our organization will permit, realizing of course that our first responsibility is to God." There was no equivocation in
his remarks: "It is our responsibility to lead students to understand clearly the
scriptural, consistent attitude we should maintain. Personally, I feel that in this instance pacifism is selfish, immoral, and anarchistic and unscriptural."[4]

With this memorandum Stacey sent out a tract by the Baptist separatist fire-
brand and imperial loyalist T. T. Shields, minister of Jarvis Street Church, Toronto.
It was Troutman, signing himself as an "anti-pacifist of Quebec," who said "I cannot give it out with a recommendation." Being located in Quebec, whose antiwar
and fascist leanings were soon going to be fully revealed, he described Stacey's stand
as "extremely weak on any university campus." He attempted to take the moral
high ground: "The arguments of pacifists and imperialists have no place in the consideration; minor questions are not even relevant; while the personal responsibility
to the Saviour is predominant. In this case, our position is not one of facts and evidences, but of relationship, it is no longer apologetic, but moral."[5]

This was the first time Troutman had taken issue with Stacey. They met up a
few days later at the beginning of staff conference at Guelph, Ontario. On 18 Sep-

tember Troutman noted, "Stacey and I had a long chat regarding the Fellowship and war and, unless I am misunderstood, we are much on the same ground while his more 'active participation' is in evidence, yet he feels that God has given us opportunities of a different nature through the war—and we must take them whether at home or overseas, we are to be his ambassadors, and nothing is to take precedence over loyalty to the Saviour."[6] Stacey had clarity and decisiveness; Charles, though less coherent, was the careful listener with deeply felt piety.

HERBERT J. TAYLOR

In early October of 1939 Stacey journeyed to Chicago and, in the course of his visit to Wheaton, called on a remarkable man. It would be difficult to overestimate the significance of Herbert J. Taylor in making possible Inter-Varsity's advance into the United States. Stacey would describe him as "a close friend, a wise counsellor, but never a dictator." Taylor was born in 1893 in the remote Upper Peninsula of Michigan, son of an entrepreneur lumberman. Professing faith in Christ at the age of sixteen at the Pickford Methodist Church, during World War I he served overseas with the YMCA, which gave him a lifelong interest in youth ministries. He returned to the United States to go into the oil and real estate business in Oklahoma. Having prospered, he settled in Chicago, working in a tea company. In 1932 he acquired the bankrupt Club Aluminum Company. He reversed its fortunes and gave 25 percent of the stock to a Christian Workers' Foundation. This was shortly after he met Stacey, and the initial profits went to start IVCF. Though he gave generously to causes such as Fuller Theological Seminary and a Methodist foundation for higher education, his main interest was four organizations that focused on youth at various stages of development: Child Evangelism, Christian Service Brigade and Pioneer Girls (for teenage boys and girls), Young Life (for high schoolers) and InterVarsity Christian Fellowship.

Being the sort of man he was, Taylor immediately took ownership of the vision that Stacey had given him. Stacey's requests grew as he responded to that interest. In October he was asking in an almost obsequious letter for money for printing two issues of the *Student News Bulletin;* the following month in response to a general appeal Taylor promised the salary of one of the three working in the United States. The day after an interview in Taylor's office on 17 January 1940, Stacey wrote somewhat breathlessly to Donald Fleming, as chair of the Canadian IVCF board, reporting that Taylor guaranteed an immediate donation of $1,000 and, starting in September, an annual gift of $5,000. For that he made three conditions: that a U.S. headquarters be set up in Chicago, the American work be independent, and that "I be set free to help in the development of the work in the United States."[7] That same day, Stacey wrote Taylor requesting immediate funding for an all-seasons dining hall cum hospitality suite for Pioneer Camp. He was feeling increasingly comfortable approaching Taylor for money, and there seemed to be a lot of it.

In the midst of all these negotiations Stacey and Yvonne's first child was born. Frederick Stephen, named after his grandfather, arrived 29 March 1940. There was both joy and sadness: sorrow that Fred was not able to share the news of his namesake, but gratitude for a safe delivery. They were now a family, though Stacey's busyness at the time gave him little time for celebration, and there was no letup in his travels and arrangements for IVCF's southward expansion. Fortunately Yvonne's mother rose to the challenge and provided backup care. And there were always summers together at Pioneer, though Stacey had mixed feelings about children being too visible while ministry was proceeding. Children could be a distraction, not only for parents but also for campers who, in common with everyone, adored babies.

One week after the birth of his first child, Stacey was at Union Station to welcome Herbert Taylor to Toronto. They proceeded to the board room of the Board of Trade in the King Edward Hotel, three blocks from the station, and discussed relations between Canada and the United States. "The growth of the Inter-Varsity Christian Fellowship in the United States has created certain problems of organization and administration," the minutes opened. Relations between Canada and the United States should continue,

Stacey Woods c. 1940 (Courtesy of IVCF-USA)

but the American branch required its own board, with two members from each board sitting on the other. There should be one common General Secretary. Starting 1 September, a Chicago office was to be set up to care for the American work, handling "finances, correspondence, payment of staff, and other matters pertaining to the United States work." That month three Americans were added to the Canadian board: John Frederick Strombeck,[8] H. J. Taylor and Charles Troutman Sr., father of Stacey's Wheaton roommate, who had also been a trustee of the college.

AN OFFICE IN CHICAGO

Stacey was to move to Chicago in time for an office setup on 1 September 1940, but his immigration clearance was delayed. Charles Troutman, as an American, was sent to Chicago instead. He arrived on 11 September and was immediately struck by the contrast between the new American operation and the time, four years earlier, when he had come to a wool yarn store at 81 Bloor Street in Toronto and thought he had made a mistake. Then

> getting courage the next morning by a phone call we found our way up an inside stairs to the dingy second floor offices. Today I drove to the Civic Office Building and parked in a great car lot, went thru the swinging doors into a great marble and gala lobby. The express elevators popped my ears going up to the 31st floor and there Bob Walker was already at work in 3112.[9]

Bob Walker was a remarkable gift by Herbert Taylor to the fledgling organization.[10] Walker had been a cub reporter in Michigan before becoming Taylor's assistant and general secretary of Taylor's Christian Workers' Foundation. He had drive and creativity, his father and uncle having invented the electric dishwasher. Stacey's immigration clearance finally came through on 23 September, and he joined Troutman and Taylor by mid-October. Muriel Clark's status took a little longer to be cleared, but she was setting up the Chicago office by early November.

In November Margaret Haines and Edward Ross, both of Philadelphia, and Davis Weyerhaeuser[11] of Tacoma, Washington, were also added to the Canadian board. On 4 January 1941, with Ross and Taylor coming up from the United States to attend the Canadian board meeting, there was a lengthy discussion as to leadership of the two movements and a final motion approved, calling for each movement to have their own general secretary commencing in September. The board then called for an independent American board: Stacey would be general secretary in the United States, provided someone else could be found to lead the Canadian movement. Soon after there were second thoughts. On 14 April 1941, at a board meeting that lasted well past midnight, Troutman recorded, "There are some misunderstandings in Canada over the U.S. proposal to have two separate works, not because of any national feeling or desire for control, but because such a plan would eliminate Stacey from Canada." The Canadians were beginning to feel keenly the possibility of losing Stacey.

Stacey provided strong leadership at a five-day staff meeting that started in Guelph (fifty miles outside Toronto) on Monday, 26 May 1941. That day, seated informally around two large tables, he led the twenty staff present in three sessions: in the morning, the purpose of the Fellowship "as related to our work"; in the afternoon on organization; and finally in the evening he touched on staff issues.[12] "As a sign of the blessing of God," Troutman noted, "these 'business' sessions have been heart searching." Stacey defined the purpose of Inter-Varsity as being first to help students "go on with God," and second, the evangelization of the campus. Staff were to be "pastors to the student group to assist them in presenting Christ to the campus. With this purpose in mind, the prayer meetings, Bible studies, and every gathering of the chapter should be subservient to this purpose."

Tuesday Stacey dealt with organizational matters, responding to the criticism he had received that Inter-Varsity was not democratic. "This is perfectly true," he countered, "as we exist only to serve students who desire help. Instead of having students concerned with a national organization, their efforts are concentrated on their own campus. While they do not have a vote in the national organization, they are autonomous on their own."[13] That evening Stacey really laid it on the staff. "Unless we are going on with God, it is not a spiritual work we are doing," he counseled them. Like Ignatius Loyola, Stacey stressed the spiritual disciplines for his workers but also emphasized the need for study, reminding them of his earlier encouragement to read a book a week.

Troutman drove Stacey to Toronto to attend his sister-in-law Jocelyn's wedding to Rex Symons on Wednesday afternoon, 29 May, missing out on a presentation by Jim Rayburn about his Young Life Campaign. Rayburn's Texas slang, Troutman noted, annoyed Cathie Nicoll, but "I believe Jim is closer to our ways than any other U.S. group I know." By now the staff were beginning to flag. To help out, Charles perpetrated a practical joke; he sent a telegram that a former staff member whom Stacey did not find easy had arrived to meet with the board. "He was in a positive dither, calling Mr Fleming and pacing the floor." "She" called through the door at dinner time, Stacey blanched, but finally discovered that the joke was on him. That Thursday staff time was spent on details about office routines, promotion and the possibility of a publication. The final day focused on the challenge ahead. Solemn commitments were made by staff with some trepidation. The budget for the United States was to be doubled and "the Canadian staff is hard hit for now. As [Stacey] was telling us of what is ahead of us a great wave of helplessness came over me and a burden of prayer for what the Lord has given us the privilege of doing," Troutman noted. "God does not work in our ways."

By now American board members had arrived, and the final gathering of the joint board was convened Saturday in Toronto. Staff made their way warily into the city. Not only had they to compete with a defense loan parade that had clogged downtown, they had other concerns. Fifteen of them made their way to the University of Toronto's Hart House for a gala evening of celebration. On arrival they were relieved to hear that only the boards were separating, and that they could continue to meet together, and university work would remain as one. Chairman Donald Fleming stated that Stacey's leadership was essential for both countries, and Stacey would continue as general secretary of each. The evening was not without its humor: the Americans were slow to rise when a toast was proposed to the King. When it came to toasting President Franklin Roosevelt, diehard Republican Strombeck refused, muttering "I won't toast that man." The new separate American board reconvened after the festivities. A subcommittee reported on a constitution, American staff were appointed for the forthcoming year, and a budget was approved in principle. Final approval of a constitution for the American InterVarsity was given 2 September. At the end of October, H. J. Taylor came back to Toronto and helped set up a publications committee, much of whose work he would subsidize. The two movements would now be on their own.

Twenty-four-year-old Mel Donald, a native of Medicine Hat, Alberta, was left in charge in Canada as assistant general secretary. Donald had been a student leader at the University of Alberta, and following graduation he became an Inter-School Christian Fellowship staffer in Edmonton. He recalled orientation at Ontario Pioneer the August he joined staff. He was told to ensure that the tuck-shop, where mattresses were left all winter, was mouse proof. There was a single day of instruction before Stacey left for Wheaton with Yvonne and fifteen-month-old Frederick Stephen. It had been a year since the family lived under one roof. The Woods family moved to a house on Madison Avenue.

The major accomplishment of the autumn of 1941 was the appearance of a new monthly magazine, which was called by Stacey *HIS*. Bob Walker was appointed executive editor 7 October and the first issue went to press a week later, launched (as Stacey would recall three years later) "on the turgid waters of religious journalism. Canada was already at war. USA was girding herself to 'the sticking point' so suddenly to be jolted into war at Pearl Harbor. Editor Robert Walker led with his chin and there was enough provocation—as well as flotsam and jetsam—in the first issue for brickbats as well as bouquets."[14] In the United States all donors received a free copy, and they were sent out to the universities in sufficient numbers for half those active in InterVarsity chapters to receive a copy. "We hope this will whet their appetite," Stacey explained. "We hope that after the third issue there will be enough subscribers to pay most of the cost of production."[15]

The editorial policy of *HIS* was threefold, as Stacey outlined it. "First, everything printed in *His* should be to the glory of God. Second, all articles should have that element of compulsion which would make them readable, for no matter how good the article, it is useless if unread. Third, each article should meet a need or solve a real problem."[16] *HIS* magazine, with its "down-to-earth realism in Christian living and student witness," arguably did more to put InterVarsity on the landscape of American evangelicalism than anything else. It was always a magazine that was close to Stacey's heart. He could be said at times to have micromanaged it. *HIS* was InterVarsity projected on a national stage and increased its influence and prestige exponentially. As Troutman said, "I cannot imagine the first two decades of InterVarsity without *His* magazine."[17]

With the uncertainties of impending conflict and the subsequent attack on Pearl Harbor, the United States was distracted, and by Christmas Eve Stacey was writing to Mel that, unlike Canada, which had done better financially, salaries were only paid up to the end of November, making for a lean holiday for staff. "I heartily sympathize with you in feeling that so much needs to be done," he responded sympathetically to Mel's frequent concerns. "I feel very much that way myself and long to run away from it all—which I guess would be cowardly on my part." In wishing that Mel would have a real rest over Christmas, he mentioned the fact that he had not had more than two weeks vacation for the past three and a half years. But he did not lose his sense of humor; at the end of a three-page letter earlier that month he wrote, "I hope that this is all I have got to write to you for today. And I guess you do too, if you're as sick of reading this as I am of droning it out. If you come to the office one morning and the dictaphone is missing don't bother writing to the Chicago office for it because it won't be returned."[18]

The financial situation did not improve immediately. By April 1942 he wrote, "things are so much in a flux in our US work that we just don't know quite where we are." He refers to his "big effort to get out of the Fellowship this year, that is, resignation to take effect in the summer," but with Charles Troutman being called up for service in the armed forces, that was now out of the question.[19] A year after Pearl Harbor, however, as the country got into a wartime rhythm, he was more positive. He told the American board, "An unprecedented number of conversions and other definite steps in spiritual progress have been reported during this Fall as compared with a similar period in previous years. The IVCF staff and students have had a sense of urgency coupled with unusual opportunities for personal conversation." There were now sixty affiliated chapters with work in an additional sixty campuses, but finances were a continuing problem. An appeal for three thousand dollars by the end of 1942 had just gone out. The letter said that 45 percent of arrears in salaries for 1941-1942 had been paid in November in spite of income being down, but there was a need for more to bring staff up to their full stipend.[20] Without backup from the Christian Workers Foundation it could have been much worse.

In 1942 Stacey deposited fifty dollars on a house at 510 Lincoln Avenue in Wheaton, where the family lived for their final two wartime years in the United States. Their second son, Charles Geoffrey, was born there 8 March 1943. Daisy Woods wrote expressing her pleasure at the meaning of Geoffrey's name, "the gift of God," and the inclusion of "Charles" also gratified her as a reminder of the Stilwell connection. On 24 July 1943 she died at the Ruhamah Rest Home in Hurstville of "chronic endocarditis," according to the death certificate, which was signed by her son-in-law.[21] She was only sixty-six, but since Fred died, her heart had slowly given way. Though he had often been an absent husband, she had grown very dependent on him. When the news came, Stacey was at the Stony Brook summer conference grounds (on Long Island) and wanted to go home for consolation but remained until the end of the session. He was a man of his word and duty trumped everything.

WHEATON CONNECTIONS

Living in Wheaton had definite advantages for Stacey, aside from inexpensive housing and a good train service into Chicago to the IVCF office. He was often invited to speak at the Wheaton College daily (and compulsory) chapel. As always in his pulpit ministry, he inspired students and became a well-known and respected figure on campus. And he was able to reach the whole Wheaton College constituency. He wrote "fellow Wheatonites" on 29 August 1942 saying,

> In our work we have looked to Wheaton for a good portion of our staff. This year five of fifteen members are Wheaton alumni. This year we are starting out with an increased staff, many, many new openings, and in new territory. We feel that this year, with men going directly to battle stations, our work takes on new significance.[22]

The link was even stronger when Ted M. Benson, Wheaton class of 1938, who did promotional work for the college, also became public relations director for IVCF.

Among other Wheatonites now with IVCF was former assistant dean of women Lois Dickason, a classmate of Charles Troutman, whom she had married earlier that year, and who took his place on staff while he was shipped to Australia by the military. Jane Hollingsworth, Wheaton class of 1940 with three years at Biblical Seminary, New York City, had just been appointed.[23] Her initiation consisted of a staff meeting at Guelph. There she inquired of Stacey what was involved in working for InterVarsity. He answered simply, "The Lord will lead you." In her southern drawl she replied, "The Lord can't lead a vacuum." To which he replied, "You're no vacuum." She was sent off to Vancouver to observe Ann Carroll at work and later the more experienced Herb Butt. It was Jane who brought inductive Bible study to InterVarsity. Her *Discovering the Gospel of Mark*, InterVarsity Press's first publication, was a landmark in making the Fellowship what Stacey had always wanted it to be, a Bible study movement. As he would say, "Jane's gift is teaching the Word, and I think it is also presenting Christ as Saviour through the Word, and in this God has blessed her ministry . . . she has not been given a gift of Bible teaching for the sake of Bible teaching, but a Bible-teaching ministry with an evangelistic emphasis."[24]

There were and would be other Wheaton graduates. Ken Taylor, class of 1938, rejoined InterVarsity in 1943, having been appointed for a year, in 1939, staff member for southwestern Ontario and Montreal.[25] As editor of *HIS* he continued for three years until he joined Good News Publishers. When Ken left staff at the beginning of 1947, Stacey wrote, "Under Ken's leadership *His* has made great progress in quality, size, and circulation, but most important of all, in effective spiritual ministry."[26] Ken Taylor later became famous as the paraphraser of the *Living Bible*.

In 1944 Stacey was speaking about student work at chapel at Faith Seminary, suburban Philadelphia, when he met Joe and Mary Lou Bayly, Wheaton graduates of 1941 and 1942. They set up an appointment and were hired on the spot. Stacey sent them up to Pioneer Camp in Ontario, and then they were assigned as a couple to the whole of New England and upper New York state, living initially in a cottage on John Bolten's Andover farm. Being classified 4-D for American selective service, Joe was exempt from call-up and provided mature leadership in a part of the country where staff were thinly spread and there was rapid growth. Three years later Stacey wrote, "I cannot say how greatly I am praising God, Joe, for the fact that you and Mary Lou are united [in] feeling that the Fellowship is God's call for you."[27]

Joe Bayly reciprocated those feelings, writing in a monthly staff report to Stacey: "It is good to be able to place complete trust in the man, under God, who leads the organisation in which one works."[28] Fourteen years later Joe Bayly was described by Stacey as "such a decent fellow, such a godly fellow, and such a worthwhile fellow, an asset to our work."[29] Joe Bayly was one of the most articulate advocates of a progressive evangelicalism. His *Gospel Blimp* allowed fundamentalists to laugh at themselves. Joe would freely admit that he owed much of his growth in ministry to his strong bond with Stacey. Stacey saw Bayly's potential and confidently freed him to use his extraordinary gifts, which were developed through much pain and great joy. Joe was enriched by his family, the wider IVCF community, *HIS* readers and the entire Christian world.

Other Wheaton graduates who joined IVCF that same year were Polly Barkhuff, class of 1936, appointed to Philadelphia, a ten-year staff veteran and Barbara Boyd's recruiter to staff, and Connie Johnston, class of 1943, daughter of longtime board member and grande dame Mrs. F. Cliffe Johnston.[30] Mrs. Johnston's upscale apartment at 927 Fifth Avenue became a venue for ministry in Manhattan.

It is fascinating that staff members who, like Stacey, had no personal experience of student life in a secular university proved so effective in ministering in an environment vastly different from that of Wheaton. Back in April 1941 Stacey and Charles Troutman had discussed the pressure Stacey was under to include Christian colleges and seminaries in InterVarsity's brief. Troutman was opposed to a "swing away from the small, struggling, discouraged, and untaught (relatively) student groups in a pagan school to the prosperous, active, taught groups of keen Christian students in Christian colleges." He saw a danger in simply becoming "recruiting grounds for Christian colleges and seminaries." But his main objection was that "it would mean the alteration of our God-given purpose. We are committed as an organization to help students to go on with God and to witness to Christ to their fellow students (devotional-evangelistic). For a Christian college, we have nothing to offer."[31]

In 1944, under the pseudonym "Charles Stilwell," Stacey wrote an important article in *HIS*, asking the question, "Should I Go to a Christian College This Fall?" It was too controversial to appear under his own surname so he used his mother's. He began his predictable answer with a description of an incident in a fraternity house of a college that was denominational but nonevangelical. A discussion was going on about "these strange specimens of college men who came from a Christian college where students didn't dance, drink or smoke, and who spoke of their Christianity as something which meant more than a nominal religious appellation." He stated emphatically, "If the Lord leads a student to a non-Christian college, God will keep that person through the vicissitudes and temptations of campus life, providing that student walks before Him in obedience." And he issued a solemn warning, italicized for emphasis: *"Watch out also against the danger of living in another world, failing to understand the world of unconverted men and women with whom ultimately you have to live, and before whom you have to witness."* He concluded with some ringing words: "For the secular campus is your mission field and your glorious opportunity. God has set you there to be His witness—His missionary—His ambassador."[32]

HAROLD JOHN OCKENGA

Stacey was becoming known within the wider evangelical community. It appears that his first serious contact with Harold Ockenga at Ockenga's home in Belmont, Massachusetts, engineered by David Adeney, who worshiped at Park Street Church, Boston, was in early June 1943. Stacey wrote the next day from Connecticut apologizing for not having helped Ockenga finish mowing his lawn but expressing thanks for the invitation to write a series of articles in *United Evangelical Action*.[33] The magazine had made its appearance in August 1942 as a mouthpiece for the National Association of Evangelicals, organized that April. Ockenga was the new president and was seeking columnists for the broadsheet.

Woods contributed a "Youth Column" for the next fourteen months. His first column introduced readers to IVCF, still relatively unknown. Some evangelicals coming to university, he said, "feel that time in college calls for a moratorium on

Christian work among the college students." IVCF on the campus, he went on, was about "ten or twelve Christian university students meeting week by week to dig into the Word of God for themselves."[34] Next column featured evangelism and the university: "While not denying the place of Christian evidences and apologetics it cannot be stressed too strongly that it is the Gospel message proclaimed in a way that will commend itself to university people and phrased in a thought-provoking intelligent manner that God uses in universities."[35] The following month he focused on IVCF and missions, and spoke of "the attitude of many truly consecrated Christian university students. They are alive to the fact that a new situation throughout the world necessitates a new type of evangelical missionary, with the finest academic and specialized training, yet a mission of true spiritual character and devotion."[36]

The column soon became a shameless promoter of IVCF. In November he emphasized that instead of being threatened "churches [are] strengthened by IVCF." "As I travel," Stacey wrote, "from campus to campus, nothing gives me greater joy than to visit men in seminary or in the pastorate and to realize with thanksgiving the part God has given the Inter-Varsity Christian Fellowship in the glory of their life work."[37] Two months later he was hammering the theological seminaries. Over the previous twenty-five years, he stated emphatically, "The church, both in pulpit and pew, has lacked conviction, has had little sense of direction or purpose and has vacilalted between rationalistic uncertainty and gross materialism." The reason? Seminaries had failed the church, their graduates "had been trained to be successful professional Christian leaders, lacking both the spirit of sacrifice and an urgent sense of the divine imperative."[38]

By February 1944 he was addressing the problem of worldliness and the difficulty presented by an evangelical subculture that majored on minors and the reaction to it when converts outside the fundamentalist subculture brought to faith through IVCF started attending church for the first time. It was a condition that he later addressed in "Taboo." And following a conference by SCM, SVM and the Council of Churches Board of Education at Wooster College where there was a notable lack of theological definition, he presented IVCF's alternative vision as "Students Face Postwar Missions." "A positive program of missionary education and training, encouraging the most gifted and highly educated to missionary work in the post-war world, should be undertaken by evangelical leaders immediately," he wrote, anticipating the IVCF Urbana missionary conferences.[39]

Stacey Woods's columns in the United Evangelical Action petered out by the summer of 1944 as he returned to Toronto. While they appeared, they had a positive effect in alerting the wider evangelical community to the new phenomenon of IVCF. They brought Stacey to a national audience but also made him a name to be reckoned with among those in the vanguard of evangelical rebirth in the 1940s. He was invited to Plymouth[40] as an expert on evangelism because of what he had written there. Plymouth 1944 cemented the bonds between Stacey, Ockenga and John Bolten, bonds decisive in the years ahead as evangelicalism moved in new directions.

BACK TO CANADA

In the summer of 1944 Mel Donald was called up by the Canadian army, leaving the movement without a leader. His time as assistant general director had been a challenging one for him and for Stacey. Inclined to be melancholic, he was critical of *HIS* magazine and was constantly expressing his fears to Stacey. Stacey was called back to Canada. In the United States during the four years Stacey had lived in Wheaton, there had been substantial progress. The budget was set at $50,000, there were nineteen staff (twelve full-time) and thirty chapters. Although he was still chair of the board, Herbert Taylor's determination to lessen the movement's dependence on his munificence had succeeded. Headquartered no longer at the Christian Workers Foundation location on Wacker St. (Chicago), the offices were now located at 64 East Lake Street.

The work in Canada had also prospered: Inter-Varsity was on thirteen campuses, in two hundred high schools, nine teacher's colleges and eighteen residences. Stacey and Yvonne with their two preschoolers settled into 77 Lawrence Ave., East, in Toronto. He had returned to Canada with the understanding that he would be a week in Canada, a week in the United States, and two weeks on the road. It was a punishing schedule made possible only by Yvonne's willingness to support him in his ministry. But the boys were to pay a heavy price for their father's long absences at a crucial stage of their development. Cobber, Stacey's longtime friend Vincent Craven, arrived from Australia the following year and boarded with the family, providing a male presence in the home. But Stacey was not often there, and when he was, he was distracted and anxious. Again, the proximity of Yvonne's mother and the nearby Symons family was a source of strength.

The return to Canada meant that Stacey could be giving direct supervision as a longtime dream of his was coming to fruition. He and Troutman had often discussed the need for a permanent training facility that would enable students to be more effective in their leadership on campus by taking them out of that environ-ment for reflection and study. Now Cameron Peck, vice chairman of the American board, had offered the use of Fairview Island in the Lake of Bays, 150 miles north of Toronto, as a site. Stacey appreciated the fact that it was an island, and isolated, though it lacked any facilities other than a rickety building and an uncertain dock. He immediately set about to make the facility usable, sending Vincent Craven to secure nails in the United States because there were none available in Canada. Sup-plies were short and the building permit was cancelled in the midst of construction. Stacey continued but was told to stop or be prosecuted. "By this time," Stacey re-called, "the Canadian board members were distraught, promising to visit me in jail!"[41] The last plank was put in place just as a summons was delivered from the mainland, held up by a sympathetic government official. "It was all a glorious ad-venture," was Stacey's verdict.

The speakers at that first summer school were diverse: Cornelius Van Til helped redeem his reputation for obscurity a decade earlier, board member J. F. Strombeck, staffers Irene Webster-Smith and Jane Hollingsworth made their contribution. Australian Christian Brethren evangelist Northcote Deck, a close friend of the Woodses (he had dedicated both of Stacey's sons to the Lord as infants) swam around the island like a porpoise as students were reading their Bibles during the early morning quiet time. It was for all who were there an unforgettable experience, and for many life-changing. Campus-in-the-Woods, as the site became known, was a significant factor in the growth and maturing of postwar Inter-Varsity, fulfilling Stacey's vision of training students to reach their universities.

Stacey told Charles Troutman all about it: "We had 98 students from 45 dif-ferent schools. In spite of very real difficulties and terrific amount of hard work God blessed in a wonderful way." During the sessions, word had come of atomic bombs being dropped on Hiroshima and Nagasaki. There was a possibility that Troutman would soon be demobilized: "If there is anything we can do to facilitate your release please let us know. Another question is once you are released how soon can you be with us."[42] There was much to do, and Stacey was looking forward to resuming the old partnership that had meant so much to the growth of the Fellow-ship from its early days. He was to be grieved and disappointed, however. The breakdown of that relationship was part of the unfolding tragedy of the next eight years when the American InterVarsity was to experience both spectacular growth and destructive division.

7

To the Whole World

STACEY WOODS WAS A TRAVELING MAN. Long trips are part of the Australian psyche, a way of compensating for geography. Being "down under" creates an insatiable desire to journey great distances. Stacey's father had ventured further and further away on his trips as an evangelist. His Christian Brethren connections made him welcome in many countries, spanning the globe in his itinerant ministry. Stacey's first trip, at twenty-one, to Texas was an adventure. He had thought on graduation he might go to India but settled for Canada. For the rest of his life he was constantly on the move, travel becoming a feature of his restless temperament. He challenged graduates never to "settle down" into a life of mindless complacency that lost all sense of adventure and discovery. His vision was global, his missionary passion worldwide, and his commitment was to stretch the horizon of InterVarsity to "the uttermost parts of the earth."

Stacey's first trip to a non-English-speaking country was made in April 1937 when he and Charles Troutman drove to Mexico. Troutman had tried unsuccessfully to start high school clubs in Lindsay and Ottawa in the months previous, and, given the long harsh Canadian winter and the lateness of spring there, a trip south seemed a welcome distraction. They drove because Charles not only thrived on long automobile journeys, he was the only one on staff who could afford a car. The driving was left to Troutman because Stacey had a congenital eye condition that made him dicey behind the wheel. Stacey chose a return to Dallas as their first stop. Crossing the Rio Grande River at Laredo, they made their way across country to Tijuana and then up the Pacific Coast to Vancouver, a trip of five weeks. They came home refreshed, with commitment to ministry restored, and hatching many plans for new InterVarsity initiatives.

OVERSEAS MISSIONS

The next time that Stacey visited Mexico was the spring of 1944. He reported to the American board that "with the development of the student missionary program in the last twelve months there has been an increasing awareness among many of our students as to the need of an evangelical witness among university students in Latin America."[1] Students at the University of Toronto had raised money, and Mel Donald was insisting on action, Stacey said. Three hundred dollars had been promised from the Pioneer Missionary Agency, and H. J. Taylor had already submitted to the Canadian board a survey which was then handed out to its American counterpart. In spite of staff cuts and a lack of funds, the trip was approved because of what was called Stacey's "magnetism and strategy."[2]

Stacey, who hated plane travel, at the last minute panicked and considered taking out a large insurance policy for his family. He set out on a journey that included three stopovers in Mexico, then on to Guatemala City; Managua, Nicaragua; San José, Costa Rica; and several cities in Colombia. In Bogota, Stacey encountered a Presbyterian missionary whose university ministry consisted, he claimed, of supervising square dances, with grace at meals the only Christian content. From Barranquilla, Colombia, he took a lumbering Pan American flying boat that only became airborne when all the passengers went to the back of the plane and fell on their knees. Stacey had two people on top of him when the flight finally took off for Kingston, Jamaica. There the pontoons had to be repaired, and Stacey had an unexpected layover of four days during which he fathered an InterVarsity movement in both high schools and universities. He then went on to the University of Havana in Cuba with its 13,000 students. This trip of Stacey's became the stuff of legends.

The number of university students in these locations was not, by today's standards, large—20,000 in Mexico, for instance. "In every center I visited," he reported, "I came into contact with born-again university students. The number was very, very small, but I believe that in many centers there is a nucleus upon which really effective student work can be built."[3] Stacey had many recommendations that would later become part of his global strategy. He wanted Spanish-speaking graduates to go to Latin America to teach English, "which would do more to establish close contact with Latin American students than any other approach."[4] He also recommended the establishment of hostels near universities as student centers where students could board. He thought that expatriates could take advantage of interest in American culture to provide classes. In those days, which seem so far away, there was a positive awareness of and appreciation for the United States in Latin America, which Stacey thought student ministry could exploit. The following year Edward Pentecost, a part-time staffer while studying at Dallas Theological Seminary, enrolled in Mexico's Universidad Nacional Autónoma to study Hispanic literature, working with the national students to organize what became El Coompañerismo Evangélico Estudiantil, Mexican InterVarsity.

This increasing awareness by students of opportunities beyond their borders was a result of Stacey's passionate commitment to overseas missions. Again, this was in reaction to the League of Evangelical Students's refusal to get involved in global issues, feeling that was better left to denominations. In June of 1936, arising out of a revival at Wheaton College earlier that year that had stressed worldwide outreach, a group of students gathered to form the Student Foreign Mission Fellowship (SFMF). Present at the meetings was Margaret Haines and a student leader named Will Norton. By 1940 there were thirty-six groups, mostly at Bible schools, Christian colleges and seminaries. Stacey watched the development and informal discussions were started about a possible merger. The negotiations were complicated owing to the different constituencies the two organizations were reaching.

DAVID ADENEY

From the very start of American InterVarsity, Stacey wanted to bring missions to the forefront of its activity, recapturing the initiative of the Student Volunteer Movement, which had been dissipated owing to liberalism. He turned, as might be expected, to the China Inland Mission for help in finding a staffer who could be a catalyst for greater student involvement in missionary activity. Bishop Frank

Houghton, then general director of CIM, suggested that David Adeney, who had just returned on the last boat to leave Japanese-occupied China before Pearl Harbor, would be an ideal candidate. David had been first missionary secretary for the Cambridge Inter-Collegiate Union while at the university and then national missionary secretary for the Inter-Varsity Fellowship executive committee. "As soon as he was appointed," Douglas Johnson notes, "he began to agitate for a more definite place in the central organization for missionary activities."[5] It was David who coined the watchword for the British Inter-Varsity Missionary Fellowship: "Evangelize to a finish, to bring back the King."[6] The following year he went to China where he met American Ruth Temple, who had arrived in the country at the age of twenty-two. They were married in 1938. A trans-Atlantic marriage gave the couple roots in both countries, typical of many missionary families.

Never one to miss an opportunity, Stacey approached David almost on arrival at Ruth's home in Minnesota. Appointed in November 1941 he remained based on his in-law's farm his first year on staff. David was used to family separations, his father having been a missionary in Romania for twenty years while his mother had raised their five sons in Bedford, England. "I am sorry things are so muddled with regard to David Adeney," Stacey apologized to Mel Donald a few weeks after his appointment and ten days before Adeney was due for a six-week visit to Canadian universities. "If he has to return to Toronto to pick up his wife," he continued, "I imagine he could remain over a couple of days to visit Western at the beginning of February."[7] At this point Ruth was pregnant with their third child, the second having died at birth in China. It was just as well the couple shared a common calling.

After two years, the second of which was spent in Boston with additional work with Ivy League schools, David set off for family in England and work with the China Inland Mission there. By that time Stacey had bonded with him, a link that would grow stronger over the years. On 1 December 1944 a union was finally consummated, combining the position of director of the Student Foreign Mission Fellowship with that of missionary secretary of InterVarsity. Will Norton, now home from Belgian Congo, provided interim leadership until, on graduation from Princeton Seminary, Christy Wilson, whom David Adeney had first contacted while he was an undergraduate at Princeton, became the first full-time appointee with SFMF and IVCF.[8] Looking back Stacey commented on "the thrill and excitement of those truly great happenings."[9]

First Missions Conference

Christy Wilson pioneered the first missionary conference, later to be called Urbana, at the University of Toronto over the new year's holidays at the end of 1946. Toronto was a suitable location: for some years there had been a prayer meeting on Friday afternoons at the Canadian School of Missions at 97 St. George Street. These developed into one held on Saturdays monthly at Knox Church. From this, with the support of Stacey Woods and the passion of Christy Wilson, grew the first missionary conference held on the campus of the University of Toronto, Friday, 27 December 1946, to Thursday, 2 January 1947.

The statistics were impressive: 575 students from 151 colleges and universities with 52 denominations represented. More than 250 indicated their willingness to serve overseas as missionaries. Between them, Woods and Wilson assembled an attractive roster of speakers. From Columbia Bible College came Robert McQuilkin, whose sermon at the 1936 Wheaton revival had sparked the original formation of SFMF; Calvin Chao of China; Gordon Holdcroft of the Independent Board of Presbyterian Missions (the Machen-initiated organization now connected to Carl McIntire's empire); Leslie Maxwell, founder of Three Hills, Alberta, Bible Institute; Bakht Singh, so-called apostle of the Indian subcontinent, whom leading Islamic interpreter Samuel Zwemer described as "one of the most influential missionary leaders of the twentieth century," and—after Stacey successfully struggled to persuade him that he could return to Park Street Church, Boston, in time for Sunday—that rising star of evangelicalism, Harold John Ockenga. As a result and providentially, as it turned out, Ockenga was given the opening place on the program.

J. Burgon Bickersteth, scion of a prominent English evangelical family and about to retire after twenty-six years as influential warden of the university's Hart House, greeted the delegates with a denunciation of Inter-Varsity's "separatism" and urged them to join the Student Volunteer Movement. Ockenga, next to speak, abandoned his prepared talk and—to quote Stacey:

> at his magnificent best, launched into an off-the-cuff defence of the importance and necessity of a biblical witness on campus. Smiting hip and thigh, he flayed liberalism and accommodation theology. He insisted on the right and necessity of Inter-Varsity to exist as an independent society. Here was reformation preaching at its best. The air was electric.[10]

Years later Stacey recalled the event not only with relish but also marked it as personally and organizationally determinative.

Some, attending as observers, were unimpressed. Stacey, Charles Troutman, Christy Wilson Jr., Joe Bayly, Tom Maxwell and Mel Donald met the final day of the conference with representatives of Student Christian Movement and the Student Volunteer Movement. They were told by one, "I came out of your meetings cursing mad." Another responded, "If this movement means what I think it means, it is a fight to the finish." "My reply," Stacey wrote, "was that I felt that their attitude was normal in that as a result of the missionary convention they would either be converted to evangelical Christianity or would leave the conference more liberal than before."[11]

Subsequently in a letter of 19 February 1947 Stacey included a confidential report that had been circulated by Student Christian Movement and the Student Volunteer Movement analyzing the conference. They appeared to be particularly dismayed at the fact that IVCF with the Student Foreign Mission Fellowship claimed the mantle of the old Student Volunteer Movement throughout the conference: "no reference was made to the 60 years' unbroken line of SVM quadrennials" or to a forthcoming missionary conference of their own to be held a year later. While "the devotion of a student and leaders," "the sense of unity," "the great use of prayer," and the "the reality of the power of God as evidenced there," were all commended, there were many more negatives: "over emotionalism, subjectivism, and high pressure salesmanship on the part of a number of speakers," "general lack of intellectual stimulation, verging at times on anti-intellectualism," "alignment with reactionary social-political forces, undercurrent suspicions of denominations as opposed to the sects," "anti-ecumenism," "inadequate presentation and analysis of missionary motivation, attitudes, and methods," "largest recruitment pressure was on behalf of independent boards," and finally "ignoring or deprecating of work done by other student organizations in the same fields."[12]

They were incensed by John Bolten's analysis of the situation in Germany and his call for someone to "look at Germany as a mission field." He had indicated that German Student Christian Movement was disaffiliated, an error that representatives asked Stacey to make a correction, but *"no correction was made"* though "he knew some of the information was wrong." Stacey when confronted by denominational and ecumenical critics had the freedom of being a foreigner and coming out of a free-church background. A lesser man, given the powerful forces with which he was contending, would have been intimidated. But not Stacey.

At the same time Stacey was anxious to appear cooperative with the university authorities, particularly in the light of a forthcoming university mission at the University of Toronto. He wrote president Sidney Smith a grateful letter for hospitality a week after the first Urbana Student Missions Convention and added, "May I respectfully suggest for your consideration a plan which has proved most effective in McGill and Queen's Universities and in which the Inter-Varsity Christian Fellowship has co-operated fully."[13] The plan consisted of each of the religious organizations bringing in their own speaker. At Queens, Inter-Varsity's choice was Gerald Gregson, then a senior Royal Air Force chaplain and later Scripture Union director in Canada, and at McGill it was the ever-available Herbert Mekeel. There is no record of Smith's reply.

INTERNATIONAL FELLOWSHIP OF EVANGELICAL STUDENTS

In many ways Inter-Varsity's first missionary conference stood strategically halfway between meetings in the summers of 1946 and 1947 in England that would bring international issues to the fore. On 25 August 1944 Douglas Johnson (always known by his initials, DJ), general secretary of the British Inter-Varsity Fellowship, who also served as recording secretary of the International Fellowship of Evangelical Students meetings in the 1930s, wrote participants (as much as he was able given Nazi occupation that still persisted in parts of Europe): "We have decided (without in any way pledging any of your Fellowships) to enter into a definite International Fellowship with our Continental friends." In the course of this ten-page letter he outlines what he had in mind at the conclusion of the war. "The framework is already present behind our International Conference (with its General Committee of delegates which elects its Executive Committee). The Constitution of the Conference will need very little modification."[14]

Stacey (with Canadian cooperation) was asked to compile suggestions, sending them on via Australia and New Zealand. Douglas Johnson, in his characteristic frank approach, listed five potential chairmen with their strengths and weakness.[15] He was anxious to avoid both the words *fundamentalist* and *evangelical* to describe the nascent movement. "There is a necessity for a *much more elastic policy* and a greater latitude than one would have for one's own National Fellowship," he cautioned. "It is very salutary for self-assured and somewhat complacent Anglo-Saxons to recognise Apostolic Christianity in very different dress from that in which they are accustomed to meet it."[16]

Stacey took his first flight across the Atlantic on 19 March 1946. "I am not at all keen on this flying business but it seems the only way one can travel with any certainty these days," he wrote Johnson. His friend John Bolten, he explained, would be attending the meeting. An explanation was in order; bringing a German to England months after the end of hostilities could be resented. "I thought it would be well if I gave you some advance information about Mr. Bolten. In doing so, I do not wish to cause you any alarm." He went on to tell Bolten's unusual story. Growing up in a godly home, his father was the leader of the free-church movement within the Lutheran state church. An officer under Hindenburg in the First World War, he had aligned himself with the steel helmet movement after the armistice, finally breaking with Hitler in 1928. He arrived in America to restart his business career, manufacturing tires at a plant in Lawrence, Massachusetts, north of Boston. Though he called himself a "Darbyite" (after J. N. Darby, founder of the Christian Brethren), he was attracted to the ministry of Harold Ockenga at Park Street Church and became a strong supporter until political differences later drove them apart. Over the next twenty-five years the Bolten-Woods partnership would be formative for both and for IFES.

On arrival in Britain, Stacey went immediately to the Scottish IVF conference at St. Andrew's. He then journeyed south to address 450 undergraduates at the English IVF conference at Oxford's Regent's Park College. Meetings of the international executive committee continued on there Monday and Tuesday, April 1-2. Two-thirds of the executive committee that had been appointed in Cambridge in 1939 were present. Chaired by Nils Dahlberg of Sweden, the brief meetings agreed that cooperating movements be asked to approve the formation of an International Fellowship of Evangelical Students, that an invitation of the United States IVCF to hold a constituent meeting in Cambridge, Massachusetts, in August 1947 be accepted, and that a draft constitution be circulated for adoption at that time.[17] This progress, and particularly the projected 1947 inaugural gathering, would not have been possible, as Johnson later admitted, without the financial backing of John Bolten and "senior supporters in the USA." The British and Scandinavian movements, which had earlier picked up the tab, were in no position to do so after the war. Again Stacey's well-heeled friends had made ministry happen. At the Oxford meetings a new slate of officers was approved. Ole Kristian Hallesby, released from Nazi prison the year before, was nominated president.[18] Nils Dahlberg would be chairman with Martyn Lloyd-Jones vice chairman. John Bolten was treasurer, and Stacey noted, "after a great deal of pressure was put on me to accept the Secretaryship of the International Movement but this I resolutely refused. A temporary compromise resulted in which Dr Douglas Johnson and I have been appointed co-secretarys until 1947."[19] Douglas Johnson was

Stacey Woods (left) and Douglas Johnson at Regent's Park College, Oxford, 2 April 1946 (Courtesy of IVCF-USA)

to have Europe, the Near East and Africa as his sphere, with Stacey taking on North America, Australasia, China and India. Conspicuously absent was Latin America.

Stacey then went on to London, met with the Biblical Research Committee, the IVF Graduates' Fellowship, and spent 13-18 April at Johnson's home in suburban Surrey. Over the next twenty-five years, no name appeared more often in Johnson's famous guest book than that of C. Stacey Woods. Johnson wrote to Stacey after the trip:

> I am very glad that you found the time in Britain useful. We will continue to collaborate as closely and as vigorously as we can. You will at least know now the circumstances which may make some of our efforts and actions look a bit odd to you on the opposite side of the water, and you have explained to us the points where it is necessary for you to do things on somewhat different lines from ours. The main thing is for us to keep our work as closely related as possible to the actual local needs and the various types of outlook of the different students in our various countries.[20]

"Dr Johnson is a genius," Stacey told the Canadian board after his visit. (They agreed reluctantly to his becoming Johnson's partner secretary for a year.) "The British I.V.F. is magnificent. Its influence on the evangelical life of Great Britain is considerable. On the whole, the movement is more mature than our work in Canada, and this is still more true when the British I.V.F. is compared with our work in the United States." Stacey now had to persuade Johnson to travel to the United States. Johnson mustered many excuses: restrictions on sterling and limited finances among them. Basically Johnson preferred to work behind the scenes.

MARTYN LLOYD-JONES

Dr. Martyn Lloyd-Jones presented a different challenge. Douglas Johnson, who was trying to get him to a conference in Norway in September, wrote (as a physician himself) to Stacey that "the Doctor," as he was affectionately known, had "a recurrence of his gastritis, probably due to nervous strain which has the effect of upsetting the tum."[21] However, the impression that Stacey had made on Lloyd-Jones had made him willing to commit himself to a North American foray the following year. Lloyd-Jones wrote to Stacey, "I believe that your visit has done untold good, and we all feel, who had the pleasure of meeting you, that we wish you could repeat it every year! I have never been so convinced of the importance of personal contacts."[22] Stacey had already set up a full itinerary for Lloyd-Jones: two services on three summer Sundays at Knox Church Toronto, and John Bolten had eagerly committed him to a further three in August at Park Street Church, Boston. "But please do not ask me to [do] too much, as I am generally pretty tired by that time of the year, and your climatic conditions can be somewhat trying," the Doctor cautioned in a December letter after he saw the full schedule that Stacey had set up.[23]

The next month Stacey was brokering with Carl F. H. Henry at Wheaton College for Lloyd-Jones to give the Jonathan Blanchard lectures, which later became *Truth Unchanged, Unchanging*, an InterVarsity Press bestseller. By now Stacey was having to rein in requests and to remind people that "his chief reason for coming to North America is to be an official delegate of the International Leaders' Conference of the International Fellowship of Evangelical Students to be held at Harvard University August 16 to 22."[24]

It would be hard to overestimate the influence that Martyn Lloyd-Jones had on Stacey Woods. There had been a reaction to the rigid Calvinism of the League of Evangelical Students. On a visit to see Wheaton classmates at Westminster Seminary in 1940, Troutman had said, "They are ready to die for the 'Reformed Faith,' but quite pleased to curse everyone else."[25] Lloyd-Jones's pulpit-centered ministry was a far cry from Stacey's Christian Brethren roots. His theology was also considerably different from what Stacey had been taught at Dallas Theological Seminary. The Doctor's amillennialism was regarded with deep suspicion and antagonism by many of American InterVarsity's supporters who considered premillennialism a test of orthodoxy. Thanks to Lloyd-Jones's gentle nudging, Stacey discovered the Puritans. When John Owen's classic *The Glory of Christ* was republished in 1949, Stacey praised it: "Here is none of the popular fundamentalist pablum which will further vitiate the taste and the ability of the reader to think and study for himself."[26] Stacey felt the Doctor had no equal as an expositor of Scripture, and Lloyd-Jones's opening of the Bible greatly influenced Stacey's own teaching and preaching, weaning it away from his earlier dispensationalism and letting the text speak for itself rather than imposing patterns on it. To the end of his life Stacey railed against "problem-centred and person-centred rather than Christ-centred Truth-centred Bible exposition, Christian doctrine that which will build people themselves up in their most Holy Faith."[27] He deplored the increasing lack of expository preaching and attributed the shallowness of contemporary evangelicalism to its disappearance. As Stacey's life drew to an end—he was preaching to the small group in Lausanne he pastored—there was the clear hallmark of the Doctor.

Stacey was also grateful to Lloyd-Jones for his statesmanlike leadership during the thirteen years he served as chair of IFES. He wrote to Iain Murray, Lloyd-Jones's biographer: "Dr Martyn Lloyd-Jones put his stamp on the movement. He gave us backbone, conviction, a refusal to compromise, a willingness to stand alone against the World Council of Churches and the World Student Christian Federation if necessary."[28] Nowhere was that skill more evident than in that first constituent meeting of IFES during those hot August days at Phillips Brooks House, Harvard University. "With consummate skill and unimaginable patience, Dr Lloyd-Jones chaired this Conference until a constitution was hammered out and an international movement was formed," Stacey recalled. A lesser man would have been intimidated by the roster of delegates: John Bolten as host and treasurer, Archbishop Howard Mowll of Sydney, Judge John J. Read of Ottawa, Herbert Taylor of Chicago, Donald Wiseman of London University.[29] And there were the young, yet to make a name for themselves, Joe Bayly, David Bentley-Taylor, René Pache and future archbishop of Sydney Donald Robinson. The Chinese movement, then experiencing revival, was represented by

Calvin Chao and Hong Sit. They represented a group that subsequently paid dearly for their faith.

There were undercurrents at the meeting that without Lloyd-Jones at the helm could have derailed it: Swedes against the other Nazi-occupied Scandinavian countries; latent hostility between Germans, French and Swiss; and "the perhaps unconscious but real desire of British Inter-Varsity to impose its philosophy of student Christian work, with student leadership as the key stone." Here Lloyd-Jones took the American view and nearly scuttled a motion that at least one of three delegates from a member movement be a student. In Boston, of all places, Douglas Johnson argued, there should be no taxation without representation! In the end Judge Read rescued the motion and it passed. The evening addresses by Lloyd-Jones were all memorable, but the final Saturday-morning message was never forgotten by those present. The text from Psalm 90 he chose as a parting injunction stayed with many of those present for the rest of their lives and set the tone for IFES for a generation: "Let thy work appear unto thy servants, and thy glory unto their children" (Ps 90:16 KJV). The group was deeply stirred. Archbishop Mowll made the suggestion, enthusiastically endorsed by general committee, that Lloyd-Jones to be a roving ambassador for IFES. It was an invitation he said he would give prayerful and careful consideration to, but subsequently turned down.

From the chair Lloyd-Jones stated the two functions of IFES: first, "to foster Christian fellowship and helpful association between existing national evangelical unions," and second, "that there was a great missionary evangelistic work to be done in the many countries where as yet there are no National Evangelical Unions and in other countries where the National Evangelical Unions are weak and need help." It was to this specific task that Stacey Woods set his sights as newly appointed general secretary of the IFES. He had already made arrangements to leave Canada in May and appointed a surrogate. He was to set up the IFES office in Philadelphia. Margaret Haines had promised her home as a temporary location for him and his family. For the next twenty-five years he gave himself to it as the cause closest to his heart. But in the meantime he was still general secretary of two national movements. His balancing of these three leadership responsibilities would be an ongoing challenge.

Unprecedented Growth

STACEY WOODS ASSESSED THE POSTWAR UNIVERSITY SCENE in his May 1946 report to the Canadian board.

> The first academic year after the war's end is almost over. It has been a year of unrest, strain, frustration and even discouragement—the more so because each of us had hoped so earnestly for peace, progress and constructive effort. Students have not been easier to reach—they seem nervously distracted, restless.[1]

There was a revolution taking place in North American postsecondary education. When Franklin Roosevelt signed the so-called GI Bill of Rights on 22 June 1944, entitling returning veterans to funding for degree study, he precipitated a revolution that would forever change the university. The University of Michigan, site of one of InterVarsity's earliest chapters, went from an enrollment of 10,000 to 30,000 in two years. Canada was no different. Within two years of the end of the war 37,000 students had registered in universities, two thousand more than the total enrollment before the war.

These students were like no other generation. Battle-hardened, older, career-oriented, anxious to make up for lost time, this generation had an intensity that raised significant issues. Charles Troutman, himself a returning veteran, commented that "in the 1930s you couldn't get a serious conversation going with college students. After the war, you couldn't stop."[2] They were probing, questioning, doubting. The old institutions had lost their authority. Stacey noted the difference: "Increasingly it would seem that God is working outside the major denominations of organized Christianity. If this be so, the role of the IVCF is increasingly important."[3]

The five years from 1945 to 1950 saw unprecedented growth and expansion for the work both in Canada and the United States. From eighteen chapters (with a similar number of contacts) when Charles Troutman was drafted in 1942, he returned from demobilization in January of 1946 to discover there were now 180 chapters. A year later numbers had almost doubled to 350. Men converted while in the service were now keen to share their faith on the college campus. Former officers in the military, used to making decisions and taking responsibility, provided a cadre of new leadership for chapters.

Ironically, as British and American concepts of student-led or staff-directed ministry were clashing at Cambridge that summer of 1947, the growth in the number of chapters in the United States was outpacing the capacity of InterVarsity to provide anything but the most cursory direction. The following year Charles Troutman wrote Stacey, then in Europe, "The chief problem which I have for next year is the number of chapters which we feel a staff member can handle."[4] A few days later he confirmed his worse fears: "In looking over the whole possible allotment for staff numbers for the next year I have been amazed by the fact that instead of having each staff member with ten or fifteen chapters to look after, the number is between 22 to 27."[5] The rapid growth of the Fellowship during the last half of the 1940s meant that increasingly the situation was becoming like that of the League that it had replaced with promises of better staff supervision. It also opened the way for alternative campus Christian ministries better able to provide help locally.

Publishing Beginnings

One mark of the growing maturity of evangelicalism was the appearance of *Hymns* in 1947. Paul Beckwith, who had been on staff since 1941, was the editor. Beckwith was familiar with the usual fundamentalist musical fare, having been, from the age of seventeen, accompanist for the singer Homer Hammontree and song leader for evangelist Billy Sunday. He had been hired originally to do promotional work for IVCF with concerts and musical evenings. During the war, because of staff shortages, he helped out with regular campus ministry. Headquartered in Chicago, he came over to Stacey's home in Wheaton and went over hymns, Paul playing, Stacey accompanying him with his good tenor voice and Yvonne providing the melody. "These were some of the happiest times of my life," Stacey is quoted as saying.[6] Out of these hymn sings came a revolution in evangelical hymnody, possible only because of teamwork between Stacey Woods and Paul Beckwith.

"Singing is having a new impact on today's Christian life," Beckwith stated in his introduction to *Hymns* ("Christian singing for the thoughtful"). "The song leader seeks to inspire reverence before God," he suggested—a far cry from what he described as the "cheerleader technique" then popular in fundamentalist circles. Pianists, he spoke from personal experience, should avoid "attention-drawing flourishes." He thanked Stacey Woods in particular for his help. *Hymns* was not only a publishing success, it also initiated a whole new musical idiom to evangelical worship. Gone was the uncritical acceptance of music as entertainment, with catchy choruses, repetitive harmonies and syrupy, sentimental ditties, many of which Beckwith himself, as Billy Sunday's pianist, was all too familiar. In 1956 the Auca martyrs sang in the jungles of Ecuador as they were about to go "through the pearly gates of splendour" number nine in *Hymns*, "We rest on Thee" to the tune Finlandia as suggested by Margaret Clarkson.[7] Clarkson, a young Canadian school teacher, wrote the Urbana 46 theme song "We Come O Christ to Thee." As number forty-nine in *Hymns*, it became widely known and appreciated.

Hymns was the first bestseller produced by the fledgling InterVarsity Press of the United States. From the time of InterVarsity's arrival in the United States, Stacey had wanted his own publishing arm. In those early years he encouraged staff on their visits to chapters to carry books appropriate for student ministry. One of them observed, "He had a way of knowing the right thing for me to read and greatly expanded my spiritual horizons with books."[8] Most of these were published by Inter-Varsity Press in the United Kingdom, established in 1936 with the appointment of Ronald Inchley as publications secretary. Its first title that year was T. C. Hammond's *In Understanding Be Men*, which became the standard doctrinal text for Inter-Varsity for at least a generation. In 1941 Stacey wrote Douglas Johnson about the possibility of editing the pamphlet *Quiet Time* so that its Anglicisms were eliminated. He received a reply suggesting that in such a case the names of the original authors be eliminated: "We should not like any of our more aged contributors to fall dead on the spot if they saw that they had actually said 'Gee, boys, I guess you sure oughta have a Q.T., come along now, yes sirree'!"[9]

With the 1946 purchase of 30 St. Mary Street in downtown Toronto, three blocks east of the university, the opening of "an all-inclusive IVCF Book and Magazine Department, which would provide publications both from Inter-Varsity and its sister organizations and affiliates," was now feasible. Stacey met with Ronald Inchley 6 May 1946, and reciprocal arrangements were confirmed the next day. Proofs were to be submitted of all IVP-UK publications. There was an immediate shipment of a thousand copies of Howard Guinness's *Sacrifice*, five hundred of *In Understanding Be Men* and the same number of *Reasoning Faith*. Other titles about to be shipped in similar quantity were *The Anchorage of Life* and *Why the Cross?* InterVarsity Press in North America was off and running. "I believe this trip accomplished a good deal in terms of arrangements for exchange of publications and printing rights, more complete understanding, exchange of leaders and speakers, all of which will be of great benefit to the Fellowship in Canada and the United States."[10]

A year later Stacey reported to the Canadian board, "The new venture of a separate Book Department has been fully justified" with book revenues of $2,553 and inventory of three thousand dollars. "Consideration is being given to the possibility of setting up an IVCF publishing house financed separately and operated as a nonprofit venture in order to republish British I.V.F. books and to commence to develop our own publications." That had been a developing dream of his from the moment that Jane Hollingsworth had complained to him back in 1943 that there were no inductive Bible study materials available, and he said to her "Well, Jane, *write* some!" Her *Discovering the Gospel of Mark*, which appeared that year as the first specifically IVCF title, was the result. In 1947 the American board, urged on by Stacey, determined that the organization "should undertake its own deliberate publishing program, replacing the somewhat haphazard activities of the preceding years." The office in Chicago organized publication and distribution; after 1951 Joe Bayly provided editorial supervision, initially from his Philadelphia office.

GROWING PAINS

The growth of IVCF in the United States necessitated Stacey's return to the United States. In retrospect it is strange that he did not move immediately to Chicago but chose instead to accept an offer by Margaret Haines to locate the IFES office in her home in Germantown, Pennsylvania, and take up residence there, with one bedroom for the parents and one for the boys. Returning to an empty 77 Lawrence Avenue East, Toronto, preparing to move to Philadelphia that late August was anticlimactic: 1947 had been one of the most memorable summers of Stacey's career. Speakers at Campus in the Woods, thanks partly to an auspicious alignment of events, included Martyn Lloyd-Jones and Douglas Johnson, along with Clarence Bouma of Calvin Seminary, Allan MacRae of Faith Seminary, rising stars Carl Henry (then at Northern Baptist Seminary, Chicago, but shortly to move to the new Fuller Theological Seminary in Pasadena, California) and Dawson Trotman, founder of the Navigators.

But all was not well on the Canadian front as Stacey was about to depart. His trusty friend Charles Stephens was giving up the chairmanship of the board after five years, and Dr. I. H. Erb, a well-known pathologist, took over at the helm. It was a time of change, and people were anxious. The budget approved for the fiscal year starting September called for an increase of 15 percent, given the increase in the number of staff appointed. The original plan had been that Stacey, after thirteen years as general secretary of the Canadian movement, would turn over the ministry on 31 August 1947 to Thomas Maxwell, a recent graduate of Knox College and an ordained Presbyterian minister, designating him associate general secretary.[11] "Giving him such a title as may be most fitting, his function to be to coordinate the various phases of the IVCF and to concentrate on one particular field, namely that of the work among university students." In addition to Maxwell, Vincent Craven would take over Inter-School Christian Fellowship and the camps, and the two of them, together with a new secretary of Scripture Union and a business manager, would run regular IVCF meetings with the board of directors and provide counsel. "I trust that the Board will believe that in making these suggestions, I have not the slightest lessening of interest or sense of responsibility or satisfaction in the IVCF of Canada. It is inevitable that as our work grows and develops there must be a greater division of labor and a measure of decentralization."[12]

Stacey was under pressure from the American board: "The Board of Directors of the IVCF of USA has requested that as soon as possible I devote a major portion of my time for the next several years to that work." Of the two organizations he felt that the Canadian IVCF "has more mature leadership than the IVCF of USA although the latter organization is now responsible for student work on some two hundred college campuses." Now, with a third general secretaryship handed to him and which he accepted not unwillingly, Stacey realized that both he and the organizations he parented had come to a crossroads. By 29 October 1947 he was still in Canada writing to H. J. Taylor, "Our work in Canada is in rather a critical position and the Board of Directors is feeling very keenly my leaving for the United States. Part of the reason for this, of course, is the resignation of Thomas Maxwell, whom we had groomed for leadership in our Canadian work. You will recall he goes out as a foreign missionary in January."[13]

On Maxwell's departure for British Guiana, Stacey turned direction of the work over to Vincent Craven. It was a short-term solution. In March 1949 Craven asked Stacey to be relieved of administration so that he could concentrate on high schools and camp work, which was his real métier. In his place the board appointed Wilber Sutherland, who had been the highly effective president of the University of British Columbia chapter, the largest in the country. The Sutherlands were an influential Christian Brethren family on Canada's west coast. Wilber had been on staff, working in the universities since graduation with a physics degree from the University of British Columbia in 1946. At the age of twenty-two he joined staff initially for two years, intending to go back to graduate studies.[14] He would continue for the next twenty-four years and be a compelling presence in student work, and later as a national figure, in Canada and beyond.

Stacey bonded with Wilber in a father-son relationship, which sowed the seeds of later problems, both personally and institutionally. As a high school student, Wilber first encountered Stacey at a Vancouver Inter-School Christian Fellowship rally and could always remember the text, John 3:30: "He must increase but I must decrease."

> Little did I anticipate in 1934, however, that this man would in 1946 ask me to join IVCF staff or that he would likewise ask Barbara Dixon to join the American IVCF and that we two would then wire him in 1948 asking in a semi-humorous way for his "blessing" on our proposed plan to strengthen the link between the two movements by our marriage![15]

In an undated letter (probably May of that year) to Stacey, then in Europe, Troutman responded: "Thanks for the information on Wilber Sutherland. I shall spend as much time as I can with him talking over things. I quite agree with you that his brilliance has sometimes gone to his head and will do what I can to help him along that score."[16] Stacey's success in cutting to the chase in quickly assessing an individual was again confirmed over subsequent years; it was Wilber's brilliance, at least in Stacey's view and that of others, that later became a problem.

Meanwhile Stacey, during the spring and summer of 1948, was busy making two trips to Europe on behalf of IFES. He arrived 22 April in Brussels, moving onto Paris, where he stayed a week, and then on to Switzerland for another week. From there he traveled to Italy and back to Belgium on 15 May. "This was a very strenuous trip and a great many university centres were visited, students interviewed and student meetings addressed. The chief purpose of this visit was to acquaint me with the situation in these countries and to prepare for our Summer conferences."[17] It was the start of a passionate attachment to Europe. For some of his travels he was accompanied by René Pache.[18]

After returning to Canada and the United States for spring board meetings and staff appointments, Stacey returned 9 July to Europe, this time to Thorup, Denmark, to meet with leaders of the four Scandinavian movements. Discussions followed about student work, and cooperation and coordination of the ministry. He then proceeded to Slagelse where three hundred students came to hear Ole Hallesby, "a wonderful old gentleman of regal and saintly bearing," "a national hero." "The purpose of this conference was student revival and the deepening of spiritual life." Greetings came from the kings and presidents of the five countries. Stacey then went on to Östersund for the Swedish conference. As he left by train Sunday evening 18 July, the entire conference came down to the station and said goodbye with a Norwegian hymn. He flew from Stockholm to Helsinki and then onto central Finland where there were 250 to 300 students. There he was "struck by the seriousness—almost sadness—of the Christian students. For them Christianity is no laughing matter." He then went on to an IFES conference in Vennes, Switzerland, that was, even more than Cambridge the year before, the real birthplace of IFES. Nearly four hundred students attended, eighty of them Germans whose leaders were trained with Stacey the week before in a castle near Basle. "The German students receive me with great joy," he commented. "Too much cannot be said for the faith and vision of Hans Bürki in this enterprise," Stacey said, reflecting on the leadership that had brought the movement together in Germany after the war.[19]

In Vennes there was again star-studded cast of speakers: Martyn Lloyd-Jones, Harold Ockenga, René Pache, Eric Sauer and Professor Bruxton of Aix-en-Provence Seminary.[20] Lloyd-Jones delivered a powerful address 9 August on "Why I believe the cross is the only way of salvation." At that point the question of Christian assurance dominated the conference. As the Doctor's biographer notes: "It is impossible to avoid the impression that this first European Conference of the IFES gave an impulse to minds and hearts which was to bear fruit in churches and mission fields across the world."[21] Three men brought it together: John Bolten as treasurer and financial backer, Douglas Johnson as organizer, and Stacey Woods with his passion. Mrs. Lloyd-Jones reported to her daughter at home: "Douglas J and Stacey W are here, there and everywhere, Stacey as Chaplinesque as ever."[22]

"Chaplinesque" was an inspired way of describing how Stacey came across at these international conferences. Like Shakespeare's Falstaff his laughter was able to expose the pomposities of the self-important and create a sense of the ridiculous over the petty irritants that always surface at international conferences. His sense of humor had a quality of puckishness that brought to mind the Bendigo prankster. It created a light-heartedness that belied the seriousness with which Stacey regarded these meetings. Such humor often fails to cross national boundaries, but Stacey's seemed to rise above cultural sensitivities. He could always see the funny side in any crisis, which defused otherwise explosive situations. It was a significant reason why people, in spite of being infuriated at Stacey on occasion, still loved him dearly and made allowance for his imperfections.

IVCF AND RACE RELATIONS

It was good that Stacey could be present for the 5 June 1948 American board meeting when the matter of race came up. Jane Hollingsworth, Southerner that she was, insisted that if all were not welcome at the monthly IVCF meeting held in Mrs. Cliffe Johnston's upscale Fifth Avenue apartment, she would take the meeting elsewhere, as she did. When Mrs. Johnston threatened to report Jane to the board, Jane replied, "There is no way that I can justify having everybody welcome except these negro students from these chapters." Mrs. Johnston had met her match—as Stacey knew when he appointed Jane to New York City. In spite of her close friendship with Johnston's daughter Connie, going back to Wheaton, there now was a breach in their friendship that was only healed twenty years later. "Stacey listened to people's complaints, made a decision as to what was right, and kept his ground," according to Jane's husband Peter Haile.[23] There was no compromise for Stacey in the matter of race relations.

The threefold statement of the board that day assured chapters in "Negro" colleges of full acceptance in IVCF, that all IVCF and SFMF conferences were nonsegregated, and initially issued a prophetic statement that "since colored people tend to relate segregation and the Christianity which we represent, we must demonstrate that in Christ there is neither black nor white." It recognized that applying this policy "could cause serious repercussions, particularly among our constituency in the south. It is the general feeling of the Board that this policy should not be the subject of propaganda, but as the Lord leads it should be put into effect on campuses and in student conferences."[24]

Later that year *HIS* featured a lengthy article by Ken Taylor that received a furious reaction from right-wing segregationist readers. Titled "Why Don't Fundamentalists Preach ALL the Gospel?" Taylor began, "As a fundamentalist, I am frightened because of what is happening in fundamentalism; and I find that I am not alone in this fear. A growing number of fundamentalists are beginning to ask astounding questions as to whether the present-day fundamentalist movement will survive."[25] Taylor argued that the fundamentalists had reacted against the social gospel and, in doing so, had been guilty of neglecting the second part of the law: "Love your neighbor as yourself" (Mt 22:39). He then pointedly drew attention to something evangelicals were reluctant to mention:

> Another serious issue upon which we have for the most part refused to take a stand is the matter of race. . . . Fundamentalist churches never discuss this matter and individual fundamentalists are frequently found in bitter attacks against the Jews and in silent toleration of the *status quo* in relation to Jim Crowism. . . . With the love of Christ overflowing from our hearts we ought not to be willing to see any group of people oppressed and economically downtrodden with the resultant detriment to health and morals. In all too many cases, the love of Christ has been suppressed by the love of money and of racial pre-eminence, although the explanation we have given to ourselves is something far different and more pleasing to our deceitful hearts.

He concluded with some strong words: "We ought to rethink the whole problem of our attitude toward race and not be afraid to overthrow fundamentalist traditions grounded on false premises. Wherever the love of Christ leads us in our thinking, there we must go without hesitation. If we are not particularly interested in the problem, we ought to be, if we are to obey the command of Christ."

"I would like to know whether Stacey Woods and Dr. Wilbur Smith read the article or knew of it, before it was published," wrote the prominent fundamentalist lawyer James E. Bennet from the heart of Wall Street.[26] "I would expect far better from either Mr. Woods or Dr. Smith." Bennet, who claimed to have spoken at 412 meetings the previous year and "considerably more this year" wanted to get "Mr Taylor on a witness stand and question him, and I am convinced that he would not be able to satisfactorily stand a cross-examination on most of the statements which he has made in this article." Bennett's letter was addressed to Robert Van Kampen, a right-wing gadfly publisher, and as an IVCF board member a burr in Stacey's saddle. Stacey, of course, knew well what Taylor was writing, agreed with it completely and was engaging in a well-known tactic of launching a trial balloon. *The Uneasy Conscience of American Fundamentalism* by Carl F. H. Henry (good friend of Stacey's and Campus-in-the-Woods guest speaker), which appeared in late 1946, had aroused both the ire and the conscience of American evangelicals. Stacey, from his outsider's perspective on racism—both Australian and American—was a fearless proponent of integration long before that became acceptable. As always, he was ahead of his time; his strong moral commitments leading the way in taking a still unpopular stand.

BACK TO THE CHICAGO SUBURBS

After less than a year in Philadelphia, Stacey found that his impulsive move there had been a mistake. "It soon became apparent," he reported to the Canadian IVCF corporation in the autumn of 1948,

> that to maintain an International office in Philadelphia, contact with the work in Canada through the Toronto office and contact with the American work through Chicago was well nigh impossible. Therefore, after prayer and careful consideration, and with the consent of the IFES Executive Committee, I am now living in Geneva, Illinois, near Chicago where the International office will be established.[27]

The choice of Geneva was significant: it was just west of Wheaton on a main commuter line into the Chicago Loop, where the InterVarsity office could be easily accessed. Geneva was also the home of Charles Troutman, whose house was known among staff for its seven bathrooms. Troutman, with independent means, did not require assistance in purchasing a house. Stacey was able to do so only with the generous help of Herbert Taylor. Stacey and Charles would take the train in together in the morning and out again at night, discussing the business of InterVarsity Christian Fellowship. Subsequently, as their relationship frayed, Stacey began to look for accommodation elsewhere and moved to Downers Grove four years later. Initially both families joined the First Methodist Church in Geneva, but by 1951 Stacey, appalled by the creeping liberalism of the denomination, connected with the Christian Brethren assembly in Wheaton. Charles took longer to make the break. Herbert Taylor, who lived in the upscale suburb of Park Ridge, northwestern Chicago, remained a teetotalling Methodist for the rest of his life.

The IVCF Chicago office, to which Stacey would commute, was still in rented premises, having moved from its original shared facility with H. J. Taylor's Christian Workers Foundation on Wacker Drive, first on 64 East Lake Street and then on 64 West Randolph Street. It soon became evi-

Stacey Woods c. 1950 (Courtesy of IVCF-USA)

dent that new space was required and a recommendation to buy was made. In 1948, with the United States IVCF's ballooning budget, a need for a consistent fundraising approach was obvious. W. E. C. Petersen, known as "the Great Dane," was hired to be stewardship director. His leadership, and a generous Weyerhaeuser donation, made possible the move in 1950 to North Astor Street, just off Lakeshore Drive in Chicago's Gold Coast, first to 1444 Lakeshore Drive until 1956, and then to 1519 Lakeshore Drive until 1965.

DIVIDED BETWEEN IVCF AND IFES

Shortly after his relocation to Chicago, Stacey began to make plans for a major trip to Europe. He would be away from the office for five and a half months in 1949. The American board heard of these plans at a 29 January meeting. Stacey was upbeat, describing the second missionary conference earlier that month when 1,300 had assembled at the University of Illinois campus in Urbana, representing 254 schools with 300 students indicating "that they would seek God's will looking forward to foreign missionary service." He noted, however, "certain criticisms of the convention and the plans to make future conferences even more successful and effective." The subscription tally of *HIS* was now at 8,000.

He was more defensive in discussing his summer itinerary: "there seemed no alternative to spending a considerable time in Europe if results already obtained were preserved and the work in Europe furthered." "He spoke," the minutes continued,

> of the possibility of the appointment of a travelling secretary for Europe which should make unnecessary, prolonged periods being spent in Europe in the future; but that this summer the training of such a secretary together with the student summer training schools and camps seemed to necessitate the General Secretary's being away for a five-month period—from the middle of April until the middle of September.[28]

At one point Herbert Taylor as chair asked members of the board to "express themselves on the advisability of the General Secretary's being away from the United States for so long a period." It was finally unanimously agreed, on assurances that the cost was covered, that the trip be approved, "but that this should be last trip to Europe to be authorized of so extended a character." The board recommended to IFES that Hans Bürki (who had taught briefly at Wheaton while his wife was enrolled there) be asked to become traveling secretary for Europe.[29]

The trip proceeded. In April, Stacey was in Britain, then on to IFES executive meetings in Norway, where Hans Bürki was duly appointed. May was spent in Germany training Hans Bürki, while in June (at the insistence of the board) he and the family (Geoffrey with measles before they left, Stephen with chicken pox as they arrived at Cherbourg) had holidays in off-season Biarritz. "This trip has had less natural attraction than any I have ever taken," he wrote to staff and corporation. "The somewhat disturbing financial news of recent weeks, together with complications in our summer program, make me long to take the next plane home."[30]

They went on to St. Brévin for two French camps, one for university students, the other for young people from the lycées. Conditions were unbelievably primitive, and those attending were initially hostile. Frank Horton, later with IFES in Paris, recalls:

> Anne Béguin [soon to be his wife, then on staff in the Midwest] was there, and said conditions were *very* primitive. She slept on straw with the women students, a ten minute walk from the campsite. During the day, to get to the toilet you had to climb a ladder and go through a window. Stacey and Yvonne did the cooking in order to leave the leadership to those who spoke French.[31]

From there they went on to Baillaigues in Switzerland for a summer training school.

Stacey returned home in mid-September to find a movement in serious disarray and in financial difficulty. From his home in Geneva he called for a day of prayer on 15 November. "Pride and self-satisfaction are so subtle," he wrote. "We may be proud of our zeal, proud of our tireless effort, proud of our self-discipline, proud of our knowledge, proud of our organization. . . . It is easy for us to become cold in heart and to perform our task mechanically without that buoyant conscious motivation of the constraining love of Christ."[32]

InterVarsity had grown exponentially during the 1940s, accelerating in the second half of the decade. Stacey had pioneered the work in the United States and brought it to its present strength. There were now 499 chapters (universities, 239; nurses, 210; Foreign Mission Fellowship, 60), 28 field staff, 15 support staff, and a budget that was to top $200,000 the next year. In Canada, where IVCF had at the age of twenty-one "come of age" and was celebrated by a glitzy new promotional brochure, things were also in disarray. With a budget of $46,000, up 25 percent from the previous year, it was considerably smaller and sensitive to the fact that Stacey was an absentee leader, and a twenty-five-year-old, just-married Wilber Sutherland was still feeling his way. Stacey wrote apologetically, "It is a long time since I have written to you, but that does not mean indifference or neglect. Our responsibilities have taken me away from Canada a great deal, but the work is going ahead and God is blessing."[33]

In an aside to the board before he left, Stacey said "that he believed the InterVarsity Christian Fellowship USA had staff members sufficiently mature to carry out the summer program under the leadership of the Associate General Secretary, Mr Charles H Troutman." When Stacey returned to Geneva to take up the reins of IVCF again, his neighbor had to make a psychological adjustment from being number one to number two. It was not an easy transition for anyone to make, particularly two like Charles Troutman and Stacey Woods. The next three years would be dominated in IVCF in the United States by the developing conflict between the two men, who had known each other since college days, pioneered a movement together and were now to find themselves in a place that neither they nor InterVarsity wanted to be.

9

Articulate Author

STACEY'S INVITATION TO THE 1944 PLYMOUTH CONFERENCE for the Advancement of Evangelical Scholarship placed him in the forefront of a rising generation of progressive academics and intellectuals. The opportunity came because of his friendship with Harold John Ockenga. The handsome minister of "historic Park Street Church on the Boston Common," not yet forty, came from a humble background—his father was a Chicago transit driver—who throughout a brilliant academic and athletic career showed outstanding leadership potential. Though elected the president of the Princeton Seminary student association in 1929, a guarantee of future high ecclesiastical preferment, "Ocky" (as he was called) went into exile with Machen, completing his final year at Westminster Seminary. He became assistant to Clarence Edward Macartney in Pittsburgh, briefly pastored a church in that city and before he turned thirty was chosen by A. Z. Conrad to succeed him at Boston's prestigious Park Street Church.

Ockenga soon attracted many civic leaders to the church, among them John Bolten Sr., who was seeking an alternative to his Christian Brethren connection. Bolten and Ockenga conceived the idea of a conference that would bring together the brightest and best of young evangelical scholarship. Bolten agreed to fund the whole enterprise, paying both travel and hotel expenses. The roster of topics at Plymouth reflected their own agenda: Clarence Bouma of Calvin Seminary insisted God was neither Republican nor capitalist, William Emmet Powers spoke of the need to recover the concept of atonement because it had "practically dropped out of the picture and even God has been reduced to a relative factor or to a mere process." John Bolten, who as a nonacademic layman felt it inappropriate to sign the manifesto, shared his passion for the church, saying that it was in danger of being "considered only another big business." Stacey had the concluding talk on evangelism.

The 1944 conference had called for a continuing "fellowship for evangelical scholars," a felt need because of their isolation. Gaps in the evangelical bibliography were discussed and assignments doled out. The following year they gathered in the same location and discussed progress. John Bolten was commended for his "consecrated generosity [which] made possible this forward movement in the interest of the Christian faith in such a critical hour." There were committees appointed to assess available "evangelical scholarly literature" and determine how "the most reputable publishers" could be encouraged to produce more. Stacey Woods and Clarence Bouma were asked to plan a third conference the following summer, but the constituent IFES assembly and Ockenga's unexpected government-sponsored trip to Germany caused a last-minute cancellation. Though no further gatherings of a similar nature were called, the formation of Fuller Theological Seminary (Ockenga was first president) and the growth of InterVarsity and IFES can be seen as recipients of the momentum it created.[1]

THE EVANGELICAL MIDDLE GROUND

Ockenga had been the prime mover in the establishment of the National Association of Evangelicals. Eschewing the narrow fundamentalism of Carl McIntire and his American Council of Churches, it occupied an evangelical middle ground. That was precisely where Stacey felt most comfortable in positioning the young IVCF in the United States. The National Association of Evangelicals dissociated itself from the shrill separatism of the right and also distanced itself from the fuzzy accommodation of the left. It welcomed evangelicals from the major denominations, who were regarded by the American Council of Christian Churches and the International Council of Christian Churches as hopelessly apostate and therefore irretrievably compromised. It also provided sanctuary for evangelicals who formed an increasingly struggling minority in the ecumenical frenzy then sweeping Protestantism.

Stacey was involved almost from the beginning of the National Association of Evangelicals as a member of its Commission on Evangelism. But when in 1947 Carl McIntire's group set aside $8,000 "in order to present the ecclesiastical point of view of the ACCC to our students" and subsequently assailed him, along with other broadly evangelical groups such as Child Evangelism (also a Herbert Taylor-financed organized, Taylor as a Methodist being a target) for having "adopted a noninvolvement attitude in the state of conflict now existing in American Christendom," Stacey became anxious.[2] In 1948 he resigned after only one year of his term on the National Association of Evangelicals's board of administration, noting that "Apparently realizing my oneness in spirit with NAE, these folk continue to do their utmost to line up with ACCC other national movements affiliated with us but outside continental United States." He described the result as potentially "completely and inexpressibly disastrous" particularly to IFES, as it was only just being established.[3] Considering that the gifted Francis Schaeffer was at the time involved with Carl McIntire in setting up the International Council of Christian Churches in Amsterdam, we realize that the threat was not a hollow one.

At the same time the World Student Christian Fellowship was issuing warnings about IFES.[4] In an October 1948 bulletin they cautioned about a group that was "biblical revivalist" (explained as Anglo-Saxon terminology) or "pietistic" (for continentals). "'Evangelicals' feel that they are a minority, which is standing for the Faith in face of all attempts to rethink it or restate it. The basic attitude is the defence of orthodoxy. Christians are believed to be able, through the work of the Holy Spirit, to attain to a correct set of affirmations." The statement went on to criticise IFES's attitude toward ecumenicity: "membership of the national fellowships in IFES is restricted to an 'evangelical' definition, whereas the national movements within the WSCF are, for the most part, open to all students who seriously desire to participate in the life of a Christian fellowship." It went on to say rather caustically that the IFES insisted on "a personal test of membership which makes certain that those who join a fellowship are 'real Christians'; membership of a Christian Church is not considered a sufficient guarantee of orthodoxy."

Stacey sent the report to Ockenga. How he got a copy is uncertain, but he had his sources and was remarkably abreast of everything going on in the Christian world. A lesser man would have been cowed into submission or craven with fear and anxiety, but Stacey was not abashed. Partly, of course, it was the result of having Douglas Johnson always behind him. But Stacey was by nature (if not by grace) a pugilist, and he enjoyed a good scrap. At times it seemed that he was *Athanasius contra mundum* but attacks of this kind seemed to galvanize him and meant that he was all the more concerned to give time to establishing the identity of IFES in Europe, albeit at the cost of effective leadership of InterVarsity in the United States.

THE IMPORTANCE OF PRINT MEDIA

It also meant that media, particularly print media, became very important for the fledgling organization. The establishment of a North American InterVarsity Press in 1947 implied that not only could British IVP publications, with their scholarship, be made available by staff to students. There would now be indigenous American publications. Notable among the imports was the path-breaking 1943 *Are the New Testament Documents Reliable?* by F. F. Bruce, a rising young Christian Brethren scholar who had just begun to lecture at Leeds University. Stacey encouraged staff to bring IVP titles on their visits to chapters. As mentioned earlier, one of them remarked, "He had a way of knowing the right thing for me to read and greatly expanded my spiritual horizons with books."[5] Joel Carpenter notes that "travelling Inter-Varsity agents, who often sold or gave away books, also introduced American students to the works of C. S. Lewis."[6] He goes on to note that "Inter-Varsity's intellectual mission reflected the passions of C. Stacey Woods." Stacey was indeed seldom seen without a book in his hand, always recommending one to hapless staff and generally encouraging an atmosphere of intellectual curiosity in IVCF. His list of "must-read" volumes received a mixed response from some staff. When he presented a list of "great classics" he expected his sons to have read (and reviewed) before he returned from his latest tour, it was not always appreciated!

But it was *HIS* magazine that became the bully pulpit of C. Stacey Woods. At its tenth anniversary, in the October 1951 issue, Stacey editorialized that "*His* was born in 1941 in the hope and with the prayer that it would be much more than a house organ promoting the interests of Inter-Varsity Christian Fellowship. It was to be the magazine of university students who belong to Christ and whose first desire is to live for Him. Hence *His* magazine."[7] Stacey was fortunate in his first editor, Bob Walker, whose subsequent stellar career more than vindicated his choice. Five years later the *HIS* circulation was 10,000, including a thousand copies sent to Canada. By 1958 it had soared to 17,500. But the influence of *HIS* was incalculable, as Lawrence Neal Jones pointed out in a 1961 Yale dissertation: "*His* fulfilled an indispensable role in the life of Inter-Varsity during the first decade of its existence. It helped to compensate for the lack of adequate financial resources, limited staff and facilities, lack of stable patterns of work, and the Inter-Varsity's lack of a popular image."[8]

The acquisition of Wilbur Smith as a consulting editor was a stroke of genius on the part of Stacey, as was the frequent use of Carl Henry. Both men were widely used: Smith, who was already appreciated as the author of the 1944 IVP title *The Man Who Lived Again* (a defense of the bodily resurrection of Jesus), spoke at the first two missionary conferences, in 1946 and 1948. Carl Henry, a regular contributor to *HIS*, was befriended early by Stacey and was used frequently in IVCF rallies in the mid-1940s when he was in Chicago at Northern Baptist Seminary. He was at Campus-in-the-Woods in 1947 and wrote *Giving a Reason for Our Hope* in 1949 for IVP, the product of Friday-night ministry with students. And his *The Uneasy Conscience of Modern Fundamentalism* sparked a whole series of articles in *HIS*, among them one by the Hungarian Ferenc Kiss, "The World and the Church," in April 1948. The article brought down the wrath of Carl McIntire, who dismissed it as communist propaganda, necessitating a defense from Stacey.

Stacey generally kept to less controversial issues, soliciting responses from other people. Typical of his approach was his reaction to an article in the 26 September 1947 Toronto *Star*, in which a Student Christian Movement conference at Lake Couchiching, Orillia, Ontario, had resolved that "there be a system of economic democracy in which the land and means of production are operated by the elected representatives of the people to meet the demands of all."[9] In the June 1948 *HIS* Stacey responded with "Is Free Enterprise Anti-Christian?" His reaction was predictable: "This statement indicates that the Student Christian Movement continues to move to the left politically, is opposed to the free enterprise system as such and is attempting to instill ideals of socialism in the minds of students." He wrote to Clarence Bouma of Calvin Theological Seminary that summer. Bouma was both a speaker at Campus-in-the-Woods and at the IFES inaugural that summer, and a participant in the Plymouth conferences. Stacey solicited an article "for our magazine *His* on Christianity and the free enterprise system, evaluating it from a Christian point of view negatively and positively and setting forth what in your judgment is the Christian attitude in this matter."[10] Using Bouma took some courage on Stacey's part: board member Bob Van Kampen had accused Bouma, an amilliennialist, of not believing in the second coming and, since he was a member of the Christian

Reformed Church, as having no time for evangelism and denying free will because of "an overbalanced emphasis on predestination."[11] After an exchange of seven letters over as many months, Bouma complied, but said (as he sent the finished article) that it had "cost me much sweat, though not blood and tears."[12] The resulting article was a significant contribution to evangelical thinking in that era, providing neither a blanket endorsement of free enterprise nor cosying up to socialism as was then popular among some left-leaning denominational officials.

Stacey also knew who to approach for articles that were beyond his expertise that could challenge students to think constructively about intellectual issues. After Stacey's former professor at Dallas, Henry Clarence Thiessen gave a stimulating lecture at the 1944 Plymouth conference, he was approached about writing for *HIS*.[13] Thiessen told Ockenga:

> Mr Stacey Woods asked me to write two articles for the Inter-Varsity magazine *His*. I was to write somewhat along the lines of my address at Plymouth but felt it questionable whether students would read an article so definitely philosophical as that address was. I, therefore, changed it very considerably.[14]

Thiessen, who died at a relatively young age, was the dean of the Wheaton Graduate School and a significant influence on many of the rising stars of the new evangelicalism. *HIS* spread that impact: Thiessen's two articles challenged readers critically to examine their metaphysics and epistemology. Cornelius Van Til, another presenter at Plymouth, also became a *HIS* contributor. After the legendary 1935 encounter at the League of Evangelical Students's annual meeting, the restoration of Van Til to favor in IVCF was sealed by an invitation to Campus-in-the-Woods. In 1948 he wrote a challenging *HIS* article on "Does the Universe Have a Mind?"

A PROLIFIC WRITER

Stacey's wrote more than sixty articles and editorials in *HIS* over thirty-five years, not counting the unattributed monthly "Campus News," which showed his inimitable style. Indeed, during the first ten years there was hardly an issue of *HIS* that he did not work over. When Joe Bayly came in 1951, a new format emerged, Stacey was preoccupied elsewhere, and he did not interfere as much. Stacey wrote quickly, putting down his thoughts on a large pad of paper or speaking into a dictaphone. The latter came naturally—he was quite fluent and had a gift for ministry particularly as a Bible teacher. Bob Fryling recalls how in the 1960s he would come from Switzerland, his home at the time, arrive at the *Sunday School Times* office in Philadelphia (where Bob's father worked and where Bob had a summer job), sit down in his cubicle with an open Bible, and churn out his Scripture study guide column without revision. Then Stacey would leave the office promptly, having completed his assignment.[15]

Several of Stacey's articles were turned into IVP pamphlets, such as his 1945 piece "Taboo?" which became a classic and changed for many the fundamentalist legalism in which they had been raised, what Stacey described as "unscriptural teaching on separation—'legality' in the guise of 'spirituality.'" He continued, "This modern legality has placed its taboo on certain practices, discreetly ignoring other—sometimes more harmful—practices. The implication is that one is 'separate' if he does not attend certain forbidden places of amusement." He went on to define worldliness: "self-indulgent attitude of the heart and mind toward life. . . . [I]t is not merely doing certain forbidden things or going to certain proscribed places. Worldliness is what we are, not just what we do. It is essentially an inner attitude, not only outward actions."[16] Just how revolutionary such a concept was for anyone brought up in the fundamentalist subculture of the 1940s may not be obvious today, but it was a liberating experience for those for whom Christianity had been identified with five don'ts: dancing, drinking, card-playing, smoking, and theater attendance. Stacey's concern was primarily evangelistic, making the gospel more attractive to the outsider and Christians less ghettoized.

Stacey's condemnation of legalism did not mean that he was antinomian. *HIS* featured several articles with strong ethical concerns. In "The Ten Commandments and the Campus," he applied the Decalogue, command by command, to students: "today in college and university we are responsible to God to obey Him, to keep His commandments." He distanced himself from dispensationalists, whom he charged "have mistakenly relegated the Ten Commandments to a past dispensation acting as if these categorical imperative of Mt Sinai no longer applied to their lives." He relied on the Anglican communion liturgy to drive home his challenge to "go to your room and set aside perhaps half an hour down on your knees and, if you care to do so, use the Church of England prayer for cleansing of heart."[17]

Four years later, Stacey was at it again: "Add to Your Faith Moral Character" represented an increasing concern as he surveyed the American scene. "The tragedy of mid-twentieth-century evangelical Christianity is that too often its ethical content is largely missing."[18] He complained that becoming a Christian was more important than being a Christian, and that many had "a one-sided, imperfect understanding of all that is involved in being a Christian." He emphasized (from 2 Pet 1:4-8, a passage that would soon become a favorite for evangelicals) the need of "adding" to our faith, concluding with the quality of brotherly love, "an active sacrificial quality toward all who are in Christ Jesus." These were oblique references to a popular 1950s Christianity that was, he maintained, shallow and superficial. They were also an implicit nod toward Christian involvement in the struggle for racial equality in America.

Readers sometimes could fill in the dots themselves. In another editorial, Stacey had spoken of the new loyalty given Christians: "This new national relationship, which supersedes all earthly nationality, unites Christians of every race and every color, for all are brothers and sisters in Christ."[19] A YMCA worker at the Mennonite Goshen College responded enthusiastically: "It is only when we are conscious of, and live the truth which you so forcefully emphasize that citizenship in the Kingdom of God becomes meaningful as a determining factor in our attitudes and behaviour. . . . Your editorial points up one area of human thought and activity in which the church has not always had a clear and consistent position."[20]

Lawrence Neale Jones, who interviewed Stacey extensively for his 1961 Yale dissertation, states emphatically that "conversations with Mr. Woods and his writings have given the writer the impression that Woods just does not give social concerns the same priority in his thinking that he gives to more pietistic concerns."[21] To what extent this is a fair comment is debatable. Certainly Stacey left it to others to make direct challenges to the systemic and endemic racism of the United States in the 1950s in which evangelicals were complicit. But for anyone knowledgeable in the biblical texts Stacey cited, the message was clear. At the same time, there was the residual pietism of his Christian Brethren heritage that he shared with most of the adult constituency represented by InterVarsity Christian Fellowship. His upbringing came out in a 1948 piece titled "The Principles of Christian Modesty," which asked about the appropriateness of a woman wearing one of the new two-piece bathing suits. He warned, "We are living in a culture which is rejecting Christian standards, in an increasing paganism and obsession with the physical at the expense of the spiritual."[22] The principle was nondebatable, the example perhaps questionable.

HIS was also an opportunity for Stacey to inform the IVCF constituency about his travels and activities as well as that of the staff. Each year the new staff roster appeared. From 1947 on there were regular updates on IFES activity. *HIS*, particularly in the early years when staff were spread thinly, provided instruction on the leadership of chapters, necessitated by the reality that a quarter of all students turned over each year. The goals and objectives of the organization were continually emphasized and reemphasized, particularly when under attack. At the beginning of the academic year in 1951, Stacey articulated that in the InterVarsity chapter there should be (1) a witness to the historic Christian faith, (2) a proclamation of the gospel of Christ by every Christian student, (3) a spiritual "kindergarten for the babes in Christ," and (4) a true "school of prophets" where young men and women in Christ may exercise their spiritual gifts for the extension of the kingdom of God and in the building by Jesus of his church. "We aim to be totally Christian, and by His enablement, to engage in 'total Christian warfare' against the world, the flesh, and the devil, to the glory of Christ our Lord and King."[23]

The photo of the head of a grinning Stacey Woods appeared above one article explaining the statement of faith that chapter executives, staff, the board of directors and the corporation were all required to assent to. Having provided its five affirmations, "This I Believe" went on to explain that the basis of faith is "an expression of the spiritual and doctrinal purpose of the organization, . . . the simplest and most concentrated enunciation of doctrine that would insure that the Fellowship, both nationally and locally, continue true to God and the Bible." He stipulated that this credo was "not a flag to be waved aloft and saluted. Rather, it is an anchor that keeps the organization from drifting from its doctrinal and scriptural moorings." The basis, he continued, is to ensure that "special speakers are truly evangelical" and at election time, when new officers are voted in, that they "fully understand and adhere to them. Furthermore, he must realize his responsibility in seeing that these principles guide chapter activities throughout the term. Just as great care should be taken as is exercised in the selection of Board and staff members of the Inter-Varsity Christian Fellowship."[24]

Of particular importance to an evangelical was the doctrine of Scripture. "In a day when almost every person and movement is tagged, labelled, and put into a theological pigeonhole the Inter-Varsity Christian Fellowship prefers to be known for its stand for the historic Christian faith—Biblical Christianity." He went on to define the word: "By the adjective *Biblical* we mean that the Scriptures are considered the objective, authoritative, inerrant, written Word of God."[25] A year later he further explained, "It is understood that divine inspiration guarantees the inerrancy of the Bible, and this extends not only to matters of faith and conduct but also to historicity because if the Bible were not true historically, its reliability in matters of faith and conduct would obviously be open to question."[26] The debate over inerrancy was twenty-five years away. Arguably the definitive statement on biblical inspiration for all evangelicals came with the IVP publication in 1957 of *Authority*, three talks Martyn Lloyd-Jones gave at the IFES quadrennial the year before at Glen Orchard, Ontario.

Generally Stacey avoided writing on doctrinal matters about which there was a difference of opinion among evangelicals, and particularly concerns that were church-related rather than parachurch. One exception to this rule—"Departing from its usual policy of avoiding doctrinal subjects, the details of which are disputed between denominations, *HIS* presents this article because Christian young people too frequently neglect or participate thoughtlessly in the communion service"—was a piece he coauthored with John Bolten in 1947. "The Importance of the Communion Service" later appeared as an offprint at Bolten's expense. It reflects the passion of two who were brought up with the weekly Sunday morning "breaking of bread." The article concluded, "It is shameful to note that in many churches today little or no place is given to the Lord's Supper. The communion is treated as a mere appendage to a service after the sermon—often on an irrelevant subject—and people are tired and anxious to hurry home to dinner. Little or no trouble is taken to fence the Lord's table from unbelievers or from believers living in open sin."[27] To make matters more interdenominational Stacey included at the bottom of the article a quote from the nineteenth-century Scottish Presbyterian mystic Robert Murray McCheyne.

THE NATURE OF THE UNIVERSITY

In all of the wide breadth of material covered by Stacey in his articles in *HIS* there is one striking omission: the nature of the university. Lawrence Jones stated, "Stacey was asked why this subject has been so neglected, 'We have been so busy at our basic task that we just haven't had time to treat this important area.'"[28] In addition to the "Charles Stilwell" article cited previously, there are in fact two *HIS* articles that deal with scholarly pursuits and the university, both coming from an outside source. One was a reprint from *Our Hope* magazine, the other a speech to the American Scientific Affiliation. Because they are unique in the Stacey Woods canon they deserve close scrutiny.

In 1954 Stacey sent an article titled "A Total Christian Ministry in Our Universities" to *Our Hope* magazine. *Our Hope* was basically the organ of Arno Gaebelein, the Christian Brethren eschatologist, so it is interesting to find it there, though at that point Arno's son Frank was trying to make the content more challenging. Jones describes it as "both a defense of IVCF's philosophy of campus ministry and an appeal for contributions." One looks in vain for any philosophic overview reminiscent of John Henry Newman's 1854 *The Idea of a University*. Though he had never been to a university and was no philosopher, it must be said in Stacey's defense that having come from Australia, having been influenced by British IVF and having begun his ministry in Canada, he was well acquainted with the university structure in a way that few American evangelicals were. Nor was he, as an outsider, infected by the prevalent anti-intellectualism of American fundamentalism.

Nevertheless again the approach he took to the university was more of a mission field than a place for a creative engagement by Christians with the culture. He wrote:

> Evangelical Christians are concerned about the universities and the university students of the United States as never before. The modern university has well been described as a microcosm or a little universe within itself. During his four years of study the student lives his life, in some respects, apart from the world; and yet he faces in essence all the problems and challenges of life itself. In university the student usually decides upon his vocation or profession. During his undergraduate days, his life philosophy, or world and life view, is determined. . . . Here so often the die is cast for time and for eternity.[29]

He continued by delineating the church's responsibility and specifically that of IVCF for "a total Christian message and ministry in the university." He said, "the university must be evangelized." "What do we mean by evangelization?" he asked, but instead of content to the evangel, he focused on packaging, methods taking precedence over message. There is admittedly a recognition that "there must also be a defence of the historic Christian faith to students who intellectually doubt the revelation of God" but he cannot resist a concluding altar call: "God is still using consecrated minorities, whether in the university or anywhere else," and what was required was "abandonment to God, obedience to His command, and a dependence upon Him and upon the method of the Holy Spirit, rather than for us to rethink Christianity in twentieth century terms and to adopt the success philosophy, techniques, and salesmanship of a materialistic age." Stacey is looking over his shoulder at three-year-old Campus Crusade for Christ, not facing directly on engaging intellectually with the modern university and its truth claims.

The American Scientific Affiliation was a grouping of evangelical (and funda-mentalist) scientists, many of whom were university and college professors. In his speech Stacey said:

> I would suggest that here is one area in which the American Scientific Affiliation can give leadership to the undergraduate university world, particularly the secular univer-sity world, and at all times insist that we as Christians start with God and His reve-lation, and that as a principle, human reason, understanding and interpretation must submit itself to "Thus saith the Lord."[30]

He challenged his listeners to seek spiritual truth as well as scientific investiga-tion: "Such an emphasis by men of science upon the Word of God, in an era pre-occupied with material existence, could have a profound effect upon today's uni-versity undergraduates, Christian and non-Christian." A well-thought-through Christian apologetic, starting with the creation mandate and seeking bases for a consistently Christian response to scientific knowledge, was missing. On the other hand the audience would have left with a challenge to live a life of biblical integrity that could not be ignored.

JOURNALISTIC EXCELLENCE

HIS magazine was Stacey Woods: his desire for artistic and journalistic excellence, his refusal to condone mediocrity, his entrepreneurial skills in its dissemination, and his wide-ranging search for writers who would challenge and simulate, and occasion-ally annoy. It was an extension of his personality. In many ways it was his prize jewel, something that he took infinite pains over. *HIS* was also one of the main reasons why InterVarsity Christian Fellowship received such a warm welcome from thinking American evangelicals and particularly among Christian students in the university. Many of us at university looked forward to its monthly appearance in our boxes in the dormitory mail room, eagerly reading it from cover to cover. Graphically, in terms of content, and spiritually, it represented a dramatic shift from a pulp jour-nalism that focused on negativism and the "how to" articles that characterized so much of the fundamentalist and evangelical press. Stacey's frenetic activity and in-novative creativity found a useful outlet in the production and dissemination of *HIS*. *HIS* opened the windows of the mind and enlarged the spirit. Evangelicals had re-discovered the university even if many of them had not fully engaged the culture.

10

A Dark Space

HIS SENIOR STAFF WERE NOT HAPPY WITH STACEY WOODS. They gathered in a cranky mood that 19 January 1950 at Lake Geneva, Wisconsin. The Covenant Harbor Bible Camp, an hour and a half's drive northwest of Chicago, had been chosen as the site of a senior staff consultation. The site was only three years old, the food excellent, but both the view across the lake and the mood were icy.

Minutes of the meeting could not disguise their unhappiness: "This work had required Stacey's absence for five months during the last two years in Europe and this was felt to be a distinct handicap to the American work. The staff unanimously urged that some arrangement be made whereby Stacey would be relieved of this responsibility and be able to concentrate on the American and Canadian work."[1] Valiantly, Stacey tried to defend the time he had spent the previous three years with IFES. He described it as "a pioneer missionary work for the encouragement of students in various countries." He went on to emphasize that though the goal was to establish national movements in many countries, this was only in the beginning stages. He cited the German movement, recently organized. But the fact was inescapable: money had to come from North America. "Canadian and US students and friends are carrying the complete financial load of this work." And the raising of this money is largely in the hands of staff. And then, as the minutes show, he added the sting: IFES's "administration is the responsibility of the general secretary."

Senior staff were not mollified. They went on to suggest the appointment of an IFES general secretary who could travel, and several undersecretaries should work with that individual. Then came the ominous and awkwardly phrased statement: "Inasmuch as the financial responsibility will still be borne by ourselves, care should be taken in entering into any relationship or arrangement which will not relieve Stacey in a great deal of these administrations."

The meeting, delayed for six months, was Charles Troutman's idea. Writing from Campus-in-the-Woods the previous summer to a Stacey ensconced in student ministry abroad and oblivious to what was happening at home, he brought disquieting news of a feeling of "desperation due to a lack of contact with each other. . . . No one is threatening to resign, but we are weathering five months of indecisiveness simply because I know too little of your commitments to others to do anything but wait for your return." Troutman went on to itemize some of the concerns: "Neither Joe [Bayly], Cleo [Buxton], nor Carl [Thomas] seem to have any idea of our policy and are constantly asking questions. These matters may be perfectly clear to you, but they are not to the rest of us and it seems to me that a session together is most necessary."[2] Bayly, Buxton and Thomas had been appointed regional secretaries in January of the previous year, reporting to Stacey through Charles Troutman as associate general secretary. Even W. E. C. Petersen, the "great Dane," a year into the job as secretary of stewardship, was unclear about his responsibilities. The new management grid was breaking down.

By way of specifics Troutman listed no less than eleven areas of concern. Several of them were warnings to Stacey that he would have done well to heed. It was obvious that with Stacey's long trips to Europe on behalf of IFES, InterVarsity's relationship to the international organization was creating stress: "You do not have your senior staff behind you on this and we must have them so, as well as on other problems involved." Another cloud on the horizon was their own relationship: "For the sake of the rest of the staff, our individual responsibilities—yours and mine, must be made crystal clear, or we are headed for confusion." There were compensations: "Joe [Bayly] has been positively infectious when these above matters have come up, in stating that our service is to the Lord and not to CSW nor CWT." But over against all the organizational frustrations, there was the overriding compensation of ministry: "The August camp has been one triumph after another for the Lord."[3]

It appears to have taken some time for Stacey to process this letter, one of the most important he ever received from staff, and probably the last one in the files that shows anything resembling the close bond that had once existed between him and Charles Troutman, sealed from their days together at Wheaton and in Canada. The usual annual call for prayer seemed to have added urgency that autumn of 1949. Stacey wrote,

> Let us pray that all of us may be given a fresh vision of Christ, that He may show us to ourselves as He knows us really to be and that as never before each of us may lay hold of God by faith both for ourselves and for the work to which He has called us. You know that as Christians our walk with God demands constant vigilance, frequent warfare or struggle against the world, the flesh, and the devil around us and within us. There are so many things that come between ourselves and the Lord, even our own unworthiness or the difficulty of our task, and so we fail to trust God and to honor Him with our faith, fail to trust Him on behalf of students.[4]

A Troubled Relationship

InterVarsity had gone through spectacular growth in the 1940s. Could the momentum now be sustained in a new decade? Was Stacey the pioneer equal to the task of administering a large organization—actually *three* organizations? Was he asking too much of himself?

In the Chicago office there was a bowl with two goldfish. One of them, sleek and golden, went about the water with a stately rhythm, gliding effortlessly among the rocks. The other was black and seemed to be constantly flitting in and out in a state of perpetual motion. The office staff soon called the regal goldfish Charles and the black activist fish Stacey.

Or, in Douglas Johnson's imagery, Stacey was "Battleship No. 1" and Charles "Battleship No. 2." He wrote to Troutman with his usual unerring insight:

> My own reading of the situation is that Battleship No. 1. is built for mighty scraps with determined and ruthless enemies and can unbendingly scatter them all! But he has never learnt the art of delegation in peace-time. Battleship No. 2. is built for more delicate duties of peacetime, "showing the flag" and ambassadorial tasks. He is good at visualising what can be done and quietly building up the Empire. (But he is probably not so good at detailed organisation and all the humdrum of service life. My guess is that he is, like our Highlanders, excellent at idealistically serving the

Cause—but not so outstanding in the quartermastering and Sergeant-Major duties! This last would constantly imitate Battleship No. I. And he would tend not to trust him on these points and therefore it would tend to cause him to accentuate the non-delegating tendency.)[5]

Delegation was but one issue that was driving a wedge between Charles Troutman and Stacey Wood. Ideally the two men should have complemented each other: Stacey the one with a grand vision going off in all directions, Charles the daily diarist with the patient attention to detail. Stacey would issue commands, come up with sharp and pithy statements dazzling with intuitive insight. But you could talk with Charles, who was a listener. When you talked to Charles, you felt you had been heard. People were often terrified by Stacey and failed to see the side of him that was paternal, perhaps avuncular, and often warmly pastoral. Charles made you feel good. The tragedy of the first half of the 1950s was that, instead of their differences being complementary they became competitive. That competition almost wrecked IVCF and caused long-lasting corporate—and individual—trauma. Out of the conflict between Troutman and Woods, as it unfolded like some Greek tragedy, a culture of disfunctionality, which lasted a long time, developed within senior staff and board as they related to the head of IVCF. Troutman (as Stacey's successor) would become the first of five presidents that left under unhappy circumstances. Only with the coming of Steve Hayner in 1989, after Stacey had long gone, were the ground rules changed and, years later, could there be a happy exit. Such was the corporate culture that the Troutman-Woods conflict created. That escalating conflict forms a kind of leitmotif to everything going on in IVCF during those three years, affecting every aspect of the ministry in subtle and not so subtle ways.

THE YEAR OF EVANGELISM

Meanwhile, out in the field, IVCF ministries continued despite the growing turmoil at the central office. "The strong work of the Holy Spirit at the local levels where staff, Christian faculty, and students were functioning was not dependent upon the national office as might have been true if the structures had followed the typical business lines of authority," Jim Nyquist recalled as one who joined staff in 1949.[6] Others joined the staff during that period, 1950 being a significant year for new entries that later made a name: Barbara Boyd, George Ensworth,[7] Charles

Hummel[8] and Paul Little.[9] Several of these came to IVCF from Biblical Seminary, New York City. Barbara recalls, "One of the remarkable gifts of God to Inter-Varsity was the openness of Stacey Woods . . . to bring women right into the center of the ministry, his openness to reach into a seminary like Biblical, which might have been questionable to others because it had no written doctrinal statement."[10] Biblical Seminary pioneered the inductive Bible study method, which became part of the IVCF canon. Popularizing it among staff was Barbara Boyd, whose Bible and Life curriculum was a major breakthrough in making the Scriptures come alive. Anne and Frank Horton became IFES appointees to Europe, and there were many other Biblical Seminary graduates among the staff.[11]

Stacey reported to the Canadian board on 4 February 1950 that "there had been on the part of the senior staff a general feeling that the time has come for more emphasis on evangelism."[12] The staff's recommendation that the fiscal (i.e., academic) year 1950-1951 should be devoted to evangelistic missions was approved unanimously by the board, as it was in the United States. Harold Ockenga was one of those approached to spearhead such an event. Stacey wrote to him asking that he block off several weeks between January until Easter 1951 for university evangelistic meetings, saying that it was "God's hour for such an evangelistic push among college students."[13] Ockenga was at the time in the midst of hosting the mid-century Billy Graham campaign that had caused considerable excitement in staid New England. Surprisingly, with all the demands of his multifaceted ministry, instead of the usual "No" at the top of the letter—Ockenga received dozens of such requests each month, almost all of them turned down—he put a "?" only later to say he was unable to oblige Woods. Graham himself came to the University of Michigan in the autumn of 1950, filling the university armory for the four days. Another utilized was Bob Munger of First Presbyterian Church in Berkeley, whose ministry at the University of California demonstrated his appeal to students.

The "Year of Evangelism" reached its peak with the arrival of Leith Samuel, who had spent the previous three years as an evangelist with Inter-Varsity Fellowship in Britain. Samuel had been recommended to Stacey by Douglas Johnson for his effective and sensitive outreach to non-Christians. Johnson had given Samuel lots of advice, outfitting him for January in Canada and telling him not to accept any honorary doctorates by American Christian colleges that were using him as a proxy for Stacey, who had turned them all down flatly. Leith Samuel flew into Montreal on a BOAC flight at 5:30 a.m. on 12 January, the day before his first mission slated for McGill University. He stayed for three months with spectacular results. In Canada he led six missions across the country. In the United States he spoke at universities in California and Michigan. In all, he estimated in his final wrap-up letter, 3,400 different students heard him speak ("adding the numbers present at the largest meeting each series"[14]), the aggregate attendance for all his meetings was 17,000, and there were 450 professed conversions.

The university administrators in each place supported the effort in ways that would be inconceivable today: Principal Cyril James at McGill University provided

Senior leaders at Campus-in-the-Woods, 1951: (standing L to R) Wilber Sutherland, Joseph Bayly, Beno Kopp(?); (sitting L to R) Charles Troutman, Stacey Woods, Jane Hollingsworth, William E. C. Petersen (Courtesy of IVCF-USA)

his office for a press conference and spoke in support of the mission to reporters present. President Sydney Smith welcomed Leith Samuel to the University of Toronto, made the suite of Chancellor Vincent Massey available for his use, and at its conclusion sent thanks on behalf of the board of governors. At the University of Western Ontario the whole lecture schedule was revised and each dean asked every class to open with an announcement. Attendance was uniformly good: 2,000 in total at the University of British Columbia, for instance. "Mr Leith Samuel seems to have been given the particular ministry of student evangelism to a degree not seen in any other man used in Canada or the United States," Wilber Sutherland reported to the board.[15] "In each case the door was left wide open on the campus for a further evangelistic effort of this nature."

Leith Samuel wrote Stacey as he sailed back to England on the Queen Elizabeth in early April 1951: "You have a great bunch of enthusiasts & I counted it a very real pleasure to have some share with them in their great work. God has been very gracious to you in the quality & number of the men & women He has given you." He recommended that the Toronto office be a regional one because IVCF was "suffering from schizophrenia, half the brain in Chicago, half in Toronto." And he concluded ominously, in reference to Stacey and Charles Troutman: "I think the work has suffered somewhat with neither of you able to give the time needed to keep things well in hand in the office. This is only a suggestion for you to consider & put in the WPB [i.e., waste paper basket] if you feel God is not in this." He sensed something was wrong but surprisingly, for a Britisher, had no awareness of Canadian sensitivities and its growing nationalism.[16]

Less successful was an invitation in June 1950 to a Latvian émigré, Dr. Karlis Leyasmeyer, engineered (with financial support provided) by Margaret Haines. After summer exposure at Campus-in-the-Woods it became apparent to senior staff that evangelism was not his gift. Stacey got caught in the middle, and Leyasmeyer was given mixed signals. Stacey failed to read correspondence between Leyasmeyer and Troutman before the executive committee met on 21 November, attempted to be diplomatic and when the executive committee terminated Leyasmeyer's appointment at the end of the academic year (now too late for him to get another appointment), Miss Haines concluded that "the IVCF has acted unethically."[17] The whole incident left a bitter taste, alienated a longtime friend and raised questions about Stacey's ability to communicate directly, make tough calls, and support his staff.

DISSATISFACTION IN THE OFFICE

On 27 April 1951 Troutman in exasperation wrote Stacey that "the only alternative for you is to spend five days a week in the office that we may carry out without confusion the work as it is coordinated through you." He stated that "some of the difficulties in the Chicago office I believe are because you, as General Secretary, have not laid out very clearly and plainly the duties and the limits of authority of each one of us."[18] This was just at the point where Keith Hunt had been brought in from Michigan to be office manager, presumably to help relieve the pressure on

Stacey and provide cohesion for the administrative functions of IVCF. Meanwhile the Canadian movement was also complaining about neglect. At a board executive meeting in early May, duties were shuffled among leaders with the arrival of the new office manager, and it was pointedly noted that "It is understood that Mr Woods will regularly spend four or five days of each month in the Toronto office."[19]

Staff meetings were held in late June that year at Campus-in-the-Woods. Troutman carefully recorded his thinking ahead of time:

> Stacey once said, "I want four or five people in the office to help me run the Fellowship." This is his statement of the British idea of hierarchy or directorship applied to North America. It is also a statement describing his nature, and God's call to him. I have been unprepared to do this. Being unwilling to take a very second-place position, I have been in a turmoil.

He then went over his options, saying that God had not terminated nor changed his call to Charles, nor had he given Charles an opening elsewhere, and that "the work with IVCF is too important to risk even a heated discussion." God "has brought me back to the place for me, which I do not like. Therefore God's place for me is as Stacey's helpmeet in the IVCF. This means doing and being everything for him which he needs to do his work, working especially in those areas where he does not wish to work."[20]

David Adeney's arrival back on staff in February 1951 provided for senior staff the perspective of a suffering IVCF in China, from which he had recently been expelled, the wisdom of experience and seniority, and a willingness to laugh at himself and not take life too seriously. He also could work with Stacey, bring the best out of him and confront him lovingly. He and his family moved into a small house on Spring Street in Geneva across from the Woodses. David's biographer notes, "As good a friend as Stacey was and as much as David truly admired him, he sometimes had to step in as peacemaker. It was a role David would have rather avoided."[21] Because Wes Gustafson (another former China missionary) was already missionary secretary, David initially was appointed to be regional secretary for the Midwest. When Wes left in 1953, as part of a general exodus, David resumed his previous responsibilities, only to return to the Far East in 1956 at Stacey's invitation to become associate general secretary for IFES.

Another development during the summer was the first use of the Prentiss Bay site in Michigan's Upper Peninsula, not far from Herbert Taylor's hometown. The land along the shores of Lake Huron had been assembled by Taylor and was now being offered to several of the organizations he supported, among them IVCF. The first "Overflow Leadership Training Camp" was held there in 1951, led by Charles Troutman, when Campus-in-the-Woods became overbooked. "Rumpus in the stumps" (as those attending called it that first primitive summer) was not regarded with favor as a permanent location by staff attending. From Campus-in-the-Woods Stacey wrote, at the end of the season, that "the site is not too satisfactory" and set up a meeting with Taylor to discuss its future.[22] They met on 30 August and developed, in spite of misgivings (not shared either by Cleo Buxton or speaker Northcote Deck who loved the place), a proposal to the executive board for the development of the site (with Taylor providing an initial $25,000 for a lodge), which later became Cedar Campus.[23] It would be another three years before Stacey's vision was developed by Keith Hunt.[24]

COMPETING STUDENT MINISTRIES

Meanwhile clouds that further threatened IVCF were gathering on the horizon. Bob Finley had been working with IVCF as a fiery evangelist, enlisting young people for overseas missionary service. He had been in China briefly before that country went Communist, went on to Korea with Bob Pierce, the founder of World Vision, and returned home after another year. Bob Finley blamed Stacey for his return, claiming that monies promised by him had not been sent ("I have been disappointed in Stacey because he has not been a man of his word"). Because of the birth of his child, Bob was unable to meet with senior staff in January 1952. Stacey was dubious about taking on Finley's vision of international students ministry because "the scope of this work was in many respects beyond that of IVCF."[25] Charles was again caught in the middle as mediator. Bob Finley went on to organize FOCUS, Fellowship of Overseas College and University Students, later known as ISI, International Students Incorporated, with Dawson Trotman of Navigators, an organization that was increasingly involved on college campuses. In January of 1952 the senior staff council determined that "there be no direct or indirect organizational [links] with Robert Finley or with the work which he represents."[26]

But it was a thirty-year-old football player from Oklahoma who changed forever the landscape of Christian ministry on college campuses. Bill Bright, a member of

First Presbyterian Church, Hollywood, was completing seminary work at Fuller Theological Seminary and Princeton Theological Seminary in 1951 when with his wife, Vonette, started a student work on the campus of UCLA. A successful confections business had launched Bright into a sales-oriented promotional style that was culturally vastly different from IVCF's understated approach. Aggressive marketing soon challenged InterVarsity's constituency to switch financial support. Their philosophy of campus evangelism was different: their approach was staff-initiated direct evangelism rather than student-led discipling. Bill Bright visited Stacey Woods at 228 Spring Street, Geneva, in early 1952 on a cross-country tour to recruit young seminarians for training in his new ministry.

Initially, there was talk of cooperation, and Stacey said he would bring it up at staff meeting. Months later Troutman wrote from Campus-in-the-Woods: "Stacey is leaving England for the student camp at Darmstadt, Germany, and (since I am on an island in Canada) I am unable to find out whether he wrote you or not concerning the decision of the senior staff council. . . . [It] has asked me to write you regarding the possibility of working together experimentally during this coming academic year in order that we might determine God's will with assurance."[27]

It soon became apparent that cooperation with either group was impossible. As Stacey reported to the American IVCF board the following autumn, "the Christian Campus Crusade, while professing a desire to cooperate with the IVCF, do[es] not hesitate to state that we are spiritually dead and that we are, at least in measure, failing in our task."[28] The irony of these attacks was obvious; history was repeating itself. IVCF had been formed as a protest against the League of Evangelical Students for not providing enough staff support and not being committed to aggressive evangelism, favoring apologetics over outreach. Now Campus Crusade for Christ was saying exactly the same thing of IVCF.

In the autumn of 1952 Stacey had other things on his mind: Yvonne was pregnant. On 13 October he rushed her to the hospital. Due to poor eyesight, it was the last time he drove a car. Jonathan Stacey was born a healthy child. Jonathan's two older brothers were nine and twelve at the time. Growing up Jonathan felt like an only child, particularly as his parents relocated to Switzerland when he was ten. In retrospect Jonathan considered that he had an easier time with his father, partly because of his own temperament but partly because Stacey's parenting became more relaxed and his expectations more realistic.[29]

"Continuing Disunity in the Fellowship"

All of this was brewing just at the time when conflict in the office situation was coming to a boil. On 14 September 1951 a letter was sent to "fellow staff members" under the joint signatures of Stacey Woods and Charles Troutman. The statement was direct and to the point:

> As we have sought the mind of God regarding recent differences, two things seem apparent. —First, that the strain of the past academic year, with insufficient time for quiet, prayer, and consultation, coupled with our almost continual absence the one from the other, has been a cause of some of the difficulty. The fact that I, Stacey, have the double task of the work in Canada and the USA, together with the IFES, has greatly contributed to the difficulty. I realize that some of you feel that a choice between the IFES and the IVCF-USA should be made. I am quite ready for this at any time. Please pray that God's plan may be made plain. Personally, I do not believe that God wants me to be window dressing or just a figurehead in either capacity. As things stand, there seems no immediate release from the present situation. Second, we realize, to some extent at least, our shortcomings, our inability, also that we are not perfect, yet we wonder if, to some extent, we do not complement one another. . . . If it is best, either or both of us are ready to resign from the IVCF, and we have seriously faced this possibility. Now does not seem God's time for such a step.[30]

It went on to itemize four specific remedial actions: (1) spending time together in prayer and fellowship, (2) complete frankness for better understanding, (3) ceasing "discussing one another with other staff members . . . if the shortcomings of CSW are reported to CT, it will be CT's duty to come to CSW about it, and to discuss policy with each other before vetting it with others." It was an astonishing letter in which Stacey particularly, as general secretary, was being unusually open and vulnerable, particularly in calling for each staffer to "pray daily for us in our relationship with one another."

Troutman had already left home when it was mailed on the Friday. One of the IVCF secretaries dropped by at the Troutman home the night before, staying past midnight, describing the contents of the letter (and office politics) to Lois. Surprisingly Lois suggested in a letter to her husband on the weekend that the joint communication had been sent without Charles's wholehearted approval and after he had left the office. She was sure it was "contrary to your wish after you and he had Tuesday together . . . such an insipid thing to send out and of course it will do nothing to help."[31] It would appear the conciliation attempt was doomed before it got off the ground. The role of this secretary would be a major issue in the coming days, particularly as she was the daughter of a significant board member. How soon Stacey realized that he had leaks in the office is not known. Anyone whose trust has been abused by an employee, particularly a trusted administrative assistant, will have sympathy for his plight.

The first meeting of the senior staff council, as constituted by the American IVCF board when it met in Muskoka the previous summer, was held in January of 1952. It was generally a productive time, with an evaluation of the year of evangelism, and "the desperate need of evangelists and suitable Bible teachers." The absence of women from the meeting was noted, with the concern that a senior woman staff member or the nurses' secretary attend for one day, "during which time the problem of the women's work will be discussed." The ratio between staff and chapters and members was also debated, with each staff member responsible for ten chapters or four hundred active members. Bayly and Troutman were to work up a statement about cooperation with other student movements. As chair of the meeting, Troutman was to be the executive officer of council "empowered to act on his own initiative." Cameron Peck, as board chairman, subsequently had Troutman send out a memo protecting the legal interests of the board and also the general secretary, countering the idea "that the Senior Staff Council was an executive body" having only an advisory capacity. "The General Secretary, as of February 1, 1952, is the liaison officer between the Board, Corporation and Executive Committee and the entire work of the Fellowship. It is his responsibility to interpret the Board policy to the organization and the organization to the Board. He is no longer, as in the present, the chief Executive Officer."[32] It was becoming apparent that a power struggle was going on between the board and senior staff—some of whom were aligned with Troutman, but an increasing number with Stacey Woods. Stacey's role had been severely restricted by the new senior staff council. The organization was coming of age.

Stacey was now aware of the need to divest himself of his Canadian portfolio. "I hung on too long," he would later admit.[33] "I have been told that it is my responsibility to provide someone to take my place when I resign," he told Troutman after an executive committee meeting he attended in Toronto in early February 1952.[34] Wilber Sutherland, who had been acting since 1948 as his surrogate, was the obvious choice, though he was only twenty-eight years old. "While there is a liking for Wilber and appreciation of his spirituality, his ability to work with students, and his ability to speak in public acceptably, there is a feeling that he is inadequate for the position," Stacey reported to Charles. Alternatives were Jim Forrester, Miller Alloway, who was a scion of a prominent evangelical business family based in Oshawa, Ontario, and Gene Thomas from the American staff.[35] Wilber and Stacey spent a whole day together after the meeting, "going over [Wilber's] disabilities and failures more frankly than I think I have with anyone in my life." After a successful western trip during which Wilber won the confidence of staff and supporters, Stacey agreed that Wilber be appointed general secretary of IVCF Canada, effective 1 October 1952.

It took a while for Stacey to react to subtle and not so subtle changes in his authority, but by late April, prior to a full board meeting, he was setting down his thoughts to Petersen and Troutman. "For the last three months one of the questions uppermost in my mind has been God's will for me and for the student work overseas and its relationship to IVCF USA." He wanted to settle the issues "apart from personalities." "Perhaps," he wrote, "in the past I have been guilty of trying to decide a principle in the light of personalities, which of course, is fundamentally wrong." His suggestion was that IVCF international work function as a department of IVCF, and "the Board of Directors at its Spring meeting would determine the amount of time I am to spend in the international department and the IFES and the amount for responsibility as General Secretary of the IVCF USA."[36]

Troutman's reaction came within a month, and it was predictable. Writing to Stacey, he spoke of "two opposing concepts held by two men working directly under you." "I see nothing possible but continued warfare." Petersen, as the one responsible for raising the budget and running the office, saw things institutionally. To Troutman IVCF was a fellowship, a "loose arrangement." "A possible solution would be to run the Chicago office as an institution and the campus work as a fellowship" or "a complete separation of the business and staff functions of the IVCF." He concluded:

> I do not feel that this matter is so much a personality problem whereby three or four rather independent characters must work closely together, but rather that it is a conflict of basic philosophies as to the means of conducting this part of God's work on American campuses. For this reason I am extremely pessimistic as to the possibility of solving anything by memos, conferences, lines of authority, appeals to the Executive Committee, limits on authority, etc.[37]

After a great deal of heat here was some light on what was driving the American IVCF apart. Stacey was torn. He actually probably sided more with Troutman and always hated ministry being run like a business. He would gladly have brought back a simpler time when the organization was new. But he was also the consummate businessman and knew that his grand visions could not happen without strong corporate underpinning. Stacey was not administratively as strong as he might have been because he could get bogged down in minutiae: his perfectionism made him a control freak. But Troutman—as his later attempt to run IVCF in the United States would prove—was hopeless operationally. Troutman spent, as he wrote on the letter, three hours discussing the matter with Stacey and "found him more institutional than Petersen."

The day before this exchange, David Adeney wrote Troutman as he waited for a train. He had just spoken to a disgruntled former IVCF office person who had told him that InterVarsity "is about to disintegrate" and had serious criticisms of Stacey. "He also says that you are going round telling all and sundry, including people who have little connection with the Fellowship, that it is quite impossible to work with Stacey."[38] In July, Stacey called a meeting at their request of the five senior staff council members then present at Campus-in-the-Woods "to consider the continuing confusion within IVCF." It anticipated a meeting called at the end of September for ten days in Chicago. The discussion was to be about "The continuing disunity in the Fellowship, especially within the Chicago office—its cause and God's cure."[39] In preparation for this meeting Troutman meticulously prepared a list of concerns ("top level disunity, business control of the IVCF, complete decentralization, Stacey's overseas activity" being the first four) and also sent a bruising memo to Stacey. The polarities were becoming ever clearer, though other issues emerged, such as Stacey's "playing staff members against each other." David Adeney spoke of "a spiritual disunity that has not been faced, but which can be resolved by prayer and confession."[40]

TROUTMAN RESIGNS

The month after these meetings Troutman had made up his mind to resign "unless the Lord in a definite way shows me to the contrary."[41] But by now board members were getting involved. In a four-page letter the father of one of the secretaries at the office made some serious charges against Stacey to Herbert Taylor, concluding that

Stacey should resign. Corporation members from afar were questioning the integrity of the general secretary. And there was a blowup at an executive meeting when one member accused the board member who had previously written Taylor that he was spreading privileged and confidential information about the inner workings of the office. The secretary herself later wrote an emotional six-page letter to Stacey asking forgiveness but raising more issues.

In mid-January 1953, Herbert Taylor invited Stacey to his home in Park Ridge, suburban Chicago. He took the inflammatory letter with him, later assuring the accuser he had taken it seriously. The conversation lasted for three hours. "Stacey admitted that he had made mistakes and that he had definite weaknesses and handicaps in his work with others," he reported.

> Stacey very frankly admitted his errors and said that he was sorry for them. We had a fine season of prayer, and all men present agreed to first give Stacey their 100% cooperation in the future, and second, to discontinue talking to others about what had happened in the past. Everyone present at the meeting felt that we had made a lot of progress and that the trend would definitely be in the right direction from here on."[42]

Taylor diplomatically expressed thanks to the board member who had accused Stacey, for his "contribution toward our being able to get the matter straightened out and get everybody working along the right lines in the future." Taylor then had his successor as chairman, Paul Westburg, meet with as many of the senior staff who were readily available. Herbert Taylor never had a finer moment in a lifetime of godly leadership and spiritual maturity.

At an executive meeting on 12 March the resignation of Charles Troutman, effective 30 June 1953, was received. Paul Westburg was surprised when it came: "I told him how surprised I was to receive his letter because I did not, in any way, anticipate such an action on his part."[43] Unresolved issues about how staff, board (particularly the chairman) and head of the organization relate to each other continued to bedevil the American IVCF for decades. How are senior staff in a Christian organization accountable to each other? What loyalty can the head of an organization expect? How do those serving a common Lord work for his glory and the peace and harmony of the organization? And ultimately what does it mean to be a *Christian fellowship*? Is it different from a business model? How do the two impinge on each other?

No one was unaffected by what transpired among the senior leadership of IVCF in the United States from 1950 to 1953 (as future events would demonstrate), certainly not the primary individuals involved. Unlike its British counterpart Inter-Varsity Fellowship, senior staff in North America had a feeling of ownership, which meant that leaving the organization seemed almost unthinkable because their identity as individuals rested on being a part of InterVarsity. Indeed after years of exciting and productive ministry with young people in the insular world of parachurch ministry, there might appear to be few attractive alternatives for ministry or employment. In Charles Troutman's case the call came from Australia, where he had eight productive years before returning to the United States. Others were not so fortunate.

And Stacey? He was bloodied but unbowed, contrite but still cantankerous. He never did completely master a besetting sin that had emerged from the conflict: gossip. "Personally," he wrote in a report to the American corporation, "I have a sense of failure during the past three years. One has spread oneself so thin, with so much diversified activity, that little has been attended as it should."

Eleven years later, when Charles Troutman was going through his own crisis as Stacey's successor in the United States, which was about to lead to his resignation, Stacey wrote as one who understood his situation from personal experience:

> I want you to know I am with you in spirit and am praying daily for you. I long desperately and pray for a restoration of that fellowship and love we both enjoyed in the 1930's. Is there anything I can do to this end? Surely this would please and glorify the Lord Jesus and should we not therefore pray and work to that end. Perhaps if we could spend some days together alone we could talk frankly and pray and perhaps God could do what we cannot do.[44]

There is no record of a reply, but in 1986 Troutman wrote to a researcher, "I am still praying that the Lord will give you the ability to portray Stacey as the brilliant and human servant of God he was."[45]

At Locarno, 1953: (L to R) Wilber Sutherland, Douglas Johnson, Hans Bürki (Courtesy of David Stewart)

At Locarno, 1953: (L to R) Stacey Woods, Paul White, Martyn Lloyd-Jones (Courtesy of David Stewart)

International Inspiration

IT WOULD BE HARD TO IMAGINE A PLACE further removed from all Stacey's recent trauma than Lake Locarno in north Italy. Swiss Scripture Union had a retreat house called Casa Tabor that was known for its beauty. Stacey found spiritual solace and recovery those days in early August 1953 amid the ripening grape harvest along the slopes, scenes made famous by artists and poets. The site had been chosen for the third general committee of IFES, preceded by the executive committee. At the meetings Stacey was among friends. He was in top form. There was little indication of the battles that had been fought during the previous months back in the United States. There he had been terribly wounded; here he was appreciated, even loved. Life seemed for him compartmentalized; he could in a remarkable way distance himself from opposition and conflict. Traveling abroad provided him with the chance to thrive in an entirely different milieu, surrounded by stimulating friends, warm Christian fellowship and gracious European hospitality.

The International Fellowship of Evangelical Students had come a long way in six years, he reported as general secretary. The second general committee held three years previously at Ridley Hall, Cambridge, had been a far less representative body. Now there was growth in Germany, an indigenous group in Denmark, a small work started in France, and a slow start in Italy. A Mexican movement applied for membership, and a beginning had been made in Latin America. In Asia there were three evangelical unions in India, a leaderless movement in Japan and groundwork laid in the Philippines. Stacey strongly advocated sensitivity to different cultures and a refusal to replicate work in one country patterned slavishly after another—a possible reference to English dominance based on superior organization, size and experience. In the midst of progress, however, treasurer John Bolten warned that there had been "insufficient activity" in the accounts. He was still subsidizing the movement from his own deep pockets.

The meeting of the executive committee began with

> a review of the character of the IFES as an organization, its personnel, and in particular the role of the General Secretary. Three viewpoints were expressed: A. That there is a need for a full-time General Secretary for the International Fellowship of Evangelical Students. B. That having surveyed available possibilities, Mr Stacey Woods appears to be the only person at present available for such a position. C. That it would be better for Mr Woods, in the event of his becoming full-time General Secretary of the IFES, to have some continuing responsibility in the IVCF-U.S.A.[1]

Stacey provided just a hint that all was not well in the United States, without letting the side down. "My own future is somewhat uncertain," he reported. "During the past six years the IVCF U.S.A. has been neglected to a considerable degree in the activities of the IFES. One person cannot adequately give leadership both to the IVCF U.S.A. and to the IFES under the present arrangement. The committee of the IVCF have asked me to concentrate upon the student work in the USA."[2] In spite of this warning the general committee proceeded to act on a recommendation of the executive committee to nominate him "to become the full-time General Secretary of the IFES, with the proviso that suitable arrangements could be made by the IVCF-U.S.A. to act in the event that Mr Woods does not accept the call to become full-time IFES General Secretary."[3] Martyn Lloyd-Jones assured the group that the implications of this for the American movement had been fully considered by the executive committee. The American delegation abstained from the vote, stating as their reason that they did not want to lose the services of their general secretary.

"When in Europe," Stacey later reported, "I felt I could make no decision until first consulting with those to whom I am responsible over here." As he sought guidance there was, as he said, "no clear guidance from the Lord one way or another." But one thing was clear:

I cannot help but believe that perhaps after having served for thirteen years as General Secretary of the IVCF-U.S.A., it might be good for the work, and might be the will of God, for someone else who is a native-born American to take over the leadership of this work, providing someone suitable can be found, and that ultimately perhaps God is calling me to have some small share in the ministry of IFES, particularly in the pioneer aspects of this work, even though this means almost beginning again from scratch organizationally, and leaving behind a great deal of that material security and stability that is represented in so established a movement as the IVCF-USA. I have therefore concluded it to be God's will that I should at this time tender my resignation to the Board of Directors of the IVCF-U.S.A., and I have done so, which resignation is to be take effect whenever it is deemed best by the Board. As God may lead the Board, I am prepared to carry on until God raises up the man of His choice for this position.[4]

Unfortunately, it was not at all clear who that person might be. With Charles Troutman gone, the alternatives were regarded with considerable uncertainty. One of them was Ralph Willoughby, who had been given a three-year leave from staff to study at Fuller Theological Seminary. He returned to accept a staff appointment and during the summer of 1953 was at Ontario Pioneer Camp (as he had been for five summers) when he suddenly became ill, was taken to Huntsville Hospital and on 27 August died, leaving the entire movement—and particularly Barbara Boyd to whom he was engaged to be married in December—in a state of shock and grief. Stacey and Paul Beckwith conducted the funeral four days later in Ann Arbor, Michigan. Barbara Boyd remembers Stacey's warm and protective love for her during those dark and terrible days. She sat through the funeral between Ralph's parents. "Stacey was always gentle, helpful, and tender," she recalled with gratitude.[5] Not an image of him that everyone shared.

EUGENE THOMAS AND "ROCKY MOUNTAIN FEVER"

Another possibility was Eugene Merlyn Thomas. Thomas was a 1946 graduate of the Colorado State College of Education, where he had come into contact with InterVarsity through *HIS* magazine. Immediately after graduation, in response to a *HIS* article, he made his way to Campus-in-the-Woods, still not (he claimed later) a convinced Christian, though he had been active in Baptist youth work and had directed gospel teams with his rich baritone voice. While teaching business in high school, he conducted Bible studies in Colorado and Wyoming, starting chapters in each school he visited. He went on to work for an insurance company, the traveling involved enabling him to do volunteer IVCF work in a wide area. He finally joined the InterVarsity staff in 1949. He was an effective communicator with non-Christians and helped prepare for the 1950-1951 "Year of Evangelism." The year after, he had acquired for InterVarsity a forty-acre property eighteen miles outside of Colorado Springs, later known as Bear Trap Ranch. Approval was given at a 23 May 1952 executive committee meeting on the condition that no national funds would be used (although it was recognized as a national program). Thomas would be responsible for fundraising and ensuring an adequate water supply.[6] Thanks to his persuasive gifts of salesmanship the money was soon forthcoming.

Eugene Thomas was a man to watch. Participating in the senior staff council, possessed of a magnetic personality and an engaging speaker, he soon developed a wide circle of influence in InterVarsity circles. The staff and board asked him to become national secretary in early 1954 in an attempt to respond to the perceived leadership vacuum. In a 12 February response to this invitation, he told Stacey:

> If it were not for the question of the work overseas, I am quite sure that my answer would be that I do not believe that it to be God's will for me at this particular time. However, I am very much interested in the work of IFES and believe it to be a tremendously important and significant work in these days. It is for this reason that I am suggesting that I become your assistant for the next year.[7]

He went on to say that he would plan to be in Chicago while Stacey was overseas that spring and autumn, but he also would be continuing his work at Bear Trap Ranch and supervising staff as regional secretary in his district. "Whether this is a step in the direction of accepting national responsibilities permanently or whether it is temporary situation, I cannot say." It was obvious that Gene Thomas was being groomed as a possible successor.

At the staff meetings following Urbana 54, there was a confrontation between Gene Thomas and Maurice Murphy that in retrospect provided insight into weaknesses in Thomas's theology. Murphy, a hulking Irishman who had been an usher at Stacey's wedding, was warmly emotional, sometimes impulsive and could be tactless. But he had theological training and was an ordained Anglican minister, which set him in contrast to Gene Thomas, who had no theological training but a winsome teaching manner, and was cool toward the organized church. Murphy raised the issue of Gene's insistence that the only biblical passages he would use were in the Gospels, particularly the Synoptics, and the only Person of the Trinity he would mention was Jesus. This Murphy regarded as unbalanced, an inverted Unitarianism, which ignored vast areas of biblical truth, dealt lightly with the Pauline doctrine of the atonement and ignored the Holy Spirit. And he appeared to be almost antinomian in his reaction against fundamentalism.

Thomas's ecclesiology also bothered Murphy. The Rocky Mountain district was beginning to confirm the view of church people that a parachurch agency such as InterVarsity was not working *alongside* the church but in opposition to it, destroying the confidence of students in their home congregations as they sought a community that would provide a continuing InterVarsity experience. At the January 1955 post-Urbana staff meeting, Stacey was asked to address the issue by several concerned senior staff. Murphy regarded his presentation as unsatisfactory, particularly when Stacey allowed staff the freedom, even if unordained (or uncertified as an elder by their assembly), to celebrate the sacraments. He tried to mollify Maurice by saying that "my statement about the Lord's Supper was somewhat loose" but regarded the way in which he had been challenged by Murphy in front of the staff as indefensible. For Murphy it was a matter of being (as Stacey said) "Mr. Valiant For Truth"; to Stacey (who had not yet recognized the gravity of the issues) it was a relational concern, that is, how to disagree agreeably and respect authority.

Maurice Murphy resigned from staff in the summer of 1955, citing as his reason a "sacerdotal tendency" in IVCF. Stacey maintained that his view of Communion was unchanged from the time twenty years earlier that he had joined staff. He wrote with feeling: "The IVCF must never become sectarian or a denomination. It is an interdenominational society working in fellowship with the evangelical churches, witnessing to the faith once for all delivered, but what is there to forbid, on occasions, such a fellowship expressing oneness with the Lord in the communion service, as a fellowship?" He concluded his farewell letter—by this time Maurice Murphy was going to Australia at the invitation of the Archbishop of Sydney—"I am sure that particularly in Sydney you will be at home."[8]

Maurice Murphy went to a suburban parish and was immediately embraced by his congregation. "The parishioners took him and his family to their hearts from the first day, and scores of them, young and old, were markedly influenced by his ministry. At the heart of all that Maurice Murphy did, was the uncompromising preaching of the gospel and clear Bible teaching." So read his obituary. At the age of forty-four, only a year into his incumbency, Maurice Murphy died of a coronary thrombosis.[9] His funeral was attended by 470 people, 200 of whom were unable to get into the church. Charles Troutman, by then the general secretary of Australian InterVarsity, shared in the service. Between Troutman and Murphy, Stacey's reputation plummeted in Australia. "Ever since we received a cable from Australia telling of Maurice's home call, we have been heavy hearted and heartsick," a contrite Stacey wrote to Belva Atkinson Murphy, who with her three young children returned to her family home in Vancouver immediately after the funeral.[10]

"Stacey Woods did not seem aware of the seriousness of the situation," Keith and Gladys Hunt wrote in their half-century history of the American IVCF. "He trusted Gene Thomas, and his own deep involvement in the work of IFES distracted him from any close supervision."[11] Thomas resigned in 1958 but by that time the virus of so-called Rocky Mountain fever had spread, student work was decimated, and churches in the area lost all confidence in IVCF. Gene Thomas continued powerfully to affect IVCF in California and particularly western Canada, strongly influencing Wilber Sutherland and being used widely there as a speaker. In 1969 he was asked to succeed Wilber as Canadian general secretary.

A year after Charles Troutman's resignation Stacey reported, "Another thing that the Lord has been doing has been to unify the staff. As you know, we have had some trouble and difficulty in recent years, but to me the growing oneness of the staff has been a fresh breath from heaven."[12] He went on to define this unity—not based on their identity as staff of IVCF but on "oneness in the Lord Jesus." He was also anxious to respond to continuing criticisms that "Inter-Varsity was too slow, that it was insufficiently aggressive evangelistically." He quoted the registrar of one seminary who preferred an unnamed Christian organization over InterVarsity "but I've got to admit that (the other organization) never sends anyone to our seminary, whereas Inter-Varsity sends a very great number of students. Therefore, whether I like it or not, I am forced to support Inter-Varsity."

InterVarsity's emphasis on discipling and training was bearing fruit. The first Missionary Training Camp, organized by David Adeney, now missionary secretary following the resignation of Wes Gustafson, had been held at Prentiss Bay. "Great enthusiasm for this type of camp has been reported, with a unanimous verdict that the site on the northern Michigan peninsula is ideal for camping purposes." A full summer program at what would become Cedar Campus was promised "which, in no way, will be in competition with Campus in the Woods." How little they knew or could anticipate the future.[13]

FRENETIC ACTIVITY

Meanwhile IFES continued to claim Stacey's time. Stacey left on board the Cunard liner *Queen Mary* on 14 April 1954, and spent time visiting student ministries in Europe, first in Paris with Frank and Anne Horton, and following the executive committee meeting, two and a half weeks in Italy, returning from Naples in mid-May. The IFES executive meeting, held in Beaconsfield, England, in an historic Quaker retreat center, was uneventful, focusing on the definition of a university and leaving the choice of qualifying schools to be chapters of national groups to local autonomy. He returned home to spend the summer at the new Bear Trap Ranch and at Campus by the Sea on Catalina Island.

At an executive meeting on 8 January 1955 Stacey's role was reviewed. For six months, Roy Horsey, as president of the board (and recently treasurer), had been studying how to bring about a more unified program for organization. He had asked Stacey to express his own feelings, while at the same time stressing that Stacey had not influenced the new ideas. With the proposed appointment of a "field secretary" (Eugene Thomas was a suggestion) and a "headquarters secretary" (Joe Bayly's name surfaced), Horsey saw Stacey's new role "as spiritual and public relations."[14] The conversation, limited to the executive, was held behind closed doors: the obvious concern was to free Stacey from administrative and field responsibilities as he had indicated that he had emotionally moved on. "I should like to be set free," he wrote Horsey, "from administrative detail in both spheres so as to be able to devote more time to the study of the Word, to writing, to speaking, to counselling with staff, and to functioning on the level of policy."[15] Horsey envisaged Stacey's new role to be advisory. During the discussion, John Bolten stated that it was important that Stacey realized he was not being kicked upstairs or downstairs. The proposal was approved unanimously, though there had been a vigorous debate. "Such an arrangement should not require my being away from the United States more than eight or nine weeks in any one year," Stacey had written to reassure Horsey. He had made his peace with IVCF-USA and could now also work for IFES with a clear conscience—though as he had indicated at the time, with two teenage sons (one now away at boarding school) he had family responsibilities to keep him home.

In 1955 Stacey made three international trips: at the beginning of the year he went to Central America, Colombia and the Caribbean. He was only home for a month before he went to Europe to attend the annual IFES executive meeting, this time at Huis ter Heide, the Netherlands. He also visited student work in Germany, Switzerland (where he called on Francis Schaeffer) and Denmark, ending up in France. In the autumn he was off to the Far East, his first visit to Asia. He visited Bill Steeper en route in Hawaii, spent a week in Japan with IFES affiliate KGK, and returned via Taiwan, the Philippines (where he visited Gwen Wong), and Honolulu (calling on Ada Lum). "My visit to the Orient was a learning experience," he later reported to the IFES general committee.

> Grave questions concerning traditional missionary work, the failure of much of the present-day approach, the failure to identify oneself with the people, the inescapable fact that too often the Gospel of Jesus Christ is being confused with our western way of life, and the fact that so many missionaries today seem to be improperly trained and to be spiritually immature and in some instances lack direction in terms of missionary goals tended to depress one and to call for a re-examination of our own approach to student work.[16]

Stacey, who had never left Canada behind and was continually advising Wilber, was brought into a situation in February 1956 that called on all his resources of pastoral (and fatherly) help. As a very young and immature teenager, a so-called third culture kid (before any attempts were made to reorient missionary children to their parents' homeland), I entered McGill University. After joining the IVCF chapter there as a freshman, I came under the influence of some unhelpful people who had issues with the organization going back twenty years. They persuaded me to resign. I fired off a letter to Toronto. Wilber Sutherland, as general secretary, arrived quickly on the scene. Unfortunately, I also forwarded three carbon copies of my letter of resignation—one of which went to Stacey, another to an uncle whose Brooklyn home had been a venue for IVCF evenings with Stacey and a third to my former headmaster, IVCF reference counselor Frank Gaebelein. It certainly got Stacey's attention.

Over the next few months Stacey wrote Wilber twice, concerned that I had not received "the fatherly counsel and loving care [I] needed."[17] "Please do not construe this as a criticism of yourself," he wrote Wilber, though it was hard to read his letters as anything else. By autumn I had come to my senses, apologized, and Stacey assured me in a warmly pastoral letter that some of my criticism of the McGill chapter had been justified. "As to the question of the group as a whole having lost contact with the rest of the university, this may well be true. It is a condition that tends to be prevalent in a great many of our Inter-Varsity chapters and constitutes one of our greatest problems," he wrote.[18] I never forgot his kindness. Many others can testify that in spite of tremendous pressure, Stacey could always reach out to the vulnerable and needy. That was the genius of the man, something never advertised because Stacey respected the privacy of the people whom he counseled.

Indeed February 1956, as Stacey was writing to me, was a time of tremendous pressure. Just to look at his itinerary for that month, typical of his life at the time, gives some idea of what he was attempting to do, his frenetic activity giving the lie to those who said he was neglecting the American movement. On 3 February he set out by air from Chicago for Richmond, Virginia, and spent the next five days both there and at two other locations: attending an IVCF conference, speaking twice at a large missions-minded, student-oriented, independent Baptist church, and addressing three IVCF chapters. He went at the end of the next week to Philadelphia, stayed overnight with Charles Hummel, and then to New York. Saturday he took the train to Buffalo, where he was the guest over the weekend of local Christian Brethren assemblies, followed by a five-day campus mission at the local state teachers college, after which there was another IVCF supporters' weekend conference. He traveled on to Toronto to speak to the Varsity Christian Fellowship chapter[19] Sunday evening at Wycliffe College, staying overnight at the Decks on South Drive, spent the following day with Wilber, and then left for Chicago that night by train. In three weeks he had stayed in seventeen different places, been on the road nineteen days and spoke (with power and conviction) on nineteen occasions. At the time he was forty-five, physically still in his prime, but that kind of pressure cannot be sustained indefinitely without real damage to body and soul. As Herbert Taylor once said when exasperated by critics of Stacey's part-time commitment to IVCF in the United States, "Half of Stacey is worth anyone else full-time."

THE FOURTH IFES GENERAL COMMITTEE

Overseas guests dominated the summer of 1956 because the Fourth IFES General Committee was being held in North America. Stacey left Campus-in-the-Woods, where he had been for much of July, to meet up in Toronto with Meg Foote, women's secretary of Inter-Varsity Fellowship (U.K.) and escort her to Bear Trap

Ranch for candidate training the final week of that month. He then crossed the continent to converge with Martyn Lloyd-Jones on Philadelphia (both preaching there Sunday 29 July), and at 1:55 the next morning Stacey saw Doctor and Mrs. Lloyd-Jones onto a westbound train at the suburban Paoli railway station. The Doctor was leaving for the Winona Lake [Indiana] Conference (where he was a guest speaker with Billy Graham). The same week Stacey gave Bible readings at nearby Morning Cheer Bible Conference. Stacey left for the Upper Peninsula to speak for eleven days at a Bible camp and dedicate the new Willoughby Lodge at Prentiss Bay. Douglas Johnson was about to arrive by plane from London at Chicago's O'Hare Airport, so Stacey hurried home. A few days later, with Dr. and Mrs. Lloyd-Jones, who had caught up with them in Chicago, they all journeyed from Chicago to Canada. The Glen Home Hotel at Glen Orchard, Ontario, was to be the venue for the Fourth IFES General Committee.

That quadrennial is noteworthy for two reasons: it placed IFES clearly in a definite theological spectrum, and Dr. Martyn Lloyd-Jones provided intellectual ballast with three memorable talks, which were later published by IVP as *Authority*. The first line has often been quoted: "If I understand the modern religious situation at all this whole question of authority is one of the most important problems confronting us."[20] He went on to refer to the World Council of Churches and the World Student Christian Federation: "The question is being asked everywhere, 'Is there any final authority?' 'Is there any objective source for this authority?' "[21] With his incisive and analytical intellect, the Doctor provided a threefold answer: the authority of Jesus Christ, the authority of the Bible, and the authority of the Holy Spirit. He pointedly referred to the evangelical triumphalism of the time in his application: "We seem to think that our influence will depend on our technique and the programme we can put forward, and that it will be the numbers, the largeness, the bigness, that will prove effective!"[22] It was a salutary, if unheeded, warning. "The Bible teaches plainly and clearly that God's own method is always through the Spirit and His authority and power."

Practically, what did this mean to IFES? Stacey reported that an invitation had been extended from the general committee of the World Student Christian Federation to that of IFES that "representative leaders of each movement meet for some days of prayer, Bible study, and discussion of theological problems which at present serve to divide the two movements." The chairman asked those present to comment on whether they experienced similar requests, and there was almost unanimous assent that in every country national movements were under pressure from member movements of the World Student Christian Federation to enter into dialogue and discussion. Furthermore, it was reported that where talks had taken place, they had proved detrimental rather than helpful to the preservation of the evangelical witness.[23]

There was the added difficulty that most members of national evangelical unions belonged to churches within the World Council of Churches and World Student Christian Federation orbit.

What to do? There was fear lest "ill-informed reports of any such proposed meetings for prayer and Bible study and discussion should cause embarrassment and difficulty." And there was particular anxiety about young member movements who needed theological clarity as they were formulating their position. Finally, with a vote of 13 to 4—a rare ballot vote in IFES history—it was agreed to respond favorably to the invitation but with certain provisions: only those appointed should attend, public and careful minutes should be taken, only the IFES executive should respond, and Martyn Lloyd-Jones, Stacey, and Douglas Johnson should be among the representatives. Johnson asked that his name be deleted.

At the same time. Stacey warned "an extremely mechanistic Fundamentalism, which expresses itself in negativism and extreme separatism, has proved to be a most sterile influence, and some in our movements believe that while holding unswervingly to the historic Christian faith, we must separate ourselves from those extremes of Fundamentalism which have brought our Lord and His cause into reproach." It was a balancing act: IFES found itself caught between Scylla of a loveless orthodoxy and the Charybdis of a creedless ecumenicity. That the fledgling movement found the right balance is due in no small part to Stacey Woods and Martyn Lloyd-Jones working so well together in tandem in those early days, supported by Douglas Johnson in the shadows. As the Doctor's daughter, Elizabeth Catherwood, declared recently, "It was amazing how such different people came together with just the right gifts and were used to create IFES."[24]

"Let us pray and plead for revival," Lloyd-Jones had counseled in his Glen Orchard talks. Now it seemed as though the longed-for revival was about to break through. The first issue of *Christianity Today*, 15 October 1956, was sent out to a quarter of a million addresses. It was an attempt to market a previously discredited evangelicalism, a vision of Billy Graham. Plans were being made by the Graham team for an evangelistic spectacular at Madison Square Garden in Manhattan.

"New York City has proved to be the graveyard of a number of evangelical student organizations," Stacey noted in a letter to Billy Graham. "It represents the largest concourse of university students in the world, one of the most pagan, and one of the most difficult. But if God should move among these students, stirring them and turning them to the Lord, it would indeed be a glorious thing."[25]

It seemed that InterVarsity was riding the crest of a wave: a resurgent evangelicalism was capturing the heart of America. Churches were full, interest in the gospel was keen. It was a good time for evangelistic rallies. And a young English vicar, invited by Stacey to lead meetings in campuses across Canada and the United States, was due to arrive shortly. John R. W. Stott would influence the universities of North America—and subsequently the worldwide ministry of IFES—in ways that Stacey could hardly have anticipated at the time.

12

Mid-Decade Malaise

"STACEY SEEMED A SOMEWHAT 'ENIGMATIC' FIGURE, and I had little personal contact with him."[1] Fifty years after the momentous university mission of 1956 that thrust John Stott onto center stage in the evangelical world, a position he would occupy for the next half-century, he acknowledged how little he had to do with the person who extended the invitation to him to come to America. While both shared a common evangelical faith, were warm and personable, and guarded their privacy, it would be hard to imagine a greater contrast in personality and interest. Stacey was the enthusiast, intense and emotional, with grand schemes and an undisciplined mind. Stott was cerebral, meticulously detailed, cautious, calculating (in a positive rather than negative sense), covering all his bases and every angle, the ultimate strategist.

Wilber Sutherland handled all the details of the Stott mission. It would appear that the idea was initiated by him and originally focused solely on Canadian universities. However, returning from a post-Urbana 54 American staff meetings he wrote Stott: "the staff generally were delighted with the thought that you might be able to visit the States and undertake two or three missions for them. . . . Mr Woods will be mentioning these in his letter."[2] The letter duly arrived three weeks later. It included an official invitation to Stott to take three university missions in the United States, and the anticipation that Stacey would discuss details when he was in the United Kingdom in April, Douglas Johnson acting as a "go-between for us."[3] A month later Stacey is apologizing for the fact that "it is unfortunate that in the United States people do not have the habit of making long range plans well ahead, as is the custom in Great Britain."[4] The plans for the mission progressed slowly.

What finally emerged was an itinerary that started at the University of Toronto on 10 November, went on after ten days to the University of Western Ontario and crossed into the United States to Ann Arbor, Michigan, in early December. The tour started up again in Winnipeg in the new year, went to the University of British Columbia during second half of January, made a brief trip to McGill University, and finished with missions at Harvard (10-17 February 1957) and the University of Illinois, concluding 1 March. The theme was "Christianity Is Christ," and six topics were provided: "Jesus of Nazareth," "The Fact of Sin," "The Death of Christ," "The Necessity of Decision," "The Cost of Discipleship," and "The Goal of Life." Accompanying Stott was to be Captain "Tony" Tyndale, who had joined Canadian staff that September. Tyndale was a Korean War veteran (Royal Dragoon Guards) with an impeccable British pedigree going back to the Bible translator. He persuaded Stott, on biblical grounds ("If a man has recently married. . . . For one year he is free to stay at home" [Deut 24:5]) to allow Tyndale to bring along his wife, then known as Penny and still in her teens, since their marriage had been celebrated by him at All Souls the previous year.

Stott left England on 4 November, sailing on the fastest liner on the North Atlantic, the SS *United States*. When the ship docked in New York, Wilber was there to greet him. After time with the Billy Graham New York Crusade Committee, they took the night train to Canada. Stacey wrote apologetically, "Your train pulled out about twenty minutes before our plane arrived."[5] The Toronto and Michigan university crusades drew large and attentive crowds, with many private interviews. Stott also met with local clergy and preached in area churches Sunday morning. After Michigan, Stott met up with Billy Graham for an evangelism conference at Princeton and then headed west to meet Stacey, a courtesy call that lasted only a day. He then spent Christmas with the Graham family in Montreat, North Carolina, and after that flew to Glen Eyrie, Colorado, headquarters of the Navigators. Stacey had assured Stott that a visit there would not be regarded as inappropriate on an Inter-Varsity sponsored trip, though the two organizations were becoming increasingly competitive in the same market.

From there Stott and the Tyndales proceeded to Winnipeg. Tony Tyndale was later to describe the University of Manitoba series as "the hardest of the missions because of satanic opposition which was also evidenced in Spiritual indifference."[6] At the University of British Columbia concerted prayer for between two and three years had made a difference: "The result was that this was a very thrilling time, and perhaps the most encouraging of the Canadian Missions." Following visits to Montreal and Ottawa, Harvard was the next major mission. Here the going was tough initially but momentum built during the week. Stott went on to join Billy Graham at his four-day Yale mission ("embarrassingly over-dramatic and clearly underintellectual" was the verdict of the *Yale Daily News*).[7] The final mission, in Urbana, at the University of Illinois, found the team quite exhausted though five hundred attended and again the response was gratifying. Stott returned to England, but in March the following year the appearance of his talks as *Basic Christianity* (which the American InterVarsity Press initially missed out on) furthered his influence and made him a household name among evangelicals.

"We think that this trip was a launching point for him personally," Gladys Hunt wrote Stott's biographer, Timothy Dudley-Smith. "His influence on the American IVCF is a significant one!"[8] It is significant that in InterVarsity and IFES circles the mantle of intellectual and spiritual leadership passed in the next ten years from Martyn Lloyd-Jones to John Stott. There were many reasons for that, age being among them. Lloyd-Jones resigned as chair of the IFES in 1959 after the Paris general committee. In 1966 a rift between those who were committed to reform and renewal within the major denominations and those who, with Lloyd-Jones, were more separatist in their ecclesiology was arguably a strong contributing factor. Most within the InterVarsity circle were, like Stott, connectionally more inclusive. Both men brought a robust confidence in Scripture, the priority of preaching and the need for careful and challenging Bible exposition to IVCF. These were all emphases that Stacey Woods prized. It was Stott who coined the word *Bibline* to indicate the depth of commitment the movement must have to Scripture.

LEADERSHIP CONCERNS

Leadership was a concern of Stacey's in these years. It was also that of the directors. After retuning from an autumn 1957 board and corporation meeting, longtime member William Kiesewetter, son-in-law of Mrs. F. Cliffe Johnston, wrote: "I have been continually upset by the instability of our staff. So little effort seems to be made to attract top-flight, permanent personnel who will man our posts as Regular Staff and Regional Secretary."[9] No one, he claimed, had come onto staff as regional secretary in the last five years, and at the same time the movement had lost Gustafson and Troutman, then in 1955 Mel Friesen, regional secretary for the West Coast, and David Adeney had gone off to the Far East. "And in the near future," he added with a note of despair, "we shall lose Gene Thomas." The responsibility must be "laid fairly largely at the door of the General Secretary who has failed to recognize the fact that this work has grown beyond the place where he can direct it himself in a one man way." He noted that Stacey had brought in someone from the central Atlantic region to provide backup: "For almost a year now, Charles Hummel has been in the Chicago office, and it is anticipated that he will take over a considerable amount of the responsibility for the day to day leadership, especially during times when Stacey is absent. However, the success of this will only be as great as Stacey allows it to be."[10] The senior staff had agreed to Hummel's appointment in January 1956 when Gene Thomas declined the post of national secretary and Stacey was desperate for a second-in-command. Hummel saw his new responsibility in that role as being "to serve the leader of our Fellowship, not to a well-defined organizational task."[11]

Stacey had been preoccupied with questions of leadership for some time. It was not only a personal cry for help. As the American InterVarsity was forced to rely on Britons with the gift of university evangelism rather than native-born Americans, and as he was attempting (however weakly) to secure his replacement so he could give himself full-time to IFES, he was asking what was basically wrong in North America that there were so few options. He ruminated out loud about an answer to that haunting question in an *Eternity* magazine article during the summer of 1956. Titled "Are Bible Schools and Seminaries Doing the Job?" it hit a raw nerve. Stacey came out swinging: "The newer crop of Christian workers lacks staying power, endurance, ability to meet discouragement, difficulty, loneliness. These newer Christian workers may be good organizers, but they seem to lack spiritual power." He referred to seminary and Bible school application forms: "If a man says he is called to serve the Lord, enters a school to be trained for Christian service, should not something more be required as an evidence of the gifts of the Holy Spirit for a particular ministry?" And what, he asked, about the quality of education Bible schools and seminaries provide: "Is the emphasis upon a student as a child of God or upon courses of instruction, semester hours for credit, and academic standing?"[12]

The article created a storm: "If you print this article in *Eternity*, we shall consider it our Christian duty to stop our ads in your paper, seeing that we will be plastered with mud," wrote the director of an Atlanta Bible school. "Such critical suggestions would accomplish more if they were sent *privately* to administrators and not broadcast to the Christian public. A critical article on InterVarsity could be written but it would be a disservice." "This article has dealt a real blow to the Bible school movement." Negative comments were however the exception, most were generally positive, some even ecstatic, at Stacey's comments. "C. Stacey Woods, a great lover of young people, has touched off something fundamental regarding the future leadership of the church at home and abroad. It is indeed time for the Bible institutes, Bible colleges, and seminaries to re-evaluate the products of their institutions and find out if they are turning out men of God or just Christian workers." Vernon Grounds of Denver Seminary responded: "He sets forth the ideal which we are desperately eager to achieve." "Stacey Woods has been very gracious in his appraisal," a Wheaton classmate wrote.[13] The article caused a lot of soul-searching in evangelical circles.

Meanwhile InterVarsity's own leadership crisis deepened. Charles Hummel doubled as acting regional secretary in the southeast. South-central, a new district, was given temporarily to Paul Little, who was also international student secretary. Jim Nyquist not only had west-central but also the Rocky Mountain district and Bear Trap Ranch, trying to rebuild after the public's confidence had been lost. "Almost everyone," Keith Hunt, a senior staff member at the time, wrote, "was responsible for more than could be done well."[14] After returning from a five-week trip to Latin America and the West Indies in late winter 1957, Stacey wrote Wilber, "I would like to begin to move away somewhat decisively during the 1957/8 academic year . . . and just put more and more on Charles Hummel's shoulders and on the Senior Staff and step back from the work myself."[15]

Further attacks came from the right flank of IVCF. The December 1957 issue of *HIS* featured an article by Dr. Ferenc Kiss of the Medical University of Budapest, wrestling with how to be salt and light as a Christian in a communist society. John Cowan of the British Christian Brethren spoke of "The Church in Russia," and to cap it all off Joe Bayly had a provocative editorial reminding readers that Jesus lived in a land occupied by a totalitarian world power.

To hear some Christians talk, or read what they write, you'd come to the logical conclusion that it was un-American, if not un-Christian, for Jesus Christ and the early
disciples to live their lives in such an environment. At the very least, they should have
"taken their stand" for democracy, for the right of free speech, for freedom from external oppression.

The inimitable separatist Cold-Warrior Carl McIntire's reaction to the issue
was fast and furious. Before many subscribers had received their copies in the mail,
he wrote in his weekly *Christian Beacon:* "This material, so attractive and disarming,
is the way the Communists would want it to appear when it is read by American
youth. . . . What has happened inside of Inter-Varsity Christian Fellowship that
such a thing as this could occur. . . . Ferenc Kiss . . . is doing a good job for the
Communists in Hungary whom he represents."[16] Two weeks later the interchange
had turned nasty. For two mornings McIntire had used his whole daily broadcast
on Philadelphia station WVCH to attack InterVarsity, *HIS* and Joe Bayly personally. He called Kiss a Communist and asked in a snide way, "Who is responsible
for putting these articles in *His?*"[17] Bayly shot back, "I am," in an undated letter,
which was then spread over the pages of the *Beacon* (breaking copyright as Bayly
noted). Bayly also referred to "a suspicion implanted by your broadcast that IVCF,
His magazine and I personally are 'pro-Communistic.' " Bayly said McIntire "did
not tell the truth," spoke against God's Word, and attacked fellow Christians before
the world. He took particular umbrage at being called "a Communist infiltrator."
Bayly was to appear on McIntire's broadcast to personally answer the charges but
withdrew when he read how vitriolic McIntire had become. "Mr. Bayly you have
been taken in, . . . a real shadow hangs over *His* magazine today," was McIntire's
parting shot.

Stacey was deeply concerned about the impact that Carl McIntire's attack might
have on IVCF, and specifically on its finances in the all-important final month of
the year. On 12 December 1957, he wrote a confidential memorandum to the corporation and staff. He noted "the extraordinary length" to which McIntire had
gone when he stated that the question was no longer *if* but *how many* Communists
were inside IVCF. In unusally harsh words, Stacey said that

> the entire presentation appears to be a tissue of falsehood, innuendo, and malicious
> intent to misrepresent our Fellowship. Apparently nothing can be done but to remain
> silent, apart from the letter that Mr Bayly has written. However one wonders how

many thousands, both by the radio and the printed page, may have been prejudiced against us and our ministry because of these untruthful presentations."[18]

But there was more to come.

WMBI, the radio station of Moody Bible Institute, was broadcasting Urbana 57 when plenary speaker Donald Grey Barnhouse of Philadelphia's Tenth Presbyterian Church (to quote the *Beacon*) started "ridiculing the fundamentalists and [saying] that anyone who came out of denominations because of modernism sinned against God."[19] The station pulled the broadcast immediately but Bob Jones Jr., at the time an ally of McIntire, wrote Stacey asking for a transcript and a copy of the October *HIS*, "a magazine which I have always found very unstimulating spiritually and intellectually and do not read habitually." Stacey, in what Jones called an "evasive" letter, said he didn't have a transcript and defended Barnhouse: "He came to our Missionary Convention to minister Christ through the Word. This I believe he did." Again the whole matter was spread over the pages of the *Christian Beacon* with the attack: "The [Urbana 57] theme, 'One Lord, One Church, One World,' is an ecumenical theme in keeping with the overall program of the World Council of Churches. It has been heard over and over again in ecumenical circles. Now it is featured by IVCF."[20] How could one respond to such invective without making matters worse?

It is easy from this distance, and with knowledge of the subsequent careers of the protagonists, to shrug this controversy off. At the time, though, it was very distressing. Joe Bayly's wife, Mary Lou, reports that Joe was aware of the fact that he was hated and that he believed an explosion at that time on the front porch of their Philadelphia home was the work of McIntire's supporters.[21] Joe's son Tim recalls how the family, who cottaged at Cape May, New Jersey, where McIntire had moved Shelton College, were literally in fear for their lives that summer, so fierce was the reaction. The interchanges with the *Beacon*, coming as they did after increasing competition with another embodiment of American fundamentalism, Campus Crusade for Christ, seemed to enervate Stacey. No longer was IVCF the glamor queen of American evangelicalism, the darling that everyone wished to court. It had distanced itself from extreme right-wing separatist fundamentalism but in so doing had created enemies and lost support. The whole fiasco created a kind of siege mentality that chipped away at that exuberant sense of direction and purpose which had been so much a part of Stacey's appeal. But, to give him his due, he stayed his ground and was not deflected in his mission. Joe Bayly never forgot how Stacey stood with him in his darkest hour.

CONFLICT WITH OTHER STUDENT MINISTRIES

Meanwhile Campus Crusade for Christ announced plans to come east and start work in the Ivy League universities. This was only a year after IVCF's Harvard mission with John Stott. With glossy publicity they solicited funds for a witness to Christ at a certain university where, it was stated categorically, there had been none previously, and yet, in point of fact, InterVarsity had been working there for years. Campus Crusade for Christ staff, it was further claimed, were infiltrating groups in order to have them change affiliation. Stacey, having met with Bill Bright to raise these issues, reiterated them in a subsequent letter, stating defensively:

> I rather expect the Inter-Varsity Christian Fellowship, to some extent, is a reflection of my own perhaps somewhat introverted and conservative point of view in which we very much hesitate to speak about a great deal of results, unless pressed, and find it best, in the long run, to work very quietly and inconspicuously. Consequently, perhaps it often has appeared that little was taking place. On the other hand, perhaps we have not always been as aggressive as we should, and I believe quite fairly we can say that we have been challenged by you and what Campus Crusade has been doing, and sincerely we rejoice in every student who has been truly born again, and for this we praise God.[22]

Bright's response, sent five weeks later ("I am just now beginning to get down to the business of answering my correspondence" after a speaking tour), was distant: "I sincerely appreciate your taking time to call these matters to my attention."[23] There the matter rested, though three years later Bill Bright was reported as telling an IVCF staff member that "Stacey was dishonest and critical of CCC and that he had never been of IVCF."[24]

Meanwhile relations between World Student Christian Federation and IFES had cooled. At the executive committee meetings in early September 1957, held in Attendorn, Germany, it was reported that the British IVF was very unhappy about the decision to meet with World Student Christian Federation representatives, and that since that time "certain new situations had arisen," namely, a rapprochement between them and the Roman Catholic church and an "open attack on the part of the WSCF on the member movements of the IFES and their doctrinal position."[25]

The reference here was to the Student Christian Movement publication by Fr. Gabriel Hebert of *Fundamentalism and the Church of God*, which began by asking whether the two movements could not work together and then caricatured evangelicalism as adding to the gospel biblical inerrancy and "a special kind of Conversion. . . . [t]hey behave like a sect. . . . [They confine] their reading to the books, pamphlets and papers published by the IVF and the Tyndale Press . . . [and] will not cooperate with SCM" and then, to add insult to injury, he identified them with Carl McIntire's International Council of Christian Churches.[26] The diatribe made dialogue impossible, and the executive committee withdrew the invitation to the World Student Christian Federation. "You will understand me," Stacey wrote to Canadian general secretary Wilber Sutherland, "when I say that personally and privately I continue to believe there is value in conversations with the WSCF, although I stand 100 per cent back of the Executive Committee's decision not to meet. Until that decision is reversed I shall continue in this course."[27]

Wilber had just come from reading a paper at a seminar at Yale University titled "The Character and Philosophy of an Evangelical Student Movement." An intense discussion followed, and Wilber's final conclusion, as he later analyzed the debate, was that "the big difference between Inter-Varsity and WSCF etc. lies in our difference of thinking concerning the Person and Work of God the Holy Spirit."[28] It was a surprising statement: some looking back could see in it the start of later ambiguities in Wilber's own theology. Others saw it simply as an interaction with Barth's neo-orthodoxy then popular at Yale. "I am interested in your comments regarding your discussion at Yale Divinity School and your own reaction," Stacey wrote him.[29]

Within a year IVP in the United Kingdom published James Packer's *"Fundamentalism" and the Word of God*. The book became the standard evangelical apologia, a classic defense of B. B. Warfield's view of inspiration, selling thirty thousand copies the first year. Unfortunately IVP in the United States again failed to pick it up. Eerdmans published it in 1960. As Packer's biographer notes, "this work moulded the thinking of evangelical students in the 1950s and early 1960s." "The result," he concludes, "was a significant growth in self-confidence within evangelicalism at this point."[30] This mood of excitement and anticipation in the British InterVarsity Fellowship—that evangelicals were coming of age and were finally being heard—was far from the feelings being generated in the American IVCF. Late in life Stacey wrote of that period in a somewhat selective and rambling history of the movement: "Inter-Varsity, after unsurpassed blessing, almost collapsed for a time." He speaks of "a mood of eviscerated dilution of the gospel voided of its demand for repentance toward God as well as faith in Jesus Christ." He generalized that "'easy believism,' 'cheap grace,' seemed the message of the decade between 1955 and 1965. Inter-Varsity suffered. Leading ministers criticized us for not getting on the bandwagon of this easy evangelistic success."[31]

STACEY'S MOVE FROM IVCF

In the midst of all this turmoil, and his own soul-searching, Stacey Woods decamped to Philadelphia. In the autumn of 1958 he moved the family from 6 Jacqueline Drive, Downers Grove (where they had been for five years, the longest stay anywhere so far), to 45 Brennan Drive in suburban Bryn Mawr, Pennsylvania. There he took up office space for IFES as he started to divest himself of the leadership of IVCF. Without any logical successor, it was a curious move. Two years later he attempted an explanation: "I moved from Chicago to Philadelphia in large part that you, Charlie [Hummel], might have a free hand in administration."[32] Charles Hummel "saw himself as a personal assistant to Stacey, not as a director of a national movement during his tenure as National Secretary," according to Keith Hunt.[33] Hummel remained (and remains) the uncelebrated hero in all of this. Without his loyalty, patience and overall goodness, neither Stacey nor the movement would have survived during that difficult period of transition. He often took the flak from exasperated staff angered that he was simply a patsy for his boss.[34] He did so quietly and without complaint, never retaining any bitterness. Stacey reported to the IFES executive committee meeting in Bjørnegard, Norway, at the end of August 1958, "that, after consultation by letter with members of the Executive Committee, he had moved his home from Chicago to Philadelphia."[35] Douglas Johnson promptly proposed a motion that the move be welcomed. It seemed to IFES that Stacey was finally going to make a move and concentrate on them. Others remained unconvinced and there was much perplexity in the American movement.

Not that it was that easy for Stacey to focus on a single ministry. Since his experience in Australia, Stacey had been advocating the use of Scripture Union reading material. Scripture Union in Canada had been coordinated since 1915 by Rupert Richardson, who refused to give up the reins until well past ninety.[36] With the arrival of Vincent Craven, Scripture Union received a further boost. Returned China Inland Mission missionary Arthur Rouse became half-time office manager for IVCF Canada and half-time coordinator of Scripture Union, working out of the IVCF office at 30 St. Mary Street in Toronto. He attempted to bring the work into the United States, where it had little success except, ironically, on the beaches of California in the 1930s as the Children's Special Service Mission. Finally, after some misunderstanding (in which Troutman had to cover for Stacey), Scripture Union was brought into the United States as a result of Stacey's move to Philadelphia. An office was shared with IFES at 2136/2138 Darby Road, and as honorary chairman Stacey was soon signing letters with yet another letterhead.

On 15 November 1958 an executive committee of Scripture Union USA was set up, and Stacey Woods was the first chairman (later known as president). The indefatigable John Bolten was enlisted as part of a United States committee for Scripture Union, along with Arthur Rouse, Claude Simmonds from Canada, and two local individuals. The Billy Graham team had first discovered Scripture Union materials when in England at Harringay in 1954. They had used them effectively for follow-up in Australia five years later. Now they introduced them in the United States where they were previously unknown in four major American cities in 1960 and 1961, including the Philadelphia crusade, which Stacey chaired. In 1961 the American Scripture Union brought in Colin Beecroft from Sydney. (He was formerly from New Zealand.) Stacey announced his resignation as chairman of Scripture Union at that time, relinquishing his responsibilities with his move to Switzerland in September 1962.

In January 1960 Stacey held his final staff conference as general secretary. It was not only a time of farewell for him, it was also an opportunity for "stirring renewal." The theme, "Inter-Varsity's Distinctive Mission in the United States Today," set an upbeat note. Stacey, Charles Hummel as national secretary, *HIS* editor Joe Bayly, missions secretary Eric Fife and the international students secretary all brought papers. Serious discussion followed. Though Stacey was profoundly discouraged by what was happening in the student work, the conference should have encouraged him to feel that he was leaving a movement that was, after twenty years, prepared to move strongly ahead on the foundation that he had laid. At the end of the conference, the staff jointly signed what became known as the "Bear Trap Statement of Faith," beginning with the ringing affirmation that "We receive the Bible in its entirety, and the Bible alone, as the Word of God written, inspired by God, and therefore the inerrant rule of faith and practice" and placing IVCF firmly in the historic doctrinal tradition of the Westminster Confession and the Anglican Thirty-nine Articles. The statement then stated a desire "to safeguard individual Christian liberty to differ in areas of doctrine not common to these formulations, provided that any interpretation is sincerely believed to arise from and is based upon the Bible." The statement enumerated specific doctrines that were currently being questioned, including one on the church as "The fellowship of Christians in the Church, which embraces Biblical doctrine, worships the true God, obeys the Lord's commands to baptize and to remember Him at the table, exercises discipline, adorns its profession by holiness and love of fellow believers, and proclaims the Christian gospel to the world." It was a ringing affirmation of where IVCF stood and a tribute to the commitments Stacey Woods had inculcated during his twenty-one year American experience. InterVarsity had come of age.

Still he persisted in his uncertainties about the future as he left. "Almost everywhere evangelical circles are in danger of succumbing to pressure to assume the superficiality of modern society," he had reported to the IFES general committee the year before.[37] "There was a mood," he commented about the approach of the 1960s, "of an eviscerated dilution of the gospel voided of its demand for repentance toward God as well as faith in Jesus Christ."[38] In this frame of mind, mistaken as it was and ignoring so many good things that were happening, it is no wonder Stacey was now looking to IFES as his new exciting frontier. It was time to start pioneering all over again.

13

American Farewell

STACEY WAS NOW ABLE TO RELIVE THE GLORY DAYS of InterVarsity when it first came to the United States. The move from Chicago to Philadelphia made him once more a pioneer. His priorities were apparent. The IFES team he now worked with most closely approximated the earlier intimacies of a fledgling movement that responded eagerly to this leadership. He was once again surrounded, as he had been, with a group of extraordinary fellow workers, most of whom would make their mark in subsequent years in the evangelical world.

ADVANCES IN LATIN AMERICA AND THE FAR EAST

Samuel Escobar was one of those bright young individuals. Samuel came from an Evangelical Union of South America church that was anxious about young people like Samuel who went off to get secular postsecondary education instead of going to Bible school. In spite of their warnings, Samuel went to Peru's prestigious San Marcos University and while a student there had a "conscious intellectual conversion experience." He attended a Baptist Church, was baptised, and joined the Baptist Student Union. The American Southern Baptists subsequently closed down the work, which was drawing fifty or sixty students, as a result of a decision made in

Richmond, Virginia. Providentially, at that point Samuel met Ruth Siemens. Ruth had started a Bible study, and the group reconnected. Ruth impressed Samuel the first time he visited her apartment, because of all the Bibles and commentaries he saw piled up on her desk. He stayed longer on that occasion than he had intended, captivated by her explanation of inductive Bible study techniques. He remembers her three-by-five-inch index cards and her excitement about the Scriptures. Together they organized the Circulo Biblico Universitario. The group grew after it showed by popular demand, not once but three times, the prohibited film *Martin Lutero*. The motion picture was violently opposed by Roman Catholics on campus, but was boosted by Marxists because of its anti-Catholicism.

Stacey first met Samuel at the Lima, Peru, airport, coming off Panagra 719 from Guayaquil, Ecuador, in the late afternoon of 14 April 1958. With him on the tarmac was Bill Aish, a Christian Brethren missionary, and Don Burns, a Wycliffe Bible Translator.[1] Stacey's incredible network of contacts across the evangelical spectrum always amazed Samuel. "He knew Fergus Macdonald [of the Free Church of Scotland, teaching in Collegio San Andres], and missionaries from EUSA. Two different people in two different worlds but both in Peru."[2]

Stacey's itinerary that first visit reads today like a who's who of later leaders, thanks to his uncanny knack of quickly spotting human potential. He began his trip with Ed Pentecost, whom Stacey had sent to Mexico in 1945 following his trip. There was the Canadian David Phillips at the Baptist Seminary in Cochabamba and Luis Perfitti in Buenos Aires.[3] Ruth Siemens had moved to São Paulo, his next stop. He called on Bob Young in Rio de Janeiro, IFES's first appointee to Latin America. Stacey was away from the United States for most of April and May 1958. "This whole journey while quite demanding was a most enlightening experience, and one has the consciousness that the Lord was present and did undertake," he wrote Wilber on his return.[4]

He returned to Latin America at the beginning of 1959 with an even more exhausting and demanding schedule, calling him to be at three ten-day leadership training camps in primitive facilities: São Paulo, Cordoba and Lima. Five languages were used, and Stacey provided "life-changing, vital messages about the Holy Spirit," according to Bob Young. Samuel Escobar remembers it because on one occasion, while having some rest and relaxation on a Brazilian beach, Stacey started whistling a tune and asked Samuel if he knew that hymn. Samuel said he had no idea. Stacey shot back: "I was teasing you. I'm teaching you a French love song."

He also enjoyed challenging Americans who would look over his shoulder on a plane and discover him reading the works of Lenin. "Stacey established connections, opened international contacts, and moved from Bible study to training leaders for Latin America and encouraging the development of a theology that was evangelical and Latin American at the same time, providing an intellectual articulation of the faith."[5] He was again away from home for seven weeks, but this time it was much more physically demanding. Almost fifty years old, and not in great physical condition, it was a challenging routine he had set for himself.

Samuel Escobar recalls his first trip to Europe that summer. Twenty-four years old at the time, he had never been on an ocean voyage before, other than between ports in his native Peru. Stacey had arranged a cheap fare. "He always knew how to get free tickets or alternatively the best rate for any trip," Samuel recalled.[6] Together with Wayne Bragg, an IFES worker in Puerto Rico, and René Padilla, an Ecuadorean entering his final year at Wheaton College, they were out on the adventure of their lives. The ship sailed out of New York harbor in late August and five days later docked at Cherbourg, France. The three set out for the train to Paris only to be told on arrival there was no room for them. Frank Horton, the IFES staff responsible for arrangements for the fifth general conference, sent them on a rail pass to see Switzerland. Meanwhile the executive committee was meeting at the Institute Biblique at Nogent sur Seine, France. After a few days, Escobar, Bragg and Padilla returned for the general committee, being held at the Fondation des États Unis.

At the 1959 Paris general committee Stacey reported on his two recent trips to Latin America. "Perhaps the most spectacular advance in our pioneer work has been in Latin America, where there is at least a very real beginning of a united student witness in every republic of South America." In Cochabamba, Bolivia, seventeen student groups from all over Latin America had met. They formed the Asociación Universitaria de Grupos Evangélicos. Two major concerns surfaced at Cochabamba: literature and leadership training.

Samuel had discovered personally the need for literature in Spanish that addressed the Latin American situation when, as an undergraduate, he was confronted by Marxists in the university. Asking for help from his pastor, he was given a Spanish translation of *Why Is Christianity True?* by American Southern Baptist theologian Edgar Mullins. Published in 1905, the book said nothing about Marxism. With Stacey's encouragement Samuel studied the subject and wrote a booklet titled *Dialogue Between Christ and Marx.* "Evangelicals needed an exposition of the faith that was both theologically sound and intellectually responsible."[7]

Professor Alex Clifford, the son of Christian Brethren missionaries in Argentina and a director of a school of languages, spoke to this same lack, and steps were taken to respond to the need of good evangelical materials in Spanish for students. Margaret Erb's Bible study guides "Foundations for Faith" were translated and then subsequently so were Martyn Lloyd-Jones's *Authority* and John Stott's *Basic Christianity*. A quarterly magazine named *Certeza*, targeting evangelical students and graduates, was being published "and has been well received."[8] *Certeza* would continued to make a significant impact until it was discontinued in 1980 due to circulation problems that made it financially no longer viable.

The other emphasis in Cochabamba was leadership training. Churches were growing in numbers but lacked leadership, and the anti-intellectualism of some expatriate missionaries didn't help. IFES filled the gap with camps all over Latin America that exhibited robust confidence in God as Creator and Lord of all truth. With his careful mentoring of men like Padilla and Escobar, Stacey set the bar high and provided a useful model encouraging an evangelicalism that was culturally sensitive to the needs of university students and graduates. Not being American himself, though having lived there for most of the past twenty years, he could understand the strong anti-American feelings of Latin Americans, though not succumbing to its appeal. "He had a great appreciation of the values of American culture," Samuel added.[9]

At Paris, Stacey also reported on encouraging news from the Far East. In the three years since the appointment of David Adeney as regional IFES secretary, there had been considerable progress. A Christmas 1958 conference held in Hong Kong was a highlight, a historic coming together of erstwhile enemies from seven countries united in a common faith. To have the Japanese movement (KGK) welcomed by Filipinos and Koreans was an achievement of grace over nationalism. "It was very clear that God had united us as one family in Christ, not only to discuss the work but to have real fellowship together," David reported.[10] Stacey added, "I believe as a result the work in the Far East has taken a large step forward."[11] IVCF in the Philippines was what IFES was all about according to Stacey. Gwen Wong and Mary Beaton pioneered a ministry that became self-sustaining that year. They had written, "Our task in the Philippines is finished. We leave behind a National Committee, a corps of national staff workers, a supportive Christian constituency, and so we are sailing for India."[12] Stacey's comment was that the Philippines provided "a classic example of the New Testament pattern of those who could found a work and then move on, instead of following the disastrous pattern of so much missionary paternalism."[13]

CHALLENGES AND TRANSITIONS

With encouragements also came challenges, and Stacey referred to difficulties IFES was encountering. IFES was being attacked from both the right and the left. The World Student Christian Federation (WSCF) continued to make overtures. "Association between the two movements would inevitably result in the loss of a clear testimony to the historic faith and to effective evangelical outreach," Stacey said, cautioning however that "the situation is more difficult because we recognize that there are sincere Christians in the WSCF and because we deplore those conditions which cause separation." But there was also a challenge from those with "a doctrinal platform essentially the same as that of the IFES and yet differ from us in method and philosophy." Campus Crusade for Christ, which he did not mention by name, had commenced new student works in countries where IFES already had a ministry, causing confusion among students. Unlike IFES, Campus Crusade was not a student movement; it was a mission *to* students. "However we must not permit this competition to hinder us in getting on with the job God has given us."[14]

Paris 1959 marked a changing of the guard: Douglas Johnson, who retired from British Inter-Varsity Fellowship five years later, resigned as IFES consulting secretary, leaving Stacey with "a sense of very great loss." Martyn Lloyd-Jones was also giving up the chairmanship. Wilber Sutherland made a motion of thanks to Lloyd-Jones for his "vigorous leadership" and the way he "stimulated precise debate on important issues." He had, the motion stated, established IFES on a "sound biblical and spiritually-vital basis."[15] The Doctor was urged to continue to attend general committees as president of IFES and to be available for counsel to the executive.

"I consider it one of the great privileges of my life to have had a degree of association with Dr. Lloyd-Jones," Stacey said.[16] The minutes record that the Doctor reciprocated, speaking of "the gratitude of those connected with the IFES for all that Mr Woods had done for the movement. He mentioned in particular his appreciation of Mr Woods' adaptability in differing situations and of the ease with which he had worked with Mr Woods." And there is a telling parenthesis: "This statement is included in the minutes at the request of the Chairman."[17]

Stacey left the 1959 Paris meetings feeling very bullish about the future of the movement. He brought a glowing report to Toronto's Knox Church missionary conference in November. He traveled on to a supporters' weekend in Montreal with the same news. Perhaps as a result of the way it was established, Canadian IVCF had always been more aware of IFES as an organization and sympathetic to Stacey's participation in its expansion. InterVarsity in the United States at the time rather resented his IFES forays and felt it snatched Stacey's leadership from them. Traditionally also America's generous missionary support has been related to individuals, and so churches have felt more connected with individual IFES staff members, usually from the United States.

In Canada, Stacey never felt the need to explain IFES or why it was so vital and he was so committed to it. Canada still retained a large part of his affection and loyalty. When he left IVCF the following summer, there were questions by the American senior staff, not all of them positive, about what continuing role he would have in the United States, but there was no such question from Canada. At one time he suggested that "possibly there should be re-established some staff relations between myself and the IVCF of Canada or some relationship on a salary basis with a view to the past many years of association in Canada and present IFES relationships."[18] Stacey had a strong emotional bond with Canada that continued until his death.

Stacey Woods c. 1960 (Courtesy of IVCF-USA)

In May 1960 Stacey attended his final meeting as general secretary of the executive committee and board of IVCF in the United States. He left almost immediately for an international Scripture Union conference in England. After side trips to Norway and France, he returned to Philadelphia with the defiant note: "between these dates [28 June to 12 August] I plan to take four weeks vacation." In late August the IFES executive committee and the literature standing committee met at Tyndale House, Cambridge. At that time Oliver Barclay of the British Inter-Varsity reported on the Pan-African Fellowship of Evangelical Students, established two years previously. The executive committee appointed a black American, Dr. Alonzo Fairbanks, as its first staff member to the continent. Fairbanks was to be located in Ibadan, Nigeria. His expense account for travel turned out to be three times his salary. Fairbanks was picking up on the remarkable volunteer work of Tony Wilmot, who initiated the work in 1955 by visiting every English-speaking university on the continent.

While he was at that 1960 executive committee meeting, Stacey received a staff application from Ruth Siemens, the missionary who had influenced Samuel Escobar as a student. Stacey once described her as "this strange, rather efficient American young lady."[19] She applied to IFES to work as staff in Brazil, where she was then living. Born in Reedley, California, she was a 1952 graduate of Chico State College nearby, having already spent three years at the Bible Institute of Los Angeles. At Chico she had been influenced by "InterVarsity literature, conferences, conversations with staff members, etc., [which] meant more to me than I could ever explain," she told Stacey.[20] In her first teaching job in Berkeley she established a small teachers Christian fellowship, and her gift at leading Bible studies was developed in a weekly class in her boarding house. She gave up her Mennonite Brethren denominational affiliation to join First Presbyterian Church, Berkeley, where Bob Munger was senior pastor. She cotaught a class for "girls from the university" with a missionary on furlough from Peru. She made her way there and soon proved to have remarkable gifts for ministry. With her appointment in 1960, Ruth Siemens began a career with IFES that was a powerful reminder of Stacey's ability to encourage women to use their giftedness in significant places of leadership.

CHARLES RETURNS TO AMERICA AND STACEY TO AUSTRALIA

That autumn IVCF in the United States was seeking a successor, and the name of Charles Troutman came up. He was flown in from Australia in November for intensive interviews and was appointed by the board to be Stacey's successor as general secretary at the end of the month. Troutman had been general secretary of Australian Inter-Varsity for seven years. He and his family were loved and appreciated by the movement. It was a very emotional tie: Lois and two of their children (Charles III and Miriam) came down with poliomyelitis in the last epidemic (1954) before Salk's vaccine eradicated the problem. "His contributions to the work here," the Australian historian Mark Hutchinson wrote, "were fundamental to its later remarkable success. He encouraged the planting of new groups, travelled extensively to encourage growth, began annual conferences, brought on new staff, worked hard on the Australia-Asia connection, and established managerial and evangelistic practices that lasted into the 1970's."[21] It is somewhat ironic that the American Troutman made the 1994 *Australian Dictionary of Evangelical Biography* but Australian Stacey Woods wasn't included, though his father was. To this day Australians regard Troutman as the American who became Australian, while Stacey is an Australian who became Americanized.

Troutman's appointment as Stacey's successor inevitably brought reflection on what he was inheriting. Charles Hummel was enthusiastic about the appointment: "You have come to the IVCF in a time of transition. On the student level a rethinking of our whole work is under way. . . . In the realm of public relations and stewardship we have largely drifted during the last decade."[22] But when Troutman arrived in the summer of 1961, he discovered a very different movement from the one he had known. He soon found the American InterVarsity "baffling and staggering and complicated." The board had recognized from the start that his gifts were in ministry, not administration. His relationship with Stacey during his three years as general secretary were difficult. The board had tried to set everything out clearly before Troutman arrived, being aware of the potential for renewed conflict. At its 30 September 1961 meeting, it expressed its desire that "C Stacey Woods be welcomed to minister to the IVCF whenever possible" and that "the IVCF will always be receptive to suggestions from C Stacey Woods, particularly regarding its part in the work of IFES." Soon, however, Stacey was writing to Troutman about "confusion with regard to my resignation."[23] There were continuing flashpoints during Troutman's brief tenure as general director of IVCF but to say that Stacey undermined him, as some (particularly in Australia) have claimed, is wide of the mark.[24] It was Troutman's own administrative limitations that undid him.

While still in Australia, Troutman helped organize Stacey's first visit there in a quarter of a century. In a January 1961 letter Stacey wrote, "I trust as in the will of God I shall be in Australia a year from now that the Lord may use me in some measure. . . . I have tentatively planned to go to India from about the middle of October to the middle of November and then return to headquarters for five weeks and travel again to the Far East Leaders' Conference and Australia."[25] True to his word (Troutman had warned him about visitors to Australia who cancel their itinerary at the last moment), Stacey first stopped off in Singapore for meetings David Adeney had carefully planned and then arrived in Sydney on Christmas Eve 1961. He was met at the airport by his sister Rosemary and her husband, Wilfred Hutchison, the administrator of the Sydney Anglican diocese. He was a man on whom Hugh Gough, who succeeded Howard Mowll as archbishop when Mowll died in 1958, and Marcus Loane, as Gough's successor in 1966, greatly depended and for whom they had a high regard.

The day after the holiday, Stacey went up to the Blue Mountains west of Sydney, where the annual Katoomba Christian Convention was in progress, and addressed meetings there. He went on to Brisbane, his father's childhood home, and gave Bible readings to the Graduates' Fellowship over the New Year's holidays. Returning to Sydney, he then attended the Inter-Varsity Fellowship conference ("usually undergraduates with some younger graduates present"),[26] speaking on the subject "Evangelism and Student Witness." The general committee of Australian Inter-Varsity followed: "We would like you to be present and to take part in the discussion. . . . Although this is primarily a business meeting it does partly serve as leadership training and frequently students receive a new vision of student work."[27] By mid-January he was bound for Adelaide and a Teachers' Christian Fellowship meeting, speaking about IFES in Southeast Asia and its interconnectedness with Scripture Union. He was only in Melbourne overnight, with no indication that he ever got up to Bendigo to see family there. He returned to his sister's home in the leafy Sydney suburb of Roseville and left the at end of January for Philadelphia. He would never again return to Australia.

MOVING IFES HEADQUARTERS

It was becoming increasingly apparent that locating the international headquarters of IFES in the United States was a mistake. In September 1961, John Bolten, the German who became a naturalized American, wrote, "There is a new mood in the world and a very strong resistance to American leadership—rightly or wrongly. Today it is quite impossible to imagine that a sovereign evangelical association of churches and societies will accept strong leadership from the United States. Unquestionably, the only way before us is for this to be a free association of member movements which themselves are sovereign."[28] The 1961 IFES executive committee "after very considerable discussion and prayer" unanimously decided to move IFES headquarters from the United States to Switzerland. "It must be emphasized that the reason behind this move was the conviction that it was God's will in the light of world conditions and the information and counsel received from every area where we are at work and in no sense represents any inherent dissatisfaction with the USA as the location for the central office. This is very much a step of faith."[29]

This move would involve a personal dislocation for the Woods family, leaving North America to take up residence on another continent. It would be a new experience for Yvonne, but it proved especially wrenching for Geoffrey, their eighteen-year-old son, who graduated in 1961 from Stony School for Boys (as it was then called) on Long Island, New York, as had his brother, Stephen, three years earlier. Geoffrey, a bit of a rebel with a reputation of being a prankster while in the school, was upset. Then a student at the University of Pennsylvania in Philadelphia, he was unhappy with the separation and would have enjoyed, it turned out later, having more opportunity to share with his parents in the move. Jonathan, nine when the change took place, was more resilient. He settled into the Swiss educational system and soon became fluent in both French and English, though again the change was not easy. Stephen was by this time at London Bible College, soon to move on to St. Louis. Stacey carried on forcefully and faithfully in spite of the difficulties his family was facing.

By moving to Lausanne, Switzerland, Stacey was not far from the ecumenical center of Geneva, but still maintained his distance in neutral but highly congenial territory. Stacey and Yvonne joined the assembly that met in rented premises on the Rue de la Tour in center city Lausanne.[30] Over the years since his father had ministered there in 1929, Stacey had maintained close links with the French-speaking Swiss Christian Brethren (Assemblées Evangéliques de Suisse Romande). Eva McCarthy, following her father's death, taught at the Bibelschule in Beatenburg, canton of Bern, and provided a steady flow of information. IFES vice-chairman René Pache, director of Emmaus Bible and Missionary Institute until his retirement in 1971, was a close friend. Albert Depeursinge, a prosperous Christian Brethren layman active in the French-speaking Swiss IVCF (Groupes Bibliques des Écoles et Universités) made space in his home for the IFES office. The Christian Brethren in the canton of Vaud were very open, and the evangelical community united around the work of Scripture Union (La ligue pour la lecture de la Bible), introduced into Switzerland in 1925 by Madame van Berchem of Nyon. There were close family links: Madame van Berchem's son-in-law Dr. Pierre de Benoit founded

Emmaus and taught there for years, and his daughter, Mademoiselle Claire Lise de Benoit, was a Scripture Union worker in the French-speaking cantons from 1944 to 1952. Stacey introduced her hymn "All is in Christ" to a wider audience through *Hymns*.

Phil Van Seters opened the office at Chandolin 8 in the summer of 1962.[31] Phil was well known to Stacey. Her father was an elder at Knox Church, Toronto, and she had worked in the IVCF office at 30 St. Mary Street for five years. Stacey was looking for someone who knew the Inter-Varsity organization and could be a bridge person with the IFES constituency in North America now that the organization was crossing the Atlantic. She knew many of the Inter-Varsity staff as her brothers had been active in leadership in the University of Toronto chapter. She came with most of her salary guaranteed as a missionary of Knox Church, which was an additional bonus. And her parents, having immigrated from the Netherlands after the First World War, had a European ethos. She still had relatives there whom she would visit.

Following an emotional sendoff from Knox Church, Phil sailed for Europe on 27 July, arrived in Lausanne ten days later and was soon busy organizing the office, which also doubled as her home, a proximity which she later found claustrophobic. She discovered that she was always on demand with chaotic office hours when Stacey was in town. Indeed the chaos was general, and Phil, like her brothers, was a highly organized person who liked her work mapped out. The other staff received their assignments through her. With Stacey gone half the year, she said, "In handling his correspondence when he's away I'm constantly having to make decisions."[32] One thing she soon stipulated was that help was essential on the financial side. In March 1964 a bookkeeper, Mitzi Megazzini, came from Italy, who soon proved very capable. Ralph Griffith arrived at about the same time, only to resign a year later, having just developed a new IFES promotional and public-relations program. ("Stacey feels quite sick about it," she reflected.) Two secretaries started in May 1964: one for French correspondence and the other English-speaking. "Where we are going to put everybody in these cramped quarters, I don't know!" Phil exclaimed to her brother in Canada.[33]

She commented, after a year of working with Stacey, that "he is hopeless in his personal relations, but he does have a tremendous vision of God and confidence in Him—and God does work through him in spite of what he is."[34] Wilber Sutherland, as her former boss, provided her with a piece of advice that remains a classic statement on how to work with Stacey Woods: "When one gets close to a person's faults that is sometimes all one can see. It's good if God enables you to see the larger picture. In Stacey's case the larger picture is very much larger indeed." To this Phil responded: "I do agree with this, and I have learned much from him, despite the fact that he exasperates me at times!"[35] Phil left staff during the summer of 1966 in order to pursue studies at Dalhousie University, Halifax, Nova Scotia. No one missed her more than Stacey: "He is increasingly nervous about my leaving . . . and says who is going to do this or that when I am gone."[36]

Yvonne Woods, meanwhile, made a home for the family at 43 route d'Oron in a condominium looking out over the mountains across the Lake of Geneva. Stacey, when he was in town, would come home for lunch. "She brightens her home with quiet edelweiss beauty, and shares her life with many travellers, who always find an open door and friendly hospitality," one visitor commented.[37] "Listening is one of her gifts, but her abundant inner strengths are as evident as the encircling mountains." Yvonne maintained an island of calm as Stacey was straddling the globe, melding a movement and providing pioneer leadership. The last lap, a final decade of work for IFES, was about to unfold. It would bring his greatest accomplishment and his loneliest challenges.

14

Global Challenges

AS MARTYN LLOYD-JONES AND HIS WIFE disembarked from the *Queen Mary* to attend the 1963 IFES general committee, they were immediately thrust into the center of controversy. Meeting them at the pier was the Doctor's fervent admirer John Bolten. Bolten had been enlisted by Billy Graham to ensure that Lloyd-Jones chaired the Berlin Congress on World Evangelization. Though it was three years away, plans were well advanced. As Bolten accompanied them to his seaside home in Gloucester, north of Boston, he used all his persuasive powers. Since the 1950 Boston crusade that launched Billy Graham, Bolten had been a major supporter of the evangelist. Would he be able now to bring the two titans of evangelicalism to sit on the same platform, and would Lloyd-Jones be willing to provide leadership for this great enterprise?

The Doctor was unimpressed. He resisted the pressure, remaining firm in his unwillingness to lend the prestige of his reputation to compromise on the cooperation with nonevangelicals and particularly Roman Catholics that was now accepted by Billy Graham as part of his broader vision. Billy Graham was then in his prime, his crusades drawing large crowds across the ecclesiastical spectrum. Lloyd-Jones, on the other hand, was increasingly separatistic. Three years later, in a dramatic session of the British Evangelical Alliance with John Stott in the chair,

Martyn Lloyd-Jones called evangelicals to leave the historic denominations. Stott, as an Anglican, took public issue with him.

IFES AND BILLY GRAHAM

The issue dominated part of the discussion at the sixth IFES general committee meeting at Nyack, New York. The meetings were held at the Nyack Missionary College of the Christian and Missionary Alliance. There, beside the Hudson River, an hour north of New York City (and not far from the IVCF Hudson House) eighty-six representatives of twenty-six national student organizations gathered, the largest attendance in the organization's seventeen years. With such a wide representation there would be many views on cooperation with the Billy Graham Evangelistic Association (BGEA), as had been evidenced by submissions from IFES member movements both pro and con.

The debate took place a month after the Anglican bishop of Hong Kong, Ronald O. Hall, had refused to allow John Stott to address students within the bounds of his diocese. Billy Graham might include nonevangelicals in his evangelistic outreach, but such freedom was not to be given to evangelicals, at least not in Hong Kong. Hall's so-called painful decision ("in loyalty to our Lord and Master Jesus Christ") was apparently on the basis of the visit being sponsored by the Hong Kong Fellowship of Evangelical Students (HKFES), which he claimed was attacking the Anglican church. Samuel Cheng, chairman of HKFES, denied this *"emphatically"* and stated, "In this great city of Hong Kong where Christians form only a small minority, it is tragic that Christian students should find their efforts to proclaim Christ opposed by others who bear the name of Christian."[1] It seemed that among the ecumenicals, there was a limit to ecumenicity.[2]

"Some evangelical unions," the minutes summarized, "had run into difficulty and very great discouragement while cooperating with Billy Graham in his campaigns. On the other hand, other national evangelical unions had experienced no problems."[3] Concerns expressed included the theology of certain sponsors, its American outlook, an inadequate followup program, and its broad base of support. Several movements additionally emphasized what they regarded as "the theological inadequacy of some of the messages in relation to our day and generation."

There was no equivocation about where Martyn Lloyd-Jones stood. He expressed considerable sympathy with those evangelical unions (some of which he had influenced) that were saying the price of what they regarded as theological compromise with Billy Graham and his ecumenical sponsors was too great. Stacey meanwhile was very much caught in the middle. Billy Graham had first spoken at Urbana 57 and was a feature of that conference for twenty-five years. He liked—as everyone did—Billy Graham's warmth, sincerity and the positive influence he had on several national movements. His campaigns had brought in many converts to IVCF chapters, particularly in Australia, but also in the United Kingdom and in North America. But there was something about the whole operation that seemed terribly American to him. Culturally the Billy Graham Evangelistic Association was more akin to Campus Crusade for Christ than it was to IFES. With its self-promotion, the arguably exaggerated reports of conversions, its diversion of so much activity and support from more apparently humdrum ministries and above all its use of stars, it seemed very American to Stacey. He once said, "I have the impression that I am judged to be somewhat anti-American by some, perhaps with justification; by others, or perhaps the same people, I am judged to be rather pro-British."[4]

When the Berlin Congress on World Evangelization was held, Stacey was present and sat next to Samuel Escobar during the proceedings. For Samuel the Bible readings at Berlin by John Stott were revolutionary and life-changing, but he recalls Stacey's reactions at some of the meetings. When George Beverley Shea, Billy Graham's iconic but sentimental soloist, sang, Stacey was less than appreciative.[5] And the arrival of the so-called Auca warriors with Rachel Saint on the platform brought an equally incisive reaction. As news cameras were flashing up at them, the Aucas seemed dazed, and Stacey said that they must have thought they were being worshiped. He hated anything that smacked of show business or entertainment in Christian ministry and witness.

So Stacey held his fire during the debate, aware both of the conscience of Martyn Lloyd-Jones as he sat through the discussion but also of the respect he also had for John Bolten and his commitment to Billy Graham. He was conscious of the debt that IVCF in the United States owed Billy Graham and his organization, Billy's presence having measurably increased Urbana's draw. Stacey had also poured staff resources into the Madison Square Garden crusade of 1957, helped the Philadelphia crusade in 1961 and was a personal friend of Billy's.

The final motion was quite mild, given the feelings that were expressed. By a vote of twenty-six in favor, three against, and no less than nine abstentions, it was agreed that while "rejoicing with [Billy Graham] in the very real blessing that had attended his ministry, yet at the same time [we express] our real concern regarding some of the questions that were raised in the General Committee." Stacey was asked to compose a letter to the Billy Graham Evangelistic Association. He had not done it by the next executive committee a year later.

SOCIAL, POLITICAL AND SPIRITUAL ISSUES

The debate about Billy Graham was only part of a wider reflection at the 1963 general committee on the influence of aspects of life in their host country. It was a time of self-examination by Americans. A 1958 volume authored by William J. Lederer and Eugene Burdick titled *The Ugly American* featured Americans as well-intentioned but bungling naive do-gooders stomping on local sensitivities in southeast Asia. Some evangelicals in the United States had a chauvinistic attachment to right-wing politics. Communism and Marxism represented an attack on capitalism and on American free-enterprise, which was regarded as superior to every other economic system in the world. Ironically, one of the spokespersons for this view was Australian Fred C. Schwartz, a contemporary and acquaintance of Stacey's, who gave up a Sydney medical practice to work with Carl McIntire's American Anti-Communist Crusade and publish and edit *Christian Economics*.

Martyn Lloyd-Jones, as president, concluded a discussion on racism with some timely words that resonate. "He warned," the minutes say,

> against a tragic misunderstanding amongst evangelical Christians today with regard to their attitude on certain social issues. He warned against any attempt to legislate regarding any particular political policy and economic theory. He also warned against the danger of associating strict conservatism in theology with a similar conservatism in politics and called upon history to support him in this position. There is nothing to indicate that because we are conservative theologically we are as a consequence conservative politically. He also suggested that as evangelical Christians it is impossible to lay down any particular political party line or to espouse any particular economic theory as being *per se* Christian. We simply cannot legislate for one another in this matter. Certain political and economic theory is outside the essence of Christianity although always the Christian must have the correct biblical attitude toward all forms of political and economic theory and practice.[6]

While the general committee was split over cooperation with Billy Graham, there was no equivocation about working in tandem with Roman Catholics, in spite of the greater openness of Vatican II, then meeting in Rome, toward so-called separated brethren. A report from Samuel Escobar and a small committee dealing with the issue sought to encourage Roman Catholics to return to the Bible, noting a trend which they rejoiced to see but also "recognized the limitations of the area of agreement," and urged member movements to "be strong in their own position, and not allow their own program to be prejudiced by any joint activity," and carefully distinguish between meeting for fellowship with Roman Catholics "who are born again" and "cooperation in the form of working together which is unscriptural." The report was accepted for distribution but was not to be regarded as official policy.

What surprised some, particularly Stacey, was the Lloyd-Jones's openness to the phenomenon of Pentecostal tongues-speaking or glossolalia then sweeping parts of the evangelical world. Earlier that year an article in *Time* magazine, titled "Blue Tongues," had appeared drawing attention to the "sobersided" Yale University IVCF chapter. "In the secular, sceptical confines of Yale University [students] report that they can pray in the spontaneous outpouring of syllables that sound like utter babble to most listeners, but has a special meaning to the 'gifted.' " Charles Troutman was asked to introduce the subject, and soon others from Germany and the Netherlands were sharing similar experiences. Martyn Lloyd-Jones raised the key question: "Can a person who is regenerated receive a further baptism of the Holy Spirit?" He concluded with a statement that displeased Stacey greatly. As the minutes read, "He then raised the question as to whether God may be speaking to us in our generation by this phenomenon and also warned against the possibility of finding ourselves fighting against God Himself if, in a general way, we condemn such phenomena and experience."[7] Concern about the charismatic issue in IFES and IVCF, so divisive, would continue to dominate the final two decades of Stacey's life. At times he seemed obsessed by it, and it cost him some longtime friendships. Meanwhile at the 1971 IFES general committee meeting, Lloyd-Jones appeared to adopt a more cautious approach.

Stacey's report to the Nyack general committee highlighted significant advances in IFES, particularly in Latin America, where the movement had increasing credibility: "Christian Latin Americans who have known of the move of the IFES office from Philadelphia to Lausanne, Switzerland, have been very happy about it." Several national movements in Latin America were received into membership: the *Alliança Biblica Universitária* (ABU) of Brazil, the Peruvian *Associatión de Grupos Evangélicos Universitarios* and the *Associatión Biblica Universitaria* of Puerto Rico and Costa Rica. In the Far East there was similar progress: KGK in Japan had seen "the emergence of much stronger student leadership." In Hong Kong, the Hong Kong Fellowship of Evangelical Students had been organized. Africa witnessed similar developments, with particular growth in the Francophone areas of West Africa. Even in Western Europe there was encouragement, though the work, especially in Italy, was "small and weak and lack[s] adequate national cohesion." Camps had been held earlier that year in Greece and Spain, and the Groupes Bibliques Universitaires (GBU) in France "has ended one of its most encouraging years of activity." Organizationally the establishment of regional offices in Hong Kong and Buenos Aires had been a success. He concluded his report with a reference to "the unfinished task": "Before us lies a great unfinished task which requires not only devotion to Christ and obedience to His law, but imagination, flexibility, and which will require us to understand one another, sympathize with one another and to serve one another."[8]

THEOLOGICAL COMPLACENCY

When the general committee adjourned Stacey stayed briefly at Hudson House. He went with several IFES staff into Manhattan to attend Sunday morning worship at the prestigious Fifth Avenue Presbyterian Church. James Sutherland Bonnell was then in his pulpit glory and delivered a polished address. Stacey however was not impressed and, on leaving, snorted: "Where was the Spirit?" The Spirit had certainly been present at Nyack. Stacey left delegates with a challenge:

> IFES is at a crossroad; because of growth and acceptance there is the danger of complacency, coldness and ineffectiveness; that in the world today there are changing patterns of world evangelism, particularly in relation to traditional forms of the foreign missionary enterprise; that evangelism must be the task of every national movement, and that above all, today is a call for a fresh commitment, a life of sacrifice and a new commissioning from God.[9]

This concern about IFES member movements becoming "complacent, cold and ineffective" would be a continuing emphasis of Stacey's final years as general secretary. The 1960s were a time of cataclysmic change, not least for Christendom (in its millennium-and-a-half post-Constantinian form), which in the West did not survive the decade. In January of 1964 Stacey was writing an anguished letter to Wilber Sutherland in Canada describing what he called a "quite a serious theological problem" that the movements involved—all on the continent of Europe—"do not know how to cope with." The issue, he said, was "the nature of truth, the nature of revelation. Unless someone helps these movements to think through these problems and solve them, we shall face some severe setbacks."[10]

The Nyack meetings had set up a special committee to look into the needs of theological students.[11] The first thing the committee had to establish was that nothing IFES did "could be a substitute for formal, theological education." However, "the care of and ministry to theological students is an integral part of the ministry of the IFES and its member movements." This was necessitated because

> the current theological and ecclesiastical climate is largely inimical to biblical Christianity and true evangelicalism. Increasingly the IFES is receiving calls for assistance to meet a problem which in some instances poses a threat to the continuation of an uncompromising witness in a local evangelical union or perhaps even threatens the integrity of a national evangelical union.

If IFES were to provide "clear, relevant leadership" it would not only make a contribution to the movement but also aid "the preservation of orthodox Christianity in our generation."[12]

Stacey had difficulty getting the whole special committee together, but he persevered because the matter was of great importance to him. Finally, after only one member joined him at Locarno, Switzerland, there was a better representation at Mainz, Germany, and he got the recommendation he wanted: hire a theological students secretary and schedule two conferences for theological students at the VBG (German-speaking Swiss IVCF) in Moscia the following year. A mail-in ballot vote was called so that arrangements could proceed quickly. Approval was promptly given for both projects. In cooperation with Park Street Church, Boston, the assistant minister responsible for its "Collegiate Club," Harold O. J. Brown, who had an impressive array of degrees from Harvard College, Harvard Divinity School and Harvard Graduate School, was invited to become theological studies secretary. IFES found itself increasingly involved in shoring up the theological commitments of its constituency.

Such was not a new venture for some of its member movements, particularly Inter-Varsity Fellowship in the United Kingdom. In 1933, T. Christie Innes, then Scottish IVF traveling secretary and later a friend of Stacey's when he was called to Knox Church, Toronto, started the Theological Colleges Prayer Fellowship, which after the war became the Theological Students Fellowship. At Locarno in 1953 the general committee had deplored the fact that "many members of National Evangelical Unions . . . after going on to a graduate theological institution, had lost their spiritual power and keen evangelical zeal, and in some cases had even abandoned a Biblical position."[13] In 1960 a Theological Students Bulletin was authorized, and two years later the magazine *Themelios* appeared, designed specifically for theological students. The theological studies secretary proposal was seen as a logical extension of these moves and was a priority for Stacey.

Somber Report

In September 1964 the executive committee met for the first time in Asia. Stacey left Geneva on 15 September, stopping off in Beirut and Jerusalem. He visited David Adeney's brother Ronald and his wife, Laura, formerly of Nurses Christian Fellowship in Canada, in Haifa and on to India, touching down at Benares and Madras, where he was met by Chandapilla, general secretary of the Union of Evangelical Students of India (UESI), IFES's affiliate in the subcontinent. Together they set off for "Highfield," the UESI training center in the Nilgiris hills.

"Highfield" was the home of the saintly and much loved IFES workers Norton and Eloise Sterrett. They had acquired the former tea plantation in the British hill station of Kotagari after a family home in Philadelphia was sold. A lovely and gracious home surrounded by trees, it was the fortieth place that they had lived in during their missionary career. They had turned Highfield into a venue for UESI students and staff throughout India and Nepal. Under their tutelage it was more than just a place for book learning; it was also a demonstration of servanthood. The Sterretts, called "Mummy" and "Daddy" by everyone, modeled Jesus' instructions quoted in a song Norton wrote for the movement: "Love one another as I have loved you."

At Highfield, Stacey reported positively on pioneer work in eleven countries[14] and with concern on theological trends in Europe, Latin America and Africa.[15] Six weeks later, in reporting to the corporation of IVCF Canada, Stacey brought a more somber report.[16] He called "1964 for the IFES a strange and perplexing year" and described events as "an attack by Satan." An expatriate couple working with students in Pakistan had to be sent home at huge expense owing to the wife having a mental breakdown. The Latin American associate general secretary John White had experienced a series of setbacks and had resigned. "This means that for the time being I shall have to be responsible for the task of coordinating our work and caring for the staff throughout that vast region." In other places IFES workers had experienced sickness and bereavement, there had been "a virulent attack upon the evangelical witness," even reaching the public press. And there had been considerable financial pressure, and staff salaries were not up to date. Positively—and Stacey always managed to stay upbeat—there had been encouragements: more literature produced, contacts behind the Iron Curtain, a Pakistani replacement for the family sent home, and a first missionary conference in the Philippines scheduled the following month.

The somberness of the report might have had something to do with the fact that Stacey, en route home from India, had acquired an infection in the Philippines. It was also a time of great distress in the American IVCF as the movement had almost imploded. In July chairman of the board Wallace Erickson had presented a paper that represented a complete volte face from Stacey's ministry approach. Over the heads of senior staff and the general secretary, he took aim at the founder: "Our staff has been taught that organizationally a fellowship has no hierarchy, no levels of authority, and if its structure were to be drawn, it would be perfectly flat. Each member of this fellowship is on the same level before God. . . . [T]here is no chain of command and no line of authority. When problems arise, they are solved by gathering the brethren together in order to seek the will of God for the solution of the problem."[17] Erickson was arguing that the word *Fellowship* be dropped and that the movement be called simply "Inter-Varsity."

Richard Wolff was brought in by Erickson over Troutman's head to streamline the operation using a business model. He then took Troutman out to lunch and seemed to suggest Troutman should hand in his resignation, which he duly offered the board in July. In the meantime Troutman tried unsuccessfully to fire Wolff. On 23 September 1964 the twelve members of the staff advisory committee wrote the American InterVarsity board and corporation that "the present situation within IVCF is so grave that the movement as we have known it is jeopardized."[18] Quick action was finally taken. Wolff left the staff, Troutman's resignation as president (a new title introduced during his time instead of general secretary) was accepted, and John Alexander, a board member who had been IVCF faculty representative at the University of Wisconsin, agreed to become president effective 1 January 1965. It had been a bruising and debilitating conflict. The wonder was that IVCF in the United States survived at all.

Stacey was overseas at the time, but as founder of the movement he figured hugely in the discussions. Charles Hummel, in an eight-page letter to board member Roy Horsey, suggested that the problems went back to 1952-1953 when Troutman and others left IVCF as Stacey's leadership became increasingly part-time. But the problems were much deeper, as Hummel conceded. Was IVCF a business, a fellowship or a mission board? Hummel offered a fourth alternative—IVCF resembled a university: "We are a university movement and in many ways our staff function with the freedom an academic person enjoys. . . . [A] college president cannot either ignore his faculty or his students . . . and hope to survive."[19]

That analogy broke down when the question of accountability was considered: ministry in IVCF (much more complex now than in the early years under Stacey) was a privilege, sacrificially supported by a constituency who expected that its missionary mandate would not be lost in endless conflict over who sets the pace, provides leadership and raises the funds, ensuring the organization adheres to its statement of faith and its mission. Was IVCF to follow a hierarchical business model or continue to be an unwieldy coming together of strong and independently minded individuals? Were there no alternative solutions? Was staff freedom absolute? How do staff relate to board members? Stacey had been the single conduit of staff to the board during his regime, and sometimes staff felt unheard and undercut. Without Stacey at the helm, there had been noticeable drift, a seeming lack of direction. But to blame the problems of IVCF on part-time leadership seemed disingenuous. The American InterVarsity had to discover a management model that took into account both sound business practices and New Testament servanthood. It would be a continuous struggle to do so. And Stacey had set the bar high.

Into this maelstrom the senior staff invited Stacey to come at Urbana 64 and attend the senior staff meetings afterward. "I have been urged to return to the United States of America," Stacey wrote Wilber Sutherland. "For a number of reasons I did not want to do this, perhaps pride was one of them. But after a good deal of thought and prayer I have decided to do so."[20] Planning and praying for Urbana 64 had kept senior staff together during the previous terrible months. The seven thousand who attended had no idea what had been going on behind the scenes. From all reports Urbana 64 was a significant time for many. The theme was "Change Witness Challenge" with a qualifier for each: *unparalleled* change, *unashamed* witness and *unquestioned* triumph. John Alexander, about to take over as president of IVCF in the United States, opened the convention. John Stott made the first of what would be six appearances at Urbana, giving five Bible readings. Stacey had been asked to provide a vision as to "What in the World Was IFES Doing" and was allowed five or six minutes each night. "The Church follows her students," he stated, stressing that every Christian student should be a Christian revolutionary.[21] He ended the final day with a challenge to students: "Oh I do hope that you'll avoid those dreadful words 'settling down.' What a dull thud they have. But God grant that you'll use the training and the strength and the ability and all the graces that God has given you to venture abroad in one way or another for Christ's and the gospel's sake."

SCHLOSS MITTERSILL

The visit of the general committee in 1963 to Highfield was fortuitous. It set Stacey thinking. Was it possible that the idea of a study center, so vital to his concept of student ministry from earliest days in Canada and subsequently in America, could be useful in the work of IFES? The concept of owning property, with all of its attendant management challenges, was fiercely resisted by many who saw it as a diversion. Such arguably had indeed been the case in Canada where Pioneer camps, founded by Howard Guinness in 1929 to provide summer ministry opportunities for students and run by IVCF, developed a whole life of their own apart from the presumed IVCF priority of university (and secondary school) outreach, no longer aiding that mission so much as proving to be an all-consuming distraction.

As if to illustrate how controversial the acquisition of property was to a member movement, at a Union of Evangelical Students of India executive meeting held in Kotagiri the year after the IFES executive committee had met there, Norton Sterrett offered to donate Highfield to the movement. It "sent sparks flying," according to one account. "Chandapilla as General Secretary of UESI was vociferous against UESI owning a piece of land."[22] Finally, out of love for the Sterretts and respect for their vision, the UESI executive passed a resolution accepting their gift. But it was a foretaste of what was to come. Stacey now had his sights set on acquiring a study center in Europe that would combine his passion for training centers with outreach to Eastern Europe. It was a vision that would dominate his final years with IFES, but it was one that was not always shared.

"Thus I entered into a new and lonely phase of ministry," Stacey said later, reflecting on the change that came into his life in 1965. Schloss Mittersill, the Austrian castle that was to become Stacey's vision for an IFES training center, was—to employ an analogy from the American novelist Herman Melville—Stacey's Moby Dick, his very own "great white whale," the nemesis that obsessed (and destroyed) aging captain Ahab, and would almost do the same for Stacey. "It was during these seven years (for five of which I was still general secretary of the IFES) that for the first time in [my] Christian ministry I was without the support of close friends."[23] Stacey's commitment to Schloss Mittersill would dominate his final years with IFES.

15

Mittersill Momentum

"IT WAS AN ANSWER TO PRAYER quietly waiting upon God that John Bolten Jr of Nürnberg got in touch with me telling me that the Schloss was up for sale."[1] That was Stacey's take on how a castle in Austria first came up on his radar. Each player in the Mittersill saga has their own perspective on how events unfolded.

For John Bolten Jr. it began in 1940 when he was a member of the Dartmouth College ski team, racing on Cannon Mountain in Franconia, New Hampshire. He heard about a "crazy" Austrian baron, Hubert Von Pantz, who wanted to recreate an Alpine village on a nearby mountain. Von Pantz convinced the town to give him the necessary permission. But he had no money. That is until he married Terry, a Lithuanian who, it was rumored, had buried four husbands. She reluctantly accepted the baron's proposal though she warned it might be "the kiss of death" for him. One of her previous marriages was to the son of the heir of the Avon homecare products. John M. McConnell Jr. had died at the age of forty-three the year before. As a result, she was a very wealthy woman. Funds for the baron's new development were no longer a problem. By this time he and John Bolten Jr. had become good friends. John bought the first ski chalet of the new development, which the baron called Mittersill—after a castle in Austria that belonged to a Sport and Shooting Club—where, along with the rich and famous, he was a shareholder. Bolten, now working in Germany, was a frequent visitor to the castle there. The castle was the rendezvous where he met his wife: their subsequent wedding in the castle chapel was the occasion when his parents met Hubert and Terry Von Pantz for the first time.

John Bolten Jr. was aware that the baron and his wife were increasingly tired of Mittersill and, as major stock holders in the company that owned the site, were thinking of selling out. They wanted a smaller castle that had belonged to the Rothschilds. And John Sr. asked, as his son remembers: " 'Why don't we buy it? We need a student center in Europe, and Austria is ideal as it is neutral between East and West.' I doubt that at first he was serious, but the more we talked about it the more interesting the idea became."[2] By this time Stacey had been brought into the discussion. And the immediate attraction for him, other than his continuing interest in developing beautiful and remote sites where ministry could happen and training courses take place, was the Eastern Europe angle. Moscia, the retreat center on Lake Maggiore for the German-speaking Swiss Inter-Varsity movement, Vereiningten Bibelgrüppen Universität (VBG), was not a realistic option for students from behind the Iron Curtain. Each had to be sponsored by a Swiss family, Switzerland was expensive, and they had no hard currency. Austria was a much better option, less expensive and the Iron Curtain was more porous.[3]

Financial and Legal Arrangements

Thus it came about that one morning Stacey and John Bolten Jr. met with Baron Hubert Von Pantz at the railroad station in Kitzbühel, Austria, and drove over the Pass Thun from Kitzbühel in Tyrol down into the valley of the river Salzach in Land Salzburg. After half an hour they saw the looming vista of an ancient pink medieval castle. The site is majestic as it guards the valley and looks out on mountains on every side and down onto the river Salzach. The Austrian Tyrol at any season is breathtakingly beautiful, but on that autumn day Stacey found it irresistible. As with many subsequent visitors, Stacey was overwhelmed by the beauty of the place, as is evident from the material that he sent out after he and John Bolten Sr. had discussed with the baron and baroness what financial arrangements were involved. It turned out that the baroness was more interested in tax relief in terms of a charitable receipt than a good price for a property that was at the time estimated to be worth $800,000. John Bolten Sr.'s tax lawyer, Sam Dennis, at the prestigious

Boston firm of Hale and Dorr (as it was known then) met with the baroness's legal counsel. Soon a deal was worked out in which both John Bolten Sr. and John Bolten Jr. would make hefty contributions, a large receipt for tax purposes would be provided for the Van Pantzes, and Stacey would make it all happen.

When IFES was constituted in 1947, a separate legal entity was created, incorporated in the state of Massachusetts, with its own officers. Harold John Ockenga was president, John Bolten Sr. treasurer, and Stacey Woods secretary. This entity was named "IFES Incorporated," usually shortened to "IFES Inc." In 1954 a change was made (the company appeared dormant at the time). John Bolten Sr. continued as treasurer but now his son, John Bolten Jr., was appointed vice president. In 1964 Stacey wrote Ockenga (still the president) suggesting that Stacey should withdraw as secretary because he was no longer resident in the United States. Stacey proposed that in his stead IFES's American representative Mel Friesen be appointed secretary. Freisen worked out of the American IFES office in Fresno, California. The relationship between IFES and IFES Inc. was murky and soon became an issue of controversy, particularly when the two moved in different directions over Schloss Mittersill. IFES Inc. was increasingly perceived as Stacey's personal fiefdom.

The move to Switzerland had been successful for IFES. Its income was now less dependent on the United States, the American proportion having dropped from 90 to 68 percent. Stacey's hope (vain, it turned out) was that it could drop to half. Even at 68 percent the American contribution was substantial and with the rising complexity of IFES legal affairs, IFES Inc. had the potential of becoming an important player. By early 1965 Stacey was writing Ockenga about "the importance of activating our corporation."[4] The pressing need for this reactivation was shortly to become apparent.

IFES Inc. met 4 December 1965 at Ockenga's Park Street Church. John Bolten Sr. and Stacey had already determined that it was this legal entity that would have to hold title for Schloss Mittersill, should IFES agree to its purchase. "The General Secretary," the minutes of that meeting record, "presented the possibility of the IFES Inc. USA purchasing on behalf of the IFES as a whole a castle in Austria known as Schloss Mittersill, Land Salzburg, Austria."[5] Because Baron Von Pantz and his wife were both American citizens with a large income, arrangements might be made whereby for a small cash payment and the issuance of tax-exempt gift certificates the property might be acquired. "The General Secretary pointed out that according to this arrangement the property at least for the time being would have to be owned and operated by the IFES Incorporated on behalf of the various ministries of the IFES particularly in Europe." At the meeting questions were raised about maintenance, and figures were given indicating that these would not be excessive. With this reassurance, IFES Inc. agreed in principle to purchasing the Schloss on behalf of IFES "on the understanding that suitable purchase arrangements can be made."

With the benefit of hindsight, it is clear that Stacey's strategy was brilliant. Three of those present were within Stacey's immediate circle of influence: Ockenga as chairman, John Bolten Sr., and Mel Friesen. John Bolten Jr. was in Germany, and the two others on the IFES Inc. board were in the Boston area and easily influenced.[6] One of them dropped out, and at the meeting three others from a wider geographic area were brought on.[7] The Mittersill project would never have gone ahead without the initial support of IFES Inc. and the financial backing of its treasurer John Bolten Sr. implicit throughout. And the support of Harold Ockenga, distracted as his letters to Stacey show him to be, was also a key factor: "I see no reason why so great an organization as the IFES should not have a center such as Schloss Mittersill. I think it would be ideal," Ockenga wrote.[8] His comment reflected his own penchant for grand visions and what could sometimes appear to his critics (among them now John Bolten Sr.) to be empire-building.

On 22 December, Stacey mailed out to the IFES executive and finance committee the first statement of his proposal in anticipation of a January meeting with the Von Pantzes. "I have almost been reluctant to pursue this matter, realizing that often a property can become more of a burden than a spiritual asset, that if we were to step out of God's will in this regard it would be a positive hindrance to our ministry. On the other hand if this were to be God's provision it could be a means of great blessing to students in Europe and to the IFES as a whole."[9]

Negative reaction was not long in coming, predictably from Australia. In a carefully reasoned statement Ian Burnard,[10] successor to Charles Troutman, and Harold Knight,[11] a leading Australian banker and financial expert, started with positives but soon mounted a withering set of objections: owning Mittersill would be costly in terms of it absorbing a disproportionate amount of the time and energies of the IFES and its staff, particularly the general secretary; it was beyond the charter of IFES; the mixing of Americans and Europeans could be dangerously provocative given the possible appearance of having "a shred of a link with the political policies of the USA"; it was a major business venture; and operating losses would be a burden to IFES.[12]

As Stacey was tearing out of the office for a 30 April London meeting of the IFES finance committee, he dictated a letter to Ockenga and John Bolten Sr. He was in overdrive and was full of plans for how to use the building. However, he warned them, IFES Inc. would have to own the property. He requested their written opinion so he could inform the other members of the corporation and get their approval. "I am hopeful," he stated, "that within a year or two, the property could be entirely self-supporting, and I do not think in the least this is a 'pipe-dream.'"[13] That is exactly what it turned out to be.

That IFES finance committee showed what Stacey conceded was "a natural and proper caution." It drew up seven caveats. "In essence the Finance Committee agrees to the acquisition of this property provided that it is in such a condition as to be suitable for the purposes envisaged and is made available to the IFES for its student ministry." IFES treasurer Jacques Beney and Stacey were sent on an inspection trip to Mittersill to arrange for an analysis of its viability as a hotel and provide an assessment of the facility by a contractor. The trip took place in mid May. They discovered that substantial work was required to make it viable. Perhaps it might have occurred to them that the baron's interest in selling the property was more than simply wanting something different. Stacey and Beney then called for two professional opinions. "We very much hope that these two reports will be concluded by about the end of July and that by the middle of August the lawyers will have worked out a possible agreement with the owners of Schloss Mittersill and we can proceed," Stacey reported.[14]

In mid-1966 an elaborate brochure was sent out from the Lausanne office providing a rationale for purchasing Mittersill accompanied by pictures of breathtaking views that would have sold the project by themselves. The raison d'être for the purchase of such a facility was given: a burgeoning student population of the 1960s necessitated a place like Mittersill if IFES was to fulfill its mandate of "teaching, training and leading" Christian students.

> There is the need for a central international training and conference centre which will set the doctrinal standards, help to maintain the biblical and evangelistic emphasis and dependence upon the Holy Spirit, and be available for national movements to send their staffs for refresher courses. A place is needed as an overall coordinating centre for training leaders for this worldwide movement.[15]

The cost was set at $100,000 in cash with another $70,000 to enlarge the dining room, rebuild the kitchen and replace equipment. Stacey set out immediately to raise the required $100,000.

The 1966 IFES executive committee met in Vevey, Switzerland, along the lake from Lausanne. The committee discussed Schloss Mittersill. They crafted a carefully worded motion, which was approved with only one negative vote. The British IVF was not happy with the purchase because it was completely contrary to the ethos of the movement. The motion read:

> The Executive Committee expresses its appreciation to the IFES, Inc. USA for its thought with regards to the possible purchase of Schloss Mittersill, and its facilities being made available to the IFES and its member movements for their student ministries upon request. We would express our approval of this possible purchase, on the understanding that this property would be operated as well as owned by the IFES Inc. and thus not become a burden on the IFES and its limited personnel; further, that in order to avoid any suggestions of luxury, or involvement in the activities of other organizations who may well wish to use this property, it be operated under some such name as the 'Schloss Mittersill Conference Centre', rather than the 'IFES Conference Centre.' In addition, because of the activities of the VBG Conference Centre at Moscia, it is felt to be most important that the activities at Schloss Mittersill should not have an adverse effect upon operations at Moscia. The IFES as such feels that it is unwise that it should own valuable property and be encumbered by its management. Therefore, the above proposal seems to be in the best interests of the IFES as a whole.[16]

In October, Stacey flew to Boston to meet with Ockenga and Bolten Sr. He sought an audience with J. Howard Pew, the oil magnate, when in Philadelphia, and with the Glenmede Trust. He had hoped to be able to sign an agreement to purchase, but that was not be. Throughout the winter there were extensive legal negotiations, all paid for (one assumes) by John Bolten Sr. At the end of 1966, for tax purposes, 750 shares, worth $800 each, of the Schloss Mittersill holding company (Sociéte Immobilière Mittersill AG) were transferred from the Van Paltzes to IFES Inc., and a receipt provided. Stacey informed members of IFES Inc. that an account had been set up in Lausanne, the balance in the SIMAG account in Zürich would be transferred there, and Dr. Marxer of Vaduz, Liechtenstein, joined the board.[17] From now on the Schloss Mittersill Club, who ran the facility, would pay a nominal rent of five thousand Swiss francs to SIMAG, which was incorporated in Liechtenstein, and that would cover all taxes. Scarce wonder everyone was confused—and continued to be—at the intricate arrangements. There were (and would continue to be) questions about whether this was an appropriate arrangement for a Christian ministry.

In the midst of all these negotiations Stacey and Yvonne set off for Wasenaar in the Netherlands, where on 4 March 1967 their oldest son Frederick Stephen was married. Stephen had met Els while a student at London Bible College. Eva McCarthy had been in favor of the union. They went to work among the Christian Brethren in Tuscany. At about the same time Geoffrey, their second son, living in Philadelphia, also married. "Yes," Stacey wrote Samuel Escobar, "I now have two daughters-in-law, and you are right, our task is almost completed. We've got number three to launch and I hope his ship will be steady and maintain the right direction."[18] Unfortunately neither marriage lasted.

On 10 March 1967, the day Stacey had anticipated for a year and a half, a large packet of documents was delivered by courier to Park Street Church from the law office of Hale and Dorr. "You will be pleased to know that the closing on the acquisition of Schloss Mittersill was concluded in New York City satisfactorily yesterday," Ockenga was informed.[19] Mariano DiGangi, soon to be leaving Tenth Presbyterian Church, Philadelphia, where he had been senior pastor, remembers vividly sitting at the supper table at 43 Route d'Oron when the news came.[20] Stacey picked up the phone and was told the transaction was now complete. It was an emotional moment. Schloss Mittersill was now the property of IFES Inc. Only Stacey Woods, with the help of John Bolten Sr. (and the silent partnership of Harold Ockenga), could have made it happen.

IFES CONCERNS ABOUT STACEY

Now came the crunch, the need to raise a substantial sum for the renovations and upgrades of the facility. There had been a major fire at Schloss Mittersill in 1938 and repairs, because of the Anschluss (Hitler's invasion of Austria that year) and the subsequent Nazi occupation, had been delayed. The kitchen needed overhauling and the middle section of the Schloss had to be remodeled for it to be appropriate for use as a student center. Money had to be raised, and Stacey set about throughout the spring and summer of 1967 to approach everyone that had given him funds to come to the aid of the Schloss, always trying to remind donors not to take from their usual giving to IVCF or IFES.

This involved sleight of hand, and Stacey was under huge pressure throughout those months to justify his leap of faith in purchasing the Schloss. The number of letters he wrote, soliciting and acknowledging gifts, is awesome. To his old friend John Howitt he wrote a full personal letter in thanks for a gift of twenty-five dollars:

> I was at Mittersill recently and am more and more encouraged with the possibilities that there are, and the way that the Lord quietly seems to be leading. I would, however value your prayer in that I have not been very well lately, having been under a great deal of strain and pressures, and have come the nearest ever to cracking up. Apparently I must stop some things or it could be serious.[21]

To John Nordquist he wrote: "I haven't been too well, as a matter of fact I have been burning the candle at both ends to too great an extent in terms of pressure, nervously."[22] Stacey was about to leave for the island of Elba, where Stacey and Yvonne had bought a home, partly to have family time with Jonathan, but also to provide a retreat from all the stress and worry of his responsibilities.

That summer Stacey's internist sent him a strongly worded statement while Stacey was at the executive committee meeting at the Netherlands. The physician indicated that Stacey was having warning signs from his cardiovascular system.[23] He went on to state that these difficulties followed periods of "extremely intense work with intercontinental trips, many committees, preaching commitments, without taking any account of intercontinental time zone changes." Stacey, at fifty-seven had, according to his doctor, passed the age where that kind of activity was supported by his own physical reality. It concluded with a note that is best given first in the original French: *"Il devrait travailler à 80%, au lieu de travailler à 130% comme il le fait actuellement."* ("He should be working at 80 percent, instead of working at 130 percent as he has actually been doing.") For almost thirty-three years Stacey had indeed been giving ministry his 130 percent. Now he was being told that he should give only 80 percent in recognition of his body's demands. It was advice that he found difficult to accept and completely contradictory to his personality. Stacey had a type-A personality and holding back was not in his nature.

It is not known how widely the internist's description of Stacey's medical situation was circulated at the executive committee of IFES in early August 1967. But as the committee met at the conference center of the Gereformeerde Kerken in Baarn, Netherlands, a replacement for him as general secretary was a matter of great concern. The committee appointed the previous year to name a successor had not met, because they had hoped up until the last moment that there would be a positive response from the candidate everyone thought was ideally suited for the job.

Michael Griffiths was an obvious choice: gifted in evangelism, spiritually passionate and a brilliant communicator with a missionary vision that had been developed as a student worker with KGK in Japan. In March, as negotiations were proceeding, Stacey had written Samuel Escobar:

> Sometimes, Samuel, I feel very discouraged, feeling that life has been too much of a failure. If only I had an assistant, someone who could understand me and work with me, to whom I could gradually turn over responsibilities, I should be grateful. I have no ambition so far as IFES is concerned, only that God's man to succeed me may appear so that I could gradually turn things over to him. The Executive Committee believes that it would be better if there were only about a twelve month period of overlap. I don't agree with this. I'd far rather have an assistant with whom I could work for about four years and then step down and let him take over. But we shall see how God leads.[24]

Stacey's idea of a lengthy overlap was not particularly appealing to someone with Griffiths's drive and creativity. He felt that experience in Canada and America had shown that as long as Stacey was around he would never be a free agent. Besides, in China Inland Mission/Overseas Missionary Fellowship he was used to sharing leadership and working closely with colleagues. He anticipated that IFES would be much more of a solo operation, given the distances between senior staff and Stacey's example. After a lengthy process of negotiation he and his wife concluded this was not God's call to them. Griffiths went on to lead the Overseas Missionary Fellowship and then the London Bible College.

Other names surfaced at Baarn once it was known that Griffiths had turned down the nomination to be Stacey's successor. Chandapilla from the Union of Evangelical Students of India had definite criteria: "Spiritual maturity, dedication to the Lord, understanding of the world, a university graduate, one who is completely in accord with the IFES and its basis and objectives, and who had already proved himself in student ministry."[25] The person also needed charisma, must be between forty and forty-five, married with children and speaking more than one language. He need not however be an administrative genius. Would the apostle Paul have qualified?

The executive went on to a YMCA center in Wuppertal, West Germany, for the meetings of the general committee. As if to add to the pressure on Stacey, there were clear signs that IFES as a whole was uneasy about the arrangement with IFES Inc. As before, Australia led the criticism. There had already been complaints from Sydney about Samuel Escobar as staff (and a confidant of Stacey's) serving on the executive committee. Now John Diesendorf rose after Stacey gave his report, expressed regret that there were not more student leaders from the new national groups present and raised four leading questions about IFES Inc. and its relationship to IFES and the running and operation of Schloss Mittersill. Stacey was asked to come up with "specific answers" to these questions, not only about IFES Inc. but also "the situation in Great Britain and Switzerland," member movements most affected about the decision about Mittersill.

In his report Stacey referred to the invitation of the executive committee the week before that he continue for another four-year term. In accepting their nomination he stated: "I believe this should be my last and that it is in the best interest of the IFES that a younger person be appointed who can adequately take over the responsibilities of this position." Without mentioning Michael Griffiths by name, he expressed "great disappointment" that he had not accepted the position and that the search must start all over again. He repeated his earlier words to Escobar, requesting an assistant who would "share the burden in connection with the many decisions that have to be made day by day in relation to our IFES ministry around the world, and who could take over the responsibility of the central office during my absences from Lausanne."[26]

It was a cry for help. Criticized openly for the first time at such an event, he left the IFES general committee a dispirited and lonely man, having paid a price of leadership. "At times," he reported, "it appears that there is the danger of some of us departing from the primary emphasis upon those principles which brought many of our movements into existence and which were accompanied by a period of great growth and spiritual blessing."[27] He had one country particularly in mind, where his ministry had begun, and about which he was now deeply troubled: Canada (see chap. 16).

Following the general committee meeting, Stacey hurried off to Elba, where Yvonne and Jonathan were staying. He spent a recuperative four weeks there. Stephen and Els joined them twice. (On the second visit, Stephen had a motorcycle accident traveling back to his ministry in Florence.) Stacey drove back over the Alps to Mittersill with Yvonne feeling steadily worse. At the local hospital a tumor was diagnosed. He took her by taxi to Munich and on to Lausanne by plane. There were many tests and 4 September she was operated on. Six days later the report from the pathologist was a relief: it was not malignant but a blood cyst the size of a baby's head. Had it burst when she was not in a hospital, she would have died. "So all in all we are deeply grateful, but I am pretty exhausted, as your can imagine," he wrote his friends Charles and Evelyn MacKechnie in Toronto.[28]

Realizing a Dream

Meanwhile the work at Mittersill commenced. John Bolten Jr. would come up many weekends from Nürnberg to supervise the renovations, which were much more extensive (and expensive) than had been envisioned. Bolten Jr. remembers, "It became quite cold, as the central heating plant was also completely revamped. We were very thankful for the fireplace in our apartment!"[29] Pipes burst because they were not drained before the first cold spell before Christmas. In reply to an anxious letter from Stacey, who was in Portland, Oregon, Anneliese Oberndorfer, a local holdover from the baron's employ, wrote to reassure him: "Alle Arbeit geht gut voran" ("As for the work it's going well").[30] There was lots to do: a new dining room to accommodate eighty-five students, a new kitchen with up-to-date equipment, the conversion of some large rooms into sleeping areas with bunk beds, the transformation of the party room to a library, and a previously unused room into an auditorium seating a hundred. Throughout that winter Stacey made frequent trips to Mittersill from Lausanne and spent time there on his own. It was at that point that he began to wrestle with his dark side.

The summer of 1968 was to be the opening of the facility, but the workmen lingered on until mid-July. A four-week IFES international training course and a three-week seminar for theological students had been scheduled. Jennifer Johnston Favré, who had come to the Lausanne office from England earlier in the year, spent the summer at Schloss Mittersill and has vivid memories, particularly of the frustration of the Americans who couldn't shower because there was almost no water available. ("The water system installed by the Nazis proved insufficient, and we shall have to spend $20,000 this autumn.") "We had a small rebellion on our hands on the part of the US students," Stacey reported to John Bolten Sr., but reassured him, "Please do not be alarmed at what I write; we had the same thing at Campus in the Woods,

Stacey and Yvonne Woods (left) with Billy and Ruth Graham at Schloss Mittersill, July 1968 (Courtesy of Yvonne Woods)

the same thing at Pioneer Camp. Obviously Satan is giving us a great deal of real opposition; far too many inexplicable difficulties have arisen."[31] The prevailing chaos affected the office staff from Lausanne, who were preparing for the IFES executive committee scheduled for late summer in Moscia. Erna Kull remembered how one time, calling Hans Bürki about the translation of a German word in a conference brochure, Stacey "started jumping up and down shouting at me to put the phone down." Hans's answer was reassuring: "What's the old shouter going on about now?"[32] Stacey was under a lot of pressure and strain.

Stacey was particularly pumped because Billy Graham was scheduled to appear, thanks to an intervention by Bolten, who was a major financial backer and friend. Graham turned down the invitation to the dedication service. ("Billy is very tired and would like to have a few days of recreation," Bolten explained to Stacey.) Graham duly arrived by rental car from Munich airport with Ruth and T. W. Wilson on 16 July, Bolten having provided Wilson with a map of central Europe. Stacey had a conversation with Billy Graham the morning Graham left, shamelessly appealing to him for the additional $20,000 for a new well. But it was particularly the ministry to Eastern Europe that he plugged.

It is now possible for students from Eastern European countries, apart from East Germany, Russia, and perhaps Rumania at the present time, to obtain visas to come to Austria, a country whose neutrality is recognized. However, they can bring virtually no money out of their country, they can only pay their travelling expenses, and each person must receive a personal invitation. Furthermore, we have to guarantee that they will return to their homeland.[33]

At the twenty-fifth anniversary of Schloss Mittersill, Yvonne reminisced:

There were twenty in that first summer from Czechoslovakia. They lapped up the teaching and spent their free time copying by hand page after page of English Bible commentaries, later to be translated into their own language at home. They all arrived safely back home just hours before the August invasion of communists troops! The door to return was then closed for the next twenty years.[34]

In some ways the dedication of Schloss Mittersill on 8 September 1968 was the crowning event of Stacey's career. The guest list included the president of Austria, the governors of the states of Salzburg and Tyrol, the minister of education and assorted evangelical leaders. Many of those invited could not attend: Martin Niemoller and Hans Rookmaaker graciously declined. Dignitaries represented both Roman Catholic and Lutheran churches. Armin Hoppler of Scripture Union made a special point of coming. The local band provided a festive atmosphere. On behalf of the staff Herr Büchmeier welcomed the guests. Anneliese Oberndorfer was much in evidence. Both Bolten couples, Sr. and Jr., welcomed arriving guests, as did Stacey. When the chapel bell finished ringing, John Bolten Jr. started the service in the new auditorium. The local Bürgermeister brought greetings. There was a prayer of dedication by the Lutheran minister at nearby Zell am See, Pastor Geisellbrecht.

First Houseparty at Schloss Mittersill, Christmas 1968 (Courtesy of Bruce Kaye)

Stacey got up and said apologetically, "I am sorry I do not speak very good German." He explained what IFES was ("39 national organizations with affiliations in some forty-three other nations, a movement of student by students and for students"). He then told the assembly "that Jesus Christ is the only answer to the world's problems." The service concluded with a rousing "Ein' feste Burg ist unser Gott" sung lustily by both Catholics and Protestants alike.

Today at Schloss Mittersill there are two marble plaques. On a wall by the chapel there is one for John Bolten Sr.: "His generosity and vision for reaching students with the gospel made this conference center possible." The dates indicate that he was eighty-nine when he died. Stacey died a year later; he was only seventy-three. On an inner wall, by the desk where guests register on arrival, there is another plaque, celebrating C. Stacey Woods: "His vision and dedication to biblical learning of students resulted in the establishment of Schloss Mittersill." These plaques recognize the leadership both men provided. But the greatest monument to them both are the lives of those for whom Mittersill has been a place of renewal, a time apart, an opportunity to discover God—exactly what Stacey envisioned it to be. They cannot begin to understand the sacrifice that was involved in making a dream take place and the toll it took on the dreamer.

16

Canadian Crisis

"Inter-Varsity is becoming theologically woolly and evangelistically ineffective."[1] Stacey was at the Berlin Congress on Evangelism the end of October 1966 when Ian Rennie, who had served on staff both in Canada and the United States in the early 1950s and was now a popular Presbyterian minister in Vancouver, caught up with him and shared his concerns. Stacey had great respect for Ian, whose family he had known from his Winnipeg visits.[2]

Change of Focus

Stacey also had deep affection and regard for the man who succeeded him. He was not the only one: Wilber Sutherland was gifted in many areas: an able communicator with an ability to share a vision, a quick and fertile mind, and leadership that had seen Inter-Varsity Canada grow significantly in the 1950s. But Stacey was becoming increasingly aware that all was not well in Canada. The state of spiritual health and vitality of Canadian Inter-Varsity, and the direction its general secretary was taking it, became a deepening anxiety for Stacey as the turbulent decade of the 1960s unfolded. It was a time of tectonic shift in the culture, and nowhere was this more evident than in postsecondary education. The rapidly growing student population, with expanding enrollment and the increasing number of universities, was having an impact.

Wilber Sutherland's address at a Yale seminar in 1958 showed that he was wrestling with the nature of Christian outreach in the university and how Inter-Varsity could respond to the culture. He had said at the time that "Inter-Varsity encourages Christians to filter out into the entire life of the university not only serving as a living, speaking witness to their growing understanding of the truth as it is in Jesus Christ but also acting as the salt of the university." He quickly added a caveat: "At the same time Inter-Varsity believes that the essential concern of these Christians in their corporate identity within the university is not the reform of the university but the proclamation to it of the Gospel."[3]

In speaking about the university in this way, Wilber was venturing into territory unfamiliar to Stacey, though his caveat would reassure him. Having refused to abandon the university as a place for Christian penetration, Stacey had difficulty in articulating what a full-orbed Christian response to it should be. His main concern, as he saw the direction Wilber Sutherland was taking, was that IVCF would be compromised both in its mission and in its message. Canadian universities, though few in number, had historically provided a powerful impetus for the modern missionary movement through the Student Volunteer Movement and the YMCA, an impulse that had dissipated and waned. Now he feared history was repeating itself in IVCF Canada.

Stacey wrote anxiously: "With regard to missionary interest, I feel, Wilber, if this dies down it will affect the movement spiritually in every way. But surely our ambition must be to help every Christian student in high school and university to face up to God's will for their lives in terms of God's call to world evangelism."[4] A 1965 survey of over a thousand Canadian missionaries across the denominational and faith-mission spectrum indicated that one-fifth of them had "received their Missionary Call" through IVCF. The first missionary conference was held at the University of Toronto in 1946. Though Canadians still attended the triennial Urbana Missions Convention at the University of Illinois in large numbers, Stacey said that "Urbana can never substitute for the grass-roots missionary emphasis in the university." And he asked why there was no longer a missionary secretary for IVCF Canada. Wilber shot back, "There is a great deal more that we can do in missions here in our work in Canada, but I think I can say that IVCF in Canada is as 'missionary minded' as it [ever] was."[5] Stacey did have a point, however. With Wilber's encouragement IVCF Canada had broadened its third (missionary) purpose ("all Christians are called to be sent") to include "fostering of convictions of Christian vocation among students." Stacey saw that statement, true as it was, as an implicit lessening of the uniqueness and urgency of the Great Commission.[6]

It all came back, in his view, to leadership. The movement, and staff especially, took their cue from Wilber. "You by nature are a student and are an intellectual," Stacey said. "The vast majority of students in university, to say nothing of those in high school, are not. My great concern for the IVCF of Canada is that its leadership will function on an intellectual level quite unintentionally and as a result there will be a neglect of those principles that made Inter-Varsity what it was."[7] He was looking back to the early days of the movement under his leadership: "My only desire is that in Inter-Varsity there can be a return to simplicity, to basics, and I believe you are the only person who can give the lead in this." The basics to which he wanted IVCF Canada to return were described as "the quiet time and the daily prayer meeting, the teaching of the Word of God, student witness, university evangelism and then involvement in the total and larger picture of world evangelism."

What Wilber may have thought as he read Stacey's letter we cannot know. In spite of his public persona, Wilber was actually a shy and a private person with a quality of insouciance that appeared to make him impervious to criticism. He was usually very gracious and appeared without malice. At the same time he never really engaged in serious debate with Stacey, perhaps because he respected him too much or knew that neither of them would change their mind. As they drifted apart, one of the few people in whom Stacey confided was no longer there for him. Nor did they have as much in common as before. Wilber was by now being influenced by people other than Stacey, having gathered around him an unusual circle of friends and confidants. Stacey felt the loss of the relationship they once had.

In spite of implicit (and not so implicit) criticism in his correspondence with Wilber, Stacey was invited to undertake a six-week trip to Canada starting the day after Christmas 1966. Finances were suffering because of a perceived lack of direction in IVCF Canada by many who were described as "old-timers." Stacey's visit might help to motivate these longtime but now alienated supporters to renew their giving. Celebrations of Canada's centennial year and Expo '67 coming to Montreal provided a great opportunity for promotion both IFES and IVCF Canada.

Stacey was given a horrendous itinerary. "When we saw the schedule," Yvonne wrote Wilber, "we were really aghast." For the first time in their married life,

Yvonne wrote without Stacey's knowledge, asking that Canada remember that "at the age of 57 he does not have the same power of recuperation and comeback as he used to possess."[8] And it turned out to be an emotional roller-coaster as Stacey kept hearing disturbing accounts of Inter-Varsity Canada as he traveled.

On 1 March 1967, the tour completed, Stacey wrote Wilber one of the most difficult letters of his life. He concluded at the end of the fourth page: "I hope this letter hasn't made you angry. In writing it I have tried to be faithful and to be a true friend."[9] The trip had renewed friendships and "stirred up memories of things past," but it had not been well planned. The lack of organization he saw as symptomatic of a movement adrift. He started with good news. Some areas of the country and some staff were doing well. He singled out Tony Tyndale in the east and Gordon Stewart in Manitoba. He was struggling to understand Marj Long, the new dynamo in Alberta, was anxious about Saskatchewan and was feeling that the work in British Columbia was going backward rather than forward.

Ontario, most affected by Wilber's new directions, received a devastating critique from Stacey: "Uncertainty, lack of vision, lack of solid direction and a general questioning of everything disturbed me greatly." He offered a reason for this drift:

> A general neglect of the exposition of the Word of God. . . . [T]he thing that appalled me most was that all too seldom was the Gospel being preached in the university. One may differ as to what we mean by the Gospel, but there seemed to be talks of Christianity and sex, Christianity and this, the Christian view of this, the Christian view of that. But even if we take it for granted that such subjects could be a launching pad for direct evangelism, it seemed obvious to me that this was not the case. . . . I do not suggest that anywhere in Canada the people are holding wrong doctrine, but they simply do not seem to be operating on Biblical and evangelistic principles.[10]

Having stated the problem as he saw it, Stacey suggested correctives. Inter-Varsity Canada needed to restore its training courses. The American interest in Campus-in-the-Woods had recently been sold to Canada, Cedar Campus having made the Canadian property less attractive to those having to cross the border. The site was already in serious disrepair, maintenance having been neglected, and with Inter-Varsity Canada's financial crunch there were no longer funds to update it. Wilber's priorities as general secretary were elsewhere. Campus-in-the-Woods had been a place where staff modeled and mentored discipleship. "Unless the staff themselves are setting examples, unless the staff are disciplined in the matter of quiet time, they are hypocrites if they try to advise this so far as the students are concerned, unless the staff are daily making new discoveries of Christ in the Scriptures."[11]

Wilber Sutherland's creative genius was now engaged in new fields. Some of the ministries that had been an integral part of Inter-Varsity Canada were being reconsidered, ignored or benignly neglected. Stacey was anxious about reports that the high school work, numbers in the clubs having nosedived since the 1950s, was now to be abandoned. A board member from Manitoba, Stacey's longtime friend Geoffrey Still, soon to be brought in briefly as executive director, witnessed what he described as "a running battle between those associated with Pioneer Camps and the other aspects of the IV ministry."[12] Stacey was already aware of this from Vincent Craven, director of Ontario Pioneer. In 1964 the IVCF Canada office moved from 30 St. Mary Street near the University of Toronto to a site out of reach of most students, ironically thanks to a legacy from the estate of Edith Read that Stacey had negotiated.[13] Wilber involved himself in a widening range of interests, the most relevant was his chairmanship of the 1970 Canadian Congress on Evangelism. Nonetheless even this raised the ire of some board members alarmed by what they saw as an absentee leader.

CREATION TWO

Creation Two, the experimental evangelistic drama company encouraged by Wilber,[14] particularly angered the conservative Christian community.[15] Performed in Toronto parks, in churches and at Grad Camp, the plays were ever more controversial, with (it was alleged) profanity, simulated sexual intercourse and speaking in tongues. That combination was guaranteed to offend at least someone, glossolalia also having become a flashpoint. As Wilber later admitted on behalf of himself and Barbara, "our natural affinity seems to be increasingly with people in the Arts—music, drama, painting, dance, literature—and with others seeking to understand and to use the modern technological communication media—film, radio, TV. It is in this direction I feel currently led."[16]

A year later Stacey sent his emissary, David Bentley-Taylor, to Canada on a fifty-six day fact-finding trip (10 October-3 December 1968). It was an exhaustive tour. David spoke ninety times, gave thirty-two lectures to non-Christians and visited twenty-two universities. The trip was chaotically organized, he met great rudeness, particularly in Victoria with a young IVCF faculty adviser, and the student groups, especially as he came east, were minuscule in attendance. At the end of his travels Wilber gave him only two hours over lunch for a concluding wrap-up consultation. Bentley-Taylor saved his observations for Stacey. The final paragraph provided a telling critique of Wilber's stewardship:

> In conclusion I am left with the impression that IVCF is a rather remarkable work of God, stronger in the west than in the east, badly needing better leadership, in some danger of holding its biblical anchors too loosely and of losing the confidence of its more rigidly evangelical friends. Anxious to count in the wild, lost world and to break from a too detached, separated attitude to current problems, it could go too far in stressing the "Creation mandate." I did not get the impression that it had already gone too far. But I suspect that Wilbur's remarkable gifts need to be differently used.[17]

On 20 September 1969, the day after intense discussions about Creation Two in the executive committee, Wilbur offered his resignation effective the end of June 1970. The next day the full board accepted it, it seems much to his surprise. "I must write to thank Wilber," Stacey dictated a memo to his secretary after a visit to Canada in December 1969, and added "also to Wilber and Barbara about Creation Two, their resignation from IFES, and their future."[18] This letter was not preserved.

In the 1960s the Canadian IVCF exposed Stacey to some of the weakness of a movement in danger of losing its vision. Stacey reflected to the 1967 general committee:

> Too easily we can be caught up in the consideration of intellectual questions which in themselves are proper, but in our concern and interest in these matters perhaps some of the more basic, elementary disciplines are in danger of being neglected. Without being anti-intellectual, mere intellectualism can become a grave danger to our university unions, and can bring about a state of fruitlessness and spiritual sterility which may result in our movements being set aside, and in God raising up other movements to maintain a witness to Christ and His salvation in the universities.[19]

It would take some time for IVCF Canada, particularly the parts most influenced by Wilber, to recover from his experimentation, but recover they did. That recovery was not without a heavy cost, a cost that Stacey shared. In the meantime Wilber had moved on. When he died in October 1997 at age seventy-three, eight hundred people from all walks of life crowded into Toronto's idiosyncratic Holy

Trinity Church for his lengthy memorial.[20] An obituary contributed to Canada's national newspaper said it all: "His mind burgeoned with ideas which his staff struggled to implement. By the time they brought the results to Wilber, he had forgotten the idea, having generated another plenitude since."[21]

In some ways Wilber Sutherland was very much like his mentor, Stacey, but he lacked the discipline of a focused or grounded mind. He was a free spirit who soared above Inter-Varsity Christian Fellowship of Canada and left it way behind. Unfortunately, in the remaining years of his life Stacey could neither forgive nor forget Wilber for what he did to Canadian IVCF. "So much promise and so much devastation," Stacey muttered once.[22]

17

Final Farewells

"HE COULD BE LIKE A FLASH OF LIGHTNING or a stick of dynamite, but there was no doubt of his ability." David Bentley-Taylor said, reflecting years later on his relationship with Stacey Woods. In December 1967 David had stopped in Lausanne at the IFES office after one of his sorties abroad as Stacey's emissary. As he watched Stacey in action, bobbing in and out from desk to desk, he was mesmerized.

> After twenty years as General Secretary he had acquired such worldwide knowledge and experience that it was risky to disagree with him. His competence amazed and delighted me: he was severe and he was inspiring, he was blunt and he was efficient, he was alarming and he had drive. I realised for the first time that he was the most complex man with whom I had ever been associated.[1]

The partnership between David Bentley-Taylor and Stacey Woods during Stacey's final years as IFES general secretary was remarkable. An Englishman with an Oxford degree, Bentley-Taylor remains one of the most brilliant missionary strategists of the twentieth century. He went to China with China Inland Mission and at Chefoo met and married a Canadian, Jessie Moore, who had cared for Yvonne Ritchie's mother in her old age. He met up with Stacey at the IFES constituent assembly in 1947: "Although he was rather roughly handled my sympathies were largely with Stacey. He did superbly. I told him so afterwards."[2]

Subsequently the Bentley-Taylors went to East Java. When his wife's ill health necessitated a return home, Bentley-Taylor became a full-time IVF missionary advocate. He was also effective in evangelism: he always carried with him in a large briefcase, which became his trademark, "one hundred talks that he could work on the hoof." In 1966, celebrating their wedding anniversary with a week in Switzerland, David and Jessie visited 43 Route d'Oron. "It proved to be a turning point for us," David later recalled. Stacey was not there, but on his return Yvonne spoke about the visit, and Stacey arranged to meet David at 39 Bedford Square, London, the IVF office. They talked a long time and finally Stacey said, "Best of all would be if you came right in and worked with me. And that is what I did," Bentley-Taylor simply added.

For the next eight years, from 1966 to 1974, Stacey "dispatched me to thirty-eight countries to contact university students and graduates." Bentley-Taylor made two eight-week trips each year and then filed insightful, lively, and thorough reports, with follow-up recommendations for Stacey. As traveling secretary at large, Stacey's designated special envoy, "we shared the same convictions and we had the same aim to promote Christian faith and obedience in Universities throughout the world."[3] Stacey looked after the logistical details, freeing David to roam. On his return he would stop off at Geneva airport and then take the train to Lausanne, reporting his adventures to Stacey.

Another significant addition to IFES staff, and someone who like David Bentley-Taylor would lead conferences at Schloss Mittersill, was Harold O. J. Brown, known as Joe. Brown joined IFES staff as theological studies secretary in the summer of 1966, having had to delay taking up his appointment in order to complete doctoral work. Stacey reported Brown's coming on staff with enthusiasm to Harold Ockenga.[4] Brown was immediately called on to lead a theological students' camp, and he settled in Pully, outside Lausanne, in the autumn. "It is the hope of the IFES," Stacey reported, "to be able to stimulate, and assist where necessary, in the development of a vital ministry and an uncompromising witness on the part of the National Evangelical Unions amongst theological students, particularly those attending nonevangelical or nonbiblical theological faculties."[5] Brown began his work by sending out a questionnaire about the theological education of IFES staff. In his report to the 1967 executive committee he concluded that "much very effective study has been accomplished by individual staff members apart from regular programs. It does not appear, however, that many of the staff have intensively studied what might be called 'modern theology' (which is not necessarily a handicap to them)." He also conceded that "non-theologians are among the most effective and valuable full-time staff." Joe Brown continued to serve as a useful resource for four more years and traveled widely, conducting seminars throughout the IFES community.

STACEY'S WORLDWIDE TRAVELS

During his final three years as general secretary Stacey did not let up in his travels. After the 1968 executive committee he went around the world, stopping off at Beirut and following up on some of David Bentley-Taylor's visits there. David had spoken of "the importance of Beirut as a centre for contacting the whole Arab world."[6] When David had made a second trip to Beirut the next January, he said that Alonso Fairbanks "should be encouraged in every way." Al had been the first IFES staff member in Africa for three years, and was now teaching at two colleges, feeling his experience as a cancer researcher was going to waste. Also in Beirut was Bob Young, a staffer with eleven years experience (six in Buenos Aires and five in California), who was also feeling frustrated. Bentley-Taylor characterized him as "a pioneer not a builder." It was Bob Young who said, "I used to find that five minutes talk with Stacey solved things which had been bothering me for years."[7] Stacey heard both Fairbanks and Young out and prescribed a week of lectures with Joe Brown.

In Madras, his next stop at Union of Evangelical Students of India headquarters, Stacey had talks with Chandapilla and made plans for Joe Brown to lead a training course. Then he flew to Singapore to arrange the 1969 executive committee meeting scheduled to meet there and proposed Samuel Escobar to be invited to lead a mission in Kuala Lumpur and Singapore beforehand. His time in Asia ended with a visit to Hong Kong, where he had lengthy sessions with Chua Wee Hian. Wee Hian had taken on from David Adeney the position as associate general secretary for East Asia. He asked about strategic priorities, and Stacey replied "that in view of student unrest and its repudiation of the previous generation, the importance of a balanced and proportionate emphasis upon student initiative and responsibility was paramount, and if this was the case, then the importance of student training could not be overemphasised."[8]

A year later Stacey also went round the world, but his time in Asia started with Pakistan. "I had not realized how very difficult the situation was for the Christian minority, how they are being discriminated against, and how it is going to be increasingly difficult for Christians in the future."[9] It was a prescient comment. He spent time with staffer David Penman.[10] Penman had been a part of celebrations that established the Pakistan Inter-Varsity Fellowship and its executive committee at the old hill station of Muree the previous August, meetings that Stacey had hoped to attend. "This is the result of many years of effort and planning so you will realise something of our great joy at the passing of this milestone," Penman wrote.[11] David Bentley-Taylor had signaled to Stacey that Penman was someone with whom it would be well to spend quality time: "I am not sure that I have in any land met a more gifted and promising missionary than this remarkable young man. I delighted in his penetrating, disciplined, and tidy mind."[12] On that trip Stacey again ended up at Hong Kong, consulting with Wee Hian, particularly about Thailand.

Later that same year Stacey was in Portugal and Spain, meeting with Ruth Siemens, anxious to ensure that she could work with the new Portuguese general secretary, and planning Mittersill training events the next summer, which she and Bentley-Taylor would lead. With each new contact Stacey's mind was racing ahead, planning, anticipating, strategizing. From Portugal he took off to meet with John Alexander and Jim McLeish in the United States. Together they set a target for American giving to IFES of $2,500 a month for various projects. Following his time in the IVCF office, in a dictabelt full of complicated instructions, he shouted "Don't let the staff ever travel TWA [Trans World Airlines]!" He was annoyed over a mixup with his travel arrangements, and it helped to explode to his stenographer, who duly typed it all up.[13]

At the beginning of 1970 Stacey was in Belgium and Holland. IFES-related movements in the Netherlands were complex, with both strong denominational loyalties and divisions. Belgium was entirely different. "My conclusion is that we can do nothing with this complicated situation until we first have a staff worker in whom we have confidence and who is sufficiently strong to build bridges, maintain his position, and forge ahead with a group."[14]

In November, Stacey spent a fortnight in Scandinavia. He found the numerical growth and spiritual strength of the IFES-related movements, particularly in Denmark and Sweden, a tremendous encouragement. There was much to be learned in the Anglo-Saxon world from their faith, he asserted. But here he also had theological concerns: "Is it possible to accept the Bible as infallible with regard to its doctrine, its ethics, its moral and spiritual teaching, and at the same time disregard the question of the authenticity of historical elements in Scripture, the space and time events."[15] In Norway's capital he had an interview with the newspaper as well as the bishop of Oslo in the state (Lutheran) church. A midafternoon dinner with his old comrade in arms, Carl Frederick Wisløff, brought back many memories. Wisløff complained, "Many of the students lack fervor, zeal, vision, sacrifice."[16]

Stacey and Yvonne were guests at Urbana 70. The theme was "Christ the Liberator," and he shared with Samuel Escobar brief daily talks on student work around the world. He called it "a remarkable event," with 12,300 present. John Stott spoke powerfully on John 13—17. Music for the first time was contemporary as well as traditional, "sung with an unmistakable beat." The multiple screen presentation by InterVarsity's 2100 Productions was a big attraction each afternoon. "The creativity of this projection proved enormously stimulating," Stacey commented. Director David Howard reminded the audience of the danger of popularity, as he reflected on the demise of the Student Volunteer Movement. The University Christian Federation, its lineal descendent after several mergers, had quietly voted itself out of existence the previous year. Urbana 70 is most remembered for the time that black activist Tom Skinner brought the crowd to their feet. His topic was "The U.S. Racial Crisis and World Evangelism." Stacey appreciated the emphasis but was anxious about what he called Skinner's demagoguery that brought a response bordering on hysteria. Overall Urbana 70 was an uplifting experience: "To sit on the platform and to look out on that vast kaleidoscope of Christian men and women who inevitably must assume Christian responsibility during this decade, to hear them sing, applaud, question, and bow in prayer, remains with me. . . . God still has His consecrated minority."[17]

He needed that encouragement, for there was also disunity. From Norton Sterrett he had an intimation of trouble over an article by Peter Wagner ("that rascal") in *Christianity Today* concerning the view of inspiration held by René Padilla and Samuel Escobar.[18] Samuel explains:

In December 1970 a group of twenty-five missionaries, pastors, IFES staff, and Seminary professors from all of Latin America gathered in Cochabamba, Bolivia, to form a Latin American Theological Fraternity. Peter Wagner, then a missionary in

Bolivia, presented a paper on church growth that was severely criticized. He also wanted us to include a reference to "inerrancy" in the foundational statement. There were only two or three Latin Americans that wanted it and it did not enter in the statement. Wagner then wrote a news release for *Christianity Today* accusing "the InterVarsity block" of fostering a "lower view of the authority of Scripture." He knew that IVCF in the States would react against us (René Padilla, Pedro Arana and myself) and so it was, and they pressed Stacey to sanction us. He did not, and in fact he defended us.[19]

Stacey was loyal to his staff, and they never forgot it. After the national staff meetings following Urbana, Stacey traveled to the Caribbean. Here he was forced to deal with the tongues movement and its affect on evangelical unity in IFES related movements.

SCHLOSS MITTERSILL

Mittersill continued to dominate Stacey's thinking. The success of the dedication 8 September 1968 was for him only a beginning of what he was convinced would be a wonderful future for the property. By the following spring he was petitioning IFES Inc. with proposals for additional facilities: a heated swimming pool, condominium apartments, a restaurant and motel rooms, all to be on adjacent property recently purchased and donated by John Bolten Sr.[20] Extensive planning with elaborate architect's designs proceeded. On 5 December 1972, after three years of work and a substantial outlay in fees, Stacey learned to his dismay that the Salzburg authorities had turned down the application. Stacey continued to think that the facility could become a first-class hotel, but this seemed idealistic and impractical to many who knew the business.

By May of 1969 Mittersill had run up a $20,000 overdraft at the bank. As with any facility of this size and complexity, there were continuing day-by-day crises, most of which ended up on Stacey's desk. This of course had been the point raised by the IFES executive committee back in 1966. Stacey was not a finance person. From 1934, he wrote Keith Hunt who later took over the Schloss from him, "I have always insisted that I am not a financial man. I don't even understand properly balanced sheets."[21] There was the problem of a succession of "Direktors" who could manage the facility. After a bad experience with the first one, Stacey had some continuity with the next two: Peter Salvisburg came 1 April 1969 and stayed to 30 September 1971, and was succeeded by Hans Jörg Töbler, who stayed for another three years. After that it was chaotic until 1979, but by then Stacey was no longer in charge. Hans Honegger wrote John Bolten Sr. that "the Schloss needs a friendly man, loving students, as a manager (not a dolled up hotel director). A man who is able to roll up his sleeves and work, when necessary."[22]

Judgment calls had to be made about fees and bookings. The Schloss was a ministry, European students (for whom it was intended) were chronically short of cash. Americans were better able to pay but they presented a problem: "without wanting to be un-American, uniformly, I found Americans the most unreliable when it comes to bookings, and we are establishing a rule now that for American bookings, they make a deposit, non-refundable, three months before the booking takes effect. We've had our fingers burned so many times, there seems to be no alternative." In the summer of 1972, Töbler's first summer as Direktor, Stacey wrote about complaints he was receiving:

> I realise this is your first summer session with the hectic student operation. It must be truly traumatic and terribly demanding. In the future things should become simpler and easier, and I want to assure you that I want to help you, to stand with you, and back you up in every way. Please, on no account take this as a personal criticism.[23]

Stacey always felt that Mittersill's dark past[24] cast a shadow over it and over him. "One had a seven-day a week stint, Mittersill most often being given the weekends," he admitted. "There were problems with management as well as constant criticism from the outside, all of which took its toll physically and spiritually."[25] Never did Stacey feel more alone: "Thus I entered a new and lonely phase of ministry . . . and for the first time I was without the support of a closely-knit, praying, cooperating committee."[26] And in a poignant moment he confessed: "And so my wife and I embarked almost like Henry Hudson on his voyage to the Arctic of Northern Canada, alone."[27]

It was at Mittersill that Stacey's demons rose up from the darkness. As he was later to say: "All the material things of this life which God gives us richly to enjoy can be used by Satan to turn us away from God. When our Lord was on earth he would enjoy a glass of wine but that same wine being used by Satan can make a person a drunkard. And Satan wants to use in his system the very best God offers to turn us away from God Himself."[28] Stacey had urged evangelicals not to succumb to the pressure of taboos in an influential 1945 *HIS* article. He had encouraged readers to abandon the strict pietistic moralism of an earlier time. Some, escaping a culture of fundamentalist legalism, fell into the trap of antinomianism, a heresy he frequently railed against. The previous generation having eschewed fermented beverages, their children were as a result often innocent about its possible addictive effects. Stacey's father, having seen the ravages of alcohol on his own father, had been strictly teetotaling. Stacey would have done well to heed the warning. The wonder of the career and influence of Stacey Woods is that, in spite of this weakness (and perhaps even because of it), God used him—and Mittersill—mightily.

The saga of finding a successor to Stacey continued. When Michael Griffiths declined the position, Stacey seemed even more irreplaceable. Many names surfaced at the 1968 executive committee at Moscia. A strong consensus in favor of Dr. Oliver Barclay of the British IVF and a member of the executive committee emerged. Barclay demurred, saying that he could not take it until 1971, and he was not at all hopeful that he would be available even then, though he could not close his mind to the possibility. Stacey was then asked whether he would be willing to serve beyond 1971, and he replied that "he could not close his mind to such a possibility." At the same time he urged that "a prayerful vigorous search should be continued to find a suitable person to take his place."[29]

The following year, having with faint hope again urged Oliver Barclay to consider the post, Stacey reversed himself on staying to 1975, stating that he had no freedom to accept such a possible extension. He might however continue on a year-to-year basis. Any need for Stacey to stay on, even on a year-to-year basis, was made unnecessary by the 1970 executive committee decision to appoint Chua Wee Hian, the young associate general secretary for East Asia, to be successor to Stacey Woods. Since Wee Hian—he chose to be called by his Chinese first names rather than the Anglicized one he had used at London Bible College—was taking a six-month study leave at Fuller Theological Seminary, Stacey agreed to stay on until 30 November 1972, when he was "to relinquish all responsibility as General Secretary." The appointment of Wee Hian was possible because Oliver Barclay, as incoming chairman, was willing "to be available for counsel and advice during the initial years of Mr Chua's service as General Secretary."[30]

As we have seen earlier, there was considerable anxiety as to whether Stacey could relinquish responsibility, given his perceived track record in leaving IVCF Canada and IVCF United States. The 1971 executive committee said that he should not be at Schloss Mittersill while there were IFES activities under the authority of his successor, though this was amended a year later as being too draconian. Balancing this measure, the committee "expressed its deep gratitude to Mr Woods for all he has done to bring about the existence of Schloss Mittersill as an IFES centre, with so much fruitful activity" and welcomed his "further services" as prime liaison between Schloss Mittersill and IFES.[31]

Stacey's final report as general secretary, delivered to the 1971 general committee at Mittersill, was a moving testimony to a ministry that he reminded delegates had begun in September of 1934. That month he had debated with Leonard Dixon, the general secretary of the Student Christian Movement of Canada, as to why a second Christian organization was needed in the universities. His answer then had been that Inter-Varsity was a biblical movement adhering strictly to the position that the Bible was without error and was entirely trustworthy. This position the SCM had refused to take. He went on to stress as his legacy:

> We are a confessional movement; we believe that the eternal truth revealed to us in Scripture exists; that it can be stated in propositions, that it is rationally understood and received, and the conversion of man is very much more than some emotional response to a message—it involves man's mind, man's will, as well as his emotion. However, the last four years have seen new student leaders coming to the fore, who in some cases appear to have little understanding or appreciation of the history of our movements.[32]

He deplored the rising tide among evangelicals, particularly in North America, of anti-intellectualism, "interpreting Scripture by Christian experience, rather than to interpret Christian experience on the basis of sound, Biblical exegesis. This is particularly noticeable where the charismatic movement has had an influence." But as he concluded, he refused to dwell on the negative but rather the unfinished task:

> Regardless of the competition and disarray in evangelical circles in so many parts of the world, regardless of tragic, unbiblical division, we can be assured that if by God's grace we advance in obedience and trust in Him alone, the hand of God will rest upon us in blessing and He will continue to give us an effective ministry.

Stacey's concern about experience-based Christianity was a theme Martyn Lloyd-Jones picked up in three addresses to the 1971 general committee. "What Is an Evangelical?" was the question he asked, challenging IFES to "reexamine our name" and not to take the word *evangelical* in its title for granted. The definition of *evangelical* is, he asserted, "the great question today, and I think you will find it to be the question you will have to face increasingly in these coming years."[33] He warned against a debilitating narrowness, an accommodating openness and an inclusive Pentecostalism. In his second lecture he laid down four guiding principles for IFES: (1) the preservation of the gospel, (2) learning from history, (3) maintaining negatives, and (4) being observant of both people's subtractions from the truth *and* their additions. His concluding talk focused on the IFES statement of faith and the difference between foundational and secondary truths. In the latter category he placed eschatology and the charismatic gifts.

Stacey Woods as IFES general secretary c. 1970 (Courtesy of IVCF-USA)

Stacey had wanted the Doctor to speak to his final general committee meeting. It was a fitting benediction for his work, summarizing and reemphasizing what he had given the movement over a quarter century, his final testimony to IFES. It was also the last trip the Doctor ever made outside of the United Kingdom. With the reminder of Lloyd-Jones's affirmations and Stacey's commitments, IFES would, they both fervently prayed, keep faith with the past as it went into the future with new leadership.

Farewell to IFES, 1972

For Stacey and Yvonne 1972 was a bridge year, a time of transition and change. In late February he set off for Madison, Wisconsin, where at the U.S. IVCF headquarters he and Stan Block, representing IFES Inc., sat down with IVCF leadership and ironed out relationships between IFES and IVCF. He went on to visit John Bolten Sr. in Massachusetts and returned home 11 March. A fortnight later Stacey and Yvonne were off to an Easter break in Elba, preparatory to Stacey setting off for six weeks on the road. Stacey first flew to Malaysia, attending the Asian regional conference. While visiting Korea he was aware of the painful division between Korean Inter-Varsity Fellowship and the United Bible Fellowship, the latter group not welcoming him. Returning, he stopped off in Portugal and Spain. The summer was spent between Elba (a month's holiday) and a training course at Schloss Mittersill.

The fall was dominated by farewells. The executive committee in Denmark at the beginning of September would be Stacey's last. It was probably at this point that Dr. Siegfried Büchholz, a German mathematics professor, came up to a board at the front of the assembly room, and asked for the names of all the people, most of them present, who reported to Stacey. As each name was called, he placed another arrow pointing to a representation of the general secretary. Finally, seeing the number of arrows directed at Stacey, he threw up his hands and said, "To have a successor we will need four people."

The discussion was about a job description for a general secretary in anticipation of Chua Wee Hian taking on the job. At times the questions appeared gratuitous. "Why had this job been created?" seemed a bit bizarre, given the circumstances in 1947 when Stacey accepted the position. But it was the era of management by objective, something that was not heard of twenty-five years earlier.

Thanks to the work of Mitzi Megazzini and Diane Bryce, the IFES office had already moved to space on Marylebone Road in London, across from Madame Tussauds, which led to some quips. Arrangements were made to maintain an office in Switzerland. Stacey offered a room in his apartment, and so the new IFES letterhead had two addresses. The meeting concluded with a unanimous "vote of thanks to the retiring General Secretary, Mr C Stacey Woods, for his twenty-six years of faithful ministry in the IFES." John Alexander, who now held Stacey's former position in the United States, "enumerated the various contributions and achievements of Mr. Woods during his years as General Secretary."[34]

During October and November Stacey stayed in London, living in John Stott's flat and helping to familiarize Wee Hian with the work of an IFES general secretary. In his final letter to the IFES constituency, Stacey spoke of retirement as "re-tire-ing." He commended Chua Wee Hian to them as "a wise and creative leader. I feel sure that you will support him by prayer as you supported me."[35]

One summer in the mid-1970s, a young woman who had been converted from a completely nonevangelical background arrived at Mittersill. She had recently attended a conference of a particular group that caused her some confusion. She was told that the organized church was totally irrelevant. Instead, she heard that Christians needed to *experience* faith, not just intellectualize it. Words had been bandied about like *relevant, real, authentic* and *cutting-edge*. She shared her questions with Stacey but also told him how this ministry had taken America by storm. She wasn't prepared for his response. He listened carefully but then snorted, "Hopelessly American! I give the organization ten years. No, on second thought, only five. It's not rooted in the word of God or the power of the Spirit. It's just a passing fancy." Becky Manley Pippert said, in looking back on that conversation, Stacey was right. It didn't last a decade. But more than that, she never forgot the lesson of what makes a ministry last: attention to the eternal.[36]

Stacey had built on a solid foundation, the Word of God and the power of the Spirit.

18

Retirement Rites

As Stacey walked away from the new IFES office at 27 Marylebone Road, the London streets seemed cold and empty on that gray November day in 1972. To ease the transition Yvonne had stopped off in London on her way home after visiting her mother in Canada. Stacey preached that final Sunday in November at the Cholmeley Evangelical Church, a Christian Brethren assembly on Archway Road in Highgate, where he had spoken the previous Sunday. He was among friends in an old, established and warm missions-minded congregation. Then Stacey and Yvonne went to have dinner nearby at the home of Oliver and Daisy Barclay, after which they flew back to Lausanne. On 30 November, twenty-six years of Stacey's life as general secretary of IFES came to an end, as did almost thirty-nine years of active student ministry.

He had plans for retirement, but much would depend on his health. His final prayer letter in early December, sent out from Madison, Wisconsin, spoke of Christmas at Mittersill. In January the Woodses would be in Egypt. In February Stacey would be teaching Isaiah in Bangalore, and March would be spent in Australia. "Then back to Lausanne for some writing and study in preparation for the summer and fall which, God willing, will be spent in Bible teaching in North

Stacey and Yvonne Woods c. 1970 (Courtesy of Yvonne Woods)

America."[1] Many of the plans they had made tentatively did not work out, including the trip to Australia. But the writing would absorb his attention during the next five years. The executive committee had encouraged him to do a history of IFES. So he would be busy.

There was, of course, the question as to where Stacey and Yvonne would retire. Stacey had lived on three continents. His older sons had settled in Philadelphia and Florence, Italy. What would hold them in Switzerland, a country with a strong currency, heavy expenses and taxation? At one point Stacey put a deposit of $10,000 on a condominium development in Philadelphia, only to lose it when they decided to stay in Lausanne. The reason was not clear: one explanation was that their apartment would not sell, the other that he was ambivalent about moving back to the United States.

One thing that made Lausanne attractive was the Christian community that gathered around them. In Frank and Anne Horton they had a longtime friendship and loyal support. After 1973 there was also the International Evangelical Church of Lausanne, which Yvonne and Stacey with Don and Martha Hoke formed that year. Don was in Lausanne as director of the International Congress on World Evangelization and discovered a need for an evangelical English-speaking work, there being only a high Anglican church and a Church of Scotland congregation whose pastor was not theologically sympathetic. The congregations never exceeded sixty, with a continual flow of people in and out of Lausanne, but they became a community that provided not only personal support but also a place where Stacey could exercise his gifts of preaching and teaching.

In retirement they were reminded of the passing of time. "Saint Eva" McCarthy was diagnosed with terminal cancer. Her last visit to them was in February 1972. She spent the year before her death challenging her friends to end well. "I have asked myself many times whether I am giving [God] the same devotion, the same loving obedience, the same keenness to put first the Kingdom of God and His right-eousness."[2] Her passing 20 March 1974 was the end of an era. In November 1977 Yvonne's mother, almost eighty-eight, died, and Yvonne was unable to get to the funeral. Stacey, who was changing planes in New York when the news came, was incommunicado, and by the time he arrived home, it was too late get to the funeral. Geoffrey flew to Australia from Philadelphia as the family representative.

Perhaps the saddest loss was that of Stacey's niece Rosemary, who was diag-nosed with cancer in 1978. It was an untimely death for a young mother with two small children, and Stacey took it very hard. Rosemary was the first of his Australian family with whom he was in proximity and close contact since he left Australia. She and her husband, Anglican minister Bruce Kaye, arrived in Basle for New Testament doctoral studies in 1967. They were at Schloss Mittersill for the first Christmas house party the next year. When Bruce took a position at Durham University, he was able to place Jonathan there, in spite of Jonathan's unusual Swiss secondary-school qualifications. Bruce and the children came to Lausanne the first Christmas after Rosemary's death. Stacey tried to get Bruce a position at a leading evangelical seminary. When he was offered the job, Bruce was surprised and quickly declined because his theological views were not those of the school's, particularly on inerrancy. He went back to Sydney, happily re-married and recently retired as secretary to the Australian general synod of the Anglican church.[3]

Stacey retired at sixty-three; Yvonne was fifty-eight. There was no lessening of Stacey's sharp mind and quick wit. David Bentley-Taylor visited them during the winter of 1974 while they were in Winnipeg and describes Stacey at the time: "He greeted me delightfully, his forcefulness and penetrating insights apparently undi-minished. He looked magnificent: grey hair, red face, strong physique, feet up on a stool. Eager to renew our relationship I talked very freely, also very carefully, and he answered me with wisdom and kindness."[4]

STACEY'S ONGOING CONCERNS

Two concerns for IFES dominated Stacey's final years: training courses and specifically Schloss Mittersill. Second and related closely was the theological integrity of the movement, particularly biblical authority not just as an article of faith but as a living dynamic for all members of IFES. This meant a continuing emphasis on the Christian life as one of daily devotion and prayer. Corporately the movement stood under the Word of God and needed consistent biblical instruction and exegesis, something in which he excelled. Although there had been concern that after all the years he had given the organization he would find it difficult to retire and would start to meddle, he was nonetheless vice-chairman, had wide experience and knowledge, and could serve as a valuable resource.

Schloss Mittersill was an ongoing concern, making serious demands on Stacey. "When we first bought Mittersill, I stepped out of all responsibility as to supervising repairs and renovations and taking care of the accounting—this was given to John Bolten Jr."[5] But Johnny (as he was often called) had fallen out with one of the IFES Inc. people.[6] John Bolten Sr. was eighty years old and deaf. Harold John Ockenga, approaching seventy and preoccupied with setting up a newly merged seminary, Gordon-Conwell, was now showing disturbing signs that his powers were waning. The withdrawal of John Bolten Jr., the youngest of the Mittersill players, was a serious blow to Stacey.

In the summer of 1974 there were changes at Schloss Mittersill. IVCF in the United States took responsibility, with staffers Keith and Gladys ("Rusty") Hunt in charge. "We have been praying," Jim Nyquist at the American InterVarsity Press wrote at the end of that summer, "that God would undertake for you in the Schloss conversion and that the ministry of that marvellous place continue and grow in years ahead. I trust that you and Yvonne are at peace that God is undertaking and that Keith and Rusty will be able to serve as God's instruments in bringing a dream and beginning and into a continuing and growing ministry."[7] Stacey left Mittersill for Elba, 29 July, having turned over responsibility to the Hunts. He returned for the Christmas Evangelistic Houseparty as program director, but he was no longer weighed down with administration. Mel Friesen, put in charge, was soon asking all sorts of questions about SIMAG (the Schloss Mittersill holding company), what vested interests there were in the Schloss, and "all the inner working of the personnel changes and conflicts."[8]

The question of the ultimate ownership of the Schloss, and the status of IFES Inc. continued to be flashpoints. A solution had been proposed that the U.S. InterVarsity, with all of its resources, assume title for Schloss Mittersill. "My conscience is still troubled," Wee Hian would subsequently write Stacey, "with the wisdom of a national movement like IVCF USA owning property in another country."[9] The European movements might misinterpret or misunderstand. He however assured Stacey that the IFES executive committee would not veto or object to such a solution. In private conversations Wee Hian made it clear that he was not supportive of Schloss Mittersill. He was cut from a different cloth than Stacey, was a consensus person and worked behind the scenes to advance his point of view. In September 1976 in preparation for an important upcoming meeting between IFES Inc. and IVCF in the United States, Stacey was again asking whether Wee Hian agreed or disagreed with the terms being drawn up: "Would you state in your letter whether you approve the transfer of the property to I.V.C.F.-U.S.A.,"[10] he specifically requested.

Schloss Mittersill was a part of Stacey's vision for IFES as an organization committed to teaching and training students in sound doctrine and a solid theological base. Stacey became increasingly anxious as he grew older than IFES not deviate from his confessional legacy. He wrote to Wee Hian expressing those concerns, relaying to him his perception that some member movements were "not Biblical and not honestly adhering to our Basis of Faith."[11] At the 1972 executive committee Stacey had expressed his anxiety that the French-speaking Swiss IFES affiliate (GBU de Suisse Romande) "was going through a very lean period in terms of spiritual growth." René Pache and Frank Horton had withdrawn. Stacey asked how IFES could help. The minutes then note that "Dr Hans Bürki disagreed with Mr Woods' analysis and he felt that the generalisations were too sweeping."[12] Bürki had considerable influence in the canton of Vaud, particularly leading marriage retreats among the clergy and being involved in counseling activities, some of which became controversial.

Stacey asked his successor anxiously, "Do you not think it is time for you to stick your neck out and insist that if a member movement will not really adhere to the Biblical and evangelistic basis of the movement, they should withdraw and another movement be started?"[13] Wee Hian bristled: "I can assure you, Stacey, that I am as rigorous as you in seeking to maintain doctrinal orthodoxy in all IFES movements. Like you, I have chosen to work quietly and to influence movements to pick leaders who are definitely conservative evangelicals. I believe that you sought to do this in the case of Canada."[14]

Hans Bürki, as a member of IFES senior staff, was particularly in Stacey's sights. Bürki was much appreciated in Latin America, and his counseling had been effective in Japan, according to staff there. Stacey had written in 1969: "Hans's training is that of a psychologist, not a theologian, and I think his theological thinking is set in this framework, and I think his objective theological teaching is existential, and I think it is a tremendous blessing, but I also think it has got to be balanced with a solid exposition of what the Bible says, not just our reaction to it."[15]

Stacey became increasingly anxious, and after his return from India in 1976 he wrote Brede Kristensen, special assistant to the IFES general secretary: "I think we need to be careful about Hans Burki."[16] Meanwhile Bürki, as a colleague of Wilber Sutherland in the old IFES days, had become highly visible in Canada.[17] In the summer of 1977 he was offered and accepted a three-year appointment as commuting director of Crossroads (now renamed Waymeet), a community in downtown Toronto that had recently divided from IVCF and was now being operated by a group of ex-staffers who had left the movement because it was seeking a different direction. "Both Hans Bürki and his wife either have been to Ontario or will be there shortly. Is there any possibility of a stop being made to this," Stacey wrote to me.[18] Without his strong leadership at the helm, there wasn't a chance. His insight and encouragement at that time were never forgotten.

Stacey also queried Wee Hian about other IFES associate general secretaries. He fired off questions: "I am very puzzled as to precisely what Samuel Escobar and René Padilla are really doing directly in relation to the IFES." Is Padilla really "doing nothing but literature, . . . high-priced stuff?" Does Samuel Escobar, now back on IFES staff, have a "precise and definite duty? Does he report directly to you?"[19] He sent off a four-page letter to René Padilla asserting that *Certeza* was no longer fulfilling the mandate that it had been given when Stacey raised the funds to launch it.[20] Shortly after this exchange Wee Hian visited Stacey, presumably in the interests of making the relationship work. He wrote on his return to London, "Thank you for those few days we could spend together in Lausanne, which were a great privilege and joy for me. . . . I am very thankful for the many things we could discuss together and I shall keep your advice and opinions in mind."[21] He had to practice patience and restraint.

Stacey's Writing

The 1972 IFES executive committee had asked Stacey to compose a history of the movement. They provided secretarial help, and he had office space now in his home. Writing would dominate the early years of his retirement. His first book, *Some Ways of God,* appeared in 1975. It was more a personal account, "a string of beads," as he described its contents. The preface was by John Alexander president of the American IVCF, who stated emphatically that "Few persons in this century have had as profound an influence for Jesus Christ on students and faculty at secular schools as have Stacey Woods." He commended the book to the Christian public, and said, "I wish every staff member would study this book and apply its message."[22] The title of the book was hardly unique, the artwork on the cover was contemporary but gimmicky and the content rambling. It was of interest to the many who loved and admired Stacey, but it hardly did justice to all that he had accomplished and the caliber of the man's leadership and creativity in his prime.

Stacey continued writing projects. He went to Toronto to research past IVCF Canada minutes in October 1975, and then on to the United States to do the same. "Esther Pedersen [his secretary from the 1950s] plans to come to me at Madison, and will go over the balance of the minutes I've not yet been able to check through," he wrote Jim Nyquist at InterVarsity Press. He had hopes that the manuscript would be ready by February for printing and distribution at Urbana 76.[23] Unfortunately, on being submitted to the IFES leadership in England when it was completed, it was regarded as unsuitable for publication and was filed. Stacey also projected a book about the parables, but was told when he submitted a chapter "We would find it very difficult to sell enough copies to make the print run economically feasible."[24]

In 1978 his history of IVCF in the United States appeared: *The Growth of a Work of God: The Story of the Early Days of Inter-Varsity Christian Fellowship.* This time Jim Nyquist, always gracious, wrote the tribute to Stacey in the introduction: "Stacey's loyalty to God's Word coupled with courage and vigor have become an integral part of the style and spiritual outlook of Inter-Varsity."[25] The story "is told," Stacey explained, "very simply and in anecdotal form," a "brief and light-handed treatment of past years" to be used by the InterVarsity family and to remind them of the convictions and goals of the early days of the movement. It is still used for IVCF staff orientation in the United States.

Throughout the early years of his retirement Stacey and Yvonne traveled widely.

They crossed the Atlantic several times a year. While they maintained their Elba hideaway, they would drop off to see the grandchildren at Stephen and Els's home in Tuscany en route, and welcome family and friends at their holiday location. "Yvonne and I are enjoying our time at Elba. Not nearly as much reading and studying as I had anticipated as there is a great deal of physical work to do outside but I think perhaps this good for me at this stage of my life, at least for a short period," he wrote a friend in 1973.[26] The Elba retreat was finally sold in 1976.

Their Easter 1976 letter brought news of a trip to India in May and June. He returned and reported to Wee Hian and Oliver Barclay, "Our time in India was an emotional, nervous and spiritual strain. Never in my life have I faced such deep divisions within the staff of a movement." In spite of all that "the Indian movement is growing; it is stable; it has a fine flock of young staff workers who give much promise for the future. Furthermore, some of the undergraduates now emerging into leadership are quite outstanding and could become superb staff workers." The trip had been hard on them physically, with the food predictably curry three times a day. The heat was horrific on the plains, but Highfield, high in the Nilgiris hills, where they were for most of the time, was very pleasant.

In November 1977 Stacey taught the General Epistles in the New Testament (James was always a favorite of his) for four weeks at the Biblical Theological Institute in Croatia.[27] "We need God's help," Yvonne wrote, "to be true, clear, uncompromising in the message but full of heavenly wisdom and discretion."[28] Set up three years earlier by Peter Kuzmič, the college was a part of Stacey's vision for Eastern Europe. Many Croatians had visited Schloss Mittersill. As one of them said, "The Schloss Mittersill fellowship was a real light in our darkness and difficulties, showing that there is no need for a sharp or artificial division between the Christian world and the rest of God's creation and that we need not be sad and unhappy in order to demonstrate our sanctification." One of the present faculty members at the school describes what he called "the spirit of Mittersill": "the fellowship, the vision, the idea behind the place and the people here making it work."[29]

Perhaps the most significant retirement trip of all was Stacey and Yvonne's 1979 triumphant tour to Canada for the fiftieth anniversary of IVCF. "Our visit to Canada," Yvonne wrote in a general letter two years later,

> stands out as a highlight. Not only was it a joy to see so many friends, who so graciously welcomed us, but it was a great privilege to travel from coast to coast for

Inter-Varsity's Jubilee year. Everywhere we were impressed by what God had done and how seed sown at Pioneer Camps, Campus-in-the-Woods and university and high school fellowships had sprouted and produced a spiritual harvest."[30]

They arrived in Toronto 12 October and set off for a dizzying round of celebrations, first in Ontario. A 19 October appearance in London, Ontario, was particularly evocative, with memories of Stacey's first Canadian base. His predecessor, Arthur Hill, came from Quebec with his niece for the occasion. Stacey and Yvonne went on to Winnipeg, out to British Columbia and then rounding back to the prairies and concluding with Atlantic Canada. They experienced "thoughtfulness and kindness" everywhere. "For me it was a wonderful experience," Stacey wrote on his return to Switzerland, "heartening, reassuring and I feel that Inter-Varsity today is stronger in terms of a witness to Christ and effective evangelism than I have known it since 1958."[31]

As if to belie that point, on 11 September 1979, just before Stacey and Yvonne arrived, the Canadian Broadcasting Corporation featured a preview of a program titled "Wilber Sutherland: A Life," which was aired nationally on 4 December, thus bracketing Stacey's visit and the jubilee celebrations. "On this program," the Canadian Broadcasting Corporation announced, "[Wilber Sutherland] describes his upbringing in the anti-sexual atmosphere of old-time Canadian fundamentalism and relates the story of his own emotional development, . . . a development that brings him now to conclude that 'sexuality rightly seen is worship.' "[32]

Because of Wilber's controversial comments on the program that appeared to advocate open marriage, his denigration of his godly mother and the references in the introduction and publicity to his IVCF connection, the program brought a firestorm on IVCF from donors and erstwhile friends. IVCF asked CBC to eliminate references to Inter-Varsity (or make clear Wilber was no longer involved) in the 4 December telecast. Wilber responded to this request saying that the movement was "attempting to rewrite history. For thirty years of Inter-Varsity's fifty years I was officially involved first as a member of a student executive and then as a member of the staff. That is a matter of public record which is not open to censorship."[33] It was a sad outburst, made all the more poignant because, in spite of all he had done for IVCF Canada, Wilber Sutherland was not a part of the jubilee. Strong feelings and a sense of betrayal, rekindled by his television appearance, made his participation problematic. He and Stacey never met during that final visit to Canada.

FINAL DAYS

Increasingly, health concerns were a preoccupation for Stacey. In the spring of 1978 he suffered a collapse. In a general letter the Woodses informed their friends: "Doctors said that forty-four years of arduous service finally caught up with him. Also there was a sort of belated post-retirement depression."[34] Trips to the Caribbean, Scandinavia, the United States and India had to be canceled. In June that year Stacey again collapsed, with trembling and dizziness. "I will take things rather easy for the next four or five months in order to sort of recharge batteries," he mentioned in a letter.[35] Stacey had an accident while boarding a bus with his big dog, Max, on 7 May 1981. Another dog attacked him from behind and Stacey was hurled to the ground, falling against the curb and breaking his left shoulder and upper arm. He was in a cast for seven and a half weeks. Miraculously, he and Yvonne were able to attend Urbana 81 but he was never completely right. A cataract operation in July 1982 was unsuccessful and he could no longer read. There followed a series of falls and in December that year he broke his back.

Amazingly he resumed his ministry at the church in Lausanne, though still wearing a body brace. "He threw himself into this with every ounce of energy left him, preaching, praying, counselling," Yvonne reported.[36] On Good Friday there was a service of meditation on the Lord's death at 43 route d'Oron. The next day, after choosing the hymns for Easter, he fell and broke his hip. An operation was planned, but his heart failed. Early on the morning of Easter, 10 April 1983, he slipped away into the presence of his resurrected Lord.

He was a man of hope to the very end. The year before he died he said in a sermon:

> To limit the Christian's hope to the return of Christ is severely to limit it. It's something much deeper than that. For instance it has to do with our eternal destiny, it has to do with life with God after death. It has to do with a new heaven and a new earth wherein dwells righteousness. It has to do with our eternal reward in heaven. It has to do with the fact that we're going to be released from the burden of earthly life. It's an all embracing theme. It begins with the return of Christ but it's far greater and more wonderful than that. It's an experiential dynamic in our lives because we're convinced the Lord Jesus is coming again, that we're going to be raised from the dead and given a resurrection body, because we've got a heavenly home, because there's going to be a new heaven and a new earth wherein dwells righteousness, because there's going to be a reward for faithfulness to the Lord Jesus Christ, because there's going

to be an eternal life with God forever and ever. These truths have got to grip us, dominate us, and be the motor that drives us forward in living for Christ.[37]

News of Stacey's death rippled out from Lausanne in ever widening circles that Easter. It became clear just how many lives he had affected and how great his influence had been. Vincent Craven heard about it at seven o'clock that morning and was immediately asked by the board of IVCF Canada to represent them at the funeral. He flew to Geneva that afternoon and met up with Chua Wee Hian at the airport. Stacey's son Stephen drove them to Lausanne.

The funeral took place at Chapelle de Villard, Chemin des Fleurettes 35, on 14 April. The church was full. Friends who knew him only in the Lausanne context were surprised at the number of international dignitaries that arrived to fill the church. Francis Schaeffer came from L'Abri. Os Guinness attended, with reminders of the longtime links between Woods and his wider family. Claude Lise de Bénoit was there, representing Scripture Union in Switzerland and worldwide. And there were many others whose lives he had touched.

Frank Horton conducted the service. Chua Wee Hian led in the opening prayer. Vincent Craven, who knew him longest, shared his memories and spoke, as Yvonne said, "from his heart to the hearts of those present." Frank Horton was to give a summary of Stacey's life and ministry, but Hans Bürki asked for that honor. Bürki also took the pastoral prayer. Frank Horton chose as his text for the message Hebrews 3:7-8: "Remember your leaders, . . . and imitate their faith." As Stacey would have wanted, there were selections from *Hymns*, "Jesus Lives and So Shall I," and "The Strife Is O'er, the Battle Done."

Following worship a small group gathered at the at la Cimetiere du Bois de Vaux, where a simple stone marks his final resting place on earth." When you put me in a coffin or lower me into the earth, that isn't the end of Stacey Woods," he said in a message two years earlier. "We are destined to live on forever and ever."[38]

Epilogue

STACEY WAS THE KIND OF MAN who would have been embarrassed by all the tributes that were given him after his death, even though they were true. He would have appreciated most the realism in Frank Horton's funeral sermon. "When Stacey liked something, he said so, beautifully. When Stacey did *not* like something, he said so, forcefully. His language could be brutal, at times even outrageous! You may be surprised to hear me say this, but the family asked me to paint a realistic rather than an idealistic picture of the man." Stacey had left instructions that those who remembered him should do so "warts and all."

At the 1983 IFES general committee David Adeney as IFES president, was asked to frame a memorial minute: "Stacey always gave people the impression of his love for the Lord Jesus and especially of his real loyalty to the principles of God's word. He would never compromise when it came to matters of truth. He held very strong convictions concerning the authority of God's word." He went on to comment on Stacey's "capacity for travel, his ability to get to know people of different cultures, his eye for those would be leaders, his tremendous skill in letter-writing." And he quoted from Stacey's final letter to him, which arrived in the mail after his death. Reflecting on Mel Friesen's passing he wrote: "It makes an emptiness in one's life from a human point of view and one wonders just how many more years the Lord will give before one hears the trumpet call to go to be with the Lord."[1]

Wilber Sutherland also sent out a moving description of the man's faith:

My abiding memory of Stacey is of his profound love of God and of his great sense
of worship. One could not pray with him without gaining an immense sense of the
greatness of God. In discussions—which used to be endless—about the key emphases of the student work he always stressed that our first concern must be the worship
of God with all our being.[2]

There was a second memorial service held for Stacey at Knox Church, Toronto, on 14 May. A group of forty, whose memories of Stacey stretched back
into the 1930s (and in Vincent Craven's case, the 1920s), attended. Donald
Fleming, then living in the Bahamas, read the lesson. The American InterVarsity
was represented by president Jim McLeish. Mel Donald, who led the service,
called for reminiscences. "A frequent note," one person observed, "was the fact
that he had an extraordinary ability to see a latent gift and then to encourage it
into full bloom. The results of his nurture are now seen in creative Christian leadership around the world."[3]

It is now almost a quarter of a century since Stacey's death. With time comes a
seasoning of the memories, a perspective on the past. Stacey Woods still evokes
strong feelings from those who knew him. Those who did not have that privilege,
hearing all the stories, the outrageous goings on, the bons mots, the legends, ask
those of us who knew him: what was he really like? Distance does not make the
response any easier. Stacey was a multilayered individual. There are some telling
comments Stacey made to Maurice Murphy, before Maurice left IVCF staff in
1955: "In each one of us there is a Dr Jekyll and Mr Hyde, or this could be expressed rather more biblically, but you know what I am driving at. We are our own
worst enemies."[4] Stacey was often his own worst enemy.

Jim Nyquist, whom Stacey called "one of the most open and sweetest Christians we have on our US staff,"[5] set up Stacey's strengths and weaknesses in parallel
columns, the former making a much longer list. His weaknesses were his critical
spirit, his tendency to gossip (a weakness he was all too aware of), the attendant
challenge to him to build up rather than tear down, and the fact that life was more
important to him than organization. On the other side of the ledger was his total
allegiance to biblical authority and respect for the work of the Holy Spirit in community. He believed passionately in the priesthood of all believers and that students could be mightily used by God. He inspired, challenged and enlisted people,

giving them a vision of what God could do through them. He abhorred superficiality. He had an awesome regard for the holiness and sovereignty of God, and was a man who wanted to see individuals growing spiritually rather than achieving organizational aggrandizement.

Stacey was painfully aware of his humanity. "We are apt to fall into the sin of criticism," he once wrote to his staff.

> I know I have failed here. Do we criticize certain Christian organizations more than we pray for them? It might be a good rule for you and me to resolve that we will not criticize anyone without first praying for him. Certain Christian colleges, certain Christian leaders, make life difficult for us. Please don't think I am singling out any one person or any one thing here. I am talking to myself.

One man who loved him was Samuel Escobar, "Sammy," as Stacey called him. In his *La chispa y la llama*, a brief history of student work in Latin America, Escobar wrote moving words of tribute to Stacey's "vision and unique ability to 'smell' and find leaders," such as "Pentecost, Siemens, Young, Bragg and dozens of others recruited by this exceptional man." He had "a vast network of friends and correspondents round the whole world and his ability to correspond with them regularly allowed him to prepare the terrain for the pioneers." "Stacey Woods was the pastor who encouraged and exhorted staff with his letters and visits." "Thank God for this exceptional man!"[6]

In relationships with IVCF staff of the United States, Stacey was criticized as manipulative, playing one off against another. The Hunts speak of his "curious mixture of admirable delegation and end-runs."[7] He could indeed sometimes delegate and then go ahead and do the assigned task himself. Partly that was his perfectionism. It also had to do with the dizzying pace of his feverish activity. He had drive and determination, a compulsive need to see things happen. His work ethic impelled him. The pace of his composition was incredible. His record was dictating eighty letters in a day. One time, coming into Chicago for four days of meetings from Lausanne, he requested "a couple of belts of dictaphone letters." As the request was passed along to staff, the reply was "two belts, yes, ten, no!"[8] On the other hand, occasionally in the rush there was a lack of clarity or charity in his correspondence.

He expected loyalty on the part of his staff, and the organization as a whole suffered when he did not receive it. Early on he wrote Mel Donald, then deputizing for him in Canada:

> If a situation arises in which a staff member disagrees with a policy or project this matter is laid before the general secretary and time is given to straighten the matter out. If, after adequate time, the difficulty cannot be settled to the satisfaction of the staff member concerned, then the said staff member, on notifying the general secretary of his intentions, may go to the board.[9]

In the United States Stacey had direct access to the board, and staff could feel unheard or short-circuited.

In their book the Hunts say, "Stacey voiced very little approval or appreciation of his staff."[10] Partly that was a matter of personality. It was also a feature of being brought up in a duty-bound Christian culture that frequently quoted Jesus' words from the King James Version: "We are unprofitable servants: we have done that which was our duty to do" (Lk 17:10). Frank Woods was proud of his son and his accomplishments, but like most fathers of that period he did not always find the words to express it. In that buttoned-up era, love was not openly talked about nor usually seen to be unconditional, either within families or among partners in ministry. Stacey had a fear of too much emotion, which may help to explain his anxieties about the charismatic movement. Things could quickly get out of hand, and too much emotional display created inevitable reaction.

And then there was Yvonne. When she was introduced to Fred Woods after their engagement had been announced, he shook her hand and said, "Yvonne, my wife and I have prayed for *you* ever since Stacey was a little boy!"[11] Stacey once described Yvonne to Becky Manley Pippert as "God's great gift to me," and he never spoke truer words. "We fit like a hand in glove." And then added, admiringly, picking up on what he had just said: "You know she fits into the same sized dress as she did the year we were married."[12] Yvonne was his star, the light in his firmament. Stacey would never have accomplished what he did without her support. There is a striking picture of her in the 13 March 1939 edition of the *London* [Ontario] *Free Press* participating in an IVCF rally in the city during their first year of marriage. For the next forty-four years she was there by his side, at least when he was home. Through all the moves they made Yvonne never complained. She provided for him the domestic security his restless spirit needed. She was a woman of intelligence, charm, energy and endless faith and confidence in God's purposes.

There were two friendships, among the many he cites in his "people that have influenced me," that stand out in his life. One is Douglas Johnson, who was always in the shadows. He never wanted his picture taken. But he was the stalwart who did not deviate from his commitment to student ministry. The other was Martyn Lloyd-Jones. The Doctor's daughter, Elizabeth Catherwood, said that her father's main responsibility was to keep Douglas and Stacey on the same line. Stacey, she observed, was "hot-hearted," a man who felt things very deeply, and his love for God was a burning passion. Perhaps that is why Lloyd-Jones, with his Welsh empathetic warmth, loved Stacey and the affection was reciprocated. To win the Doctor's respect, as Stacey had, was high commendation. In turn he described Martyn Lloyd-Jones as "my patron saint."

Stacey attracted vigorous men of purpose and drive, people like himself. When he came to Canada there was still in Toronto a corps of highly motivated and generous businessmen of deep evangelical conviction who came alongside Stacey. In America there was Herbert J. Taylor, who provided the financial means for Inter-Varsity to move forward. He was not alone, but the years he chaired the board were times of relative peace for the organization. Later difficulties came, as Stacey said, when the preponderance of board members were academics, "thinkers not doers." He saw this trend, particularly when chairpersons were chosen, as the reason why both Canada and the United States went through a difficult time in the 1960s.

IFES was always, throughout his twenty-six years as general secretary, closest to his heart. In it he could express his gifts of pioneering, envisioning and strategizing on a global scale. His achievements here are ultimately his most enduring monument. He was able to bring together a unique combination of talents and experience to create one of the most effective missionary movements of modern times. The breadth of his knowledge, the reach of his contacts and the catholicity of his interests meant that he established immediate rapport in most of the many countries he visited on his journeys.

At the end of his life Stacey Woods, whose inspired Bible teaching moved thousands, spoke weekly to a small group in a borrowed church in Lausanne. He seemed preoccupied about his future:

> There's going to be a royal presentation in heaven. And we're going to be presented. We'll no longer have a sinful nature but one perfectly clean, inward and outward. There will no longer be a sinful environment. We won't have to worry about our

clothes for the Lord Jesus will provide us with the robe of His righteousness. We'll each be wearing a crown, the crown of righteousness He gives us. We shall be holy without blemish in every respect, ready to meet our God and Father. I can imagine the heavenly choir singing, "Worthy is the Lamb who was slain."[13]

As on earth, so in heaven: Stacey's rich tenor voice made and will make its own unique contribution to the swelling praise and worship of the Lamb who was slain.

Notes

Preface
[1]Throughout this book, Canadian and British spelling of Inter-Varsity will use a hyphen, but the U.S. version will not. InterVarsity in the United States first dropped the hyphen under the leadership of President Gordon MacDonald (1985-1987), when a new IVCF logo was designed and approved. The IVCF board amended the articles of incorporation on June 6, 1997, to change the name of the corporation from Inter-Varsity Christian Fellowship of the United States of America to InterVarsity Christian Fellowship/USA.

Introduction
[1]The thirteen gathered at Plymouth Rock in addition to Woods were Harold John Ockenga of Park Street Church, Boston; Carl Henry, then of Northern Baptist Seminary, Chicago; Everett Harrison, then at Dallas Theological Seminary (these three were involved in setting up Fuller Theological Seminary three years later); Clarence Bouma, Calvin Seminary, Grand Rapids; Merrill Tenney and Henry Thiessen, Wheaton College; P. B. Fitzwater, Moody Bible Institute, Chicago; Terrelle Crum, Providence Bible Institute, Rhode Island; Leonard Lewis, president, Gordon College, Boston; Allan MacRae, Faith Seminary, then in Wilmington; William Emmett Powers, Eastern Baptist Seminary, Philadelphia; and Cornelius Van Til, Westminster Theological Seminary, Philadelphia. John Bolten Sr., Andover, Massachusetts, was the host.

Chapter 1: Bendigo Brethren Boyhood
[1]Minutes of the 113th meeting of the committee, 25 September 1872, St. Paul's church, Sandhurst. Courtesy of Ian Smith, parish archivist, St. Paul's Cathedral, Bendigo.

[2]"The Young Believers Question Box: The After-Death Condition of the Redeemed," *Believers Magazine* 371 (November 1921): 118-19.

[3]Historically, Christian Brethren have preferred the word *assembly* rather than *church*, so this book will use the word *assembly* for local faith communities.

[4]Stacey Woods, *Some Ways of God* (Downers Grove, Ill.: InterVarsity Press, 1977), p. 15.

[5]George Grove (1845-1910) arrived with his wife and family in Brisbane from England in 1885 and had a peripatetic existence, living primarily in Melbourne but also in Tasmania.

[6]Woods, *Some Ways of God*, p. 15.

[7]The quartz kings were George Lansell, who died, in 1906 and Ernst Mueller in 1910.

[8]David Bentley-Taylor, *Adventures of a Christian Envoy* (UCCF Booklets, 1992), p. 5. Also found in the InterVarsity Christian Fellowship Records 374.4, in the Billy Graham Center archives, Wheaton College, Wheaton, Ill.

[9]*Bendigo Advertiser*, 18 August 1914, quoted in Frank Cusack, *Bendigo: A History*, rev. ed. (Bendigo, Australia: Lerk & McClure, 2002), p. 236.

[10]George Mackay, *Annals of Bendigo*, 3: 413, quoted in Frank Cusack, *Bendigo: A History*, rev. ed. (Bendigo, Australia: Lerk & McClure, 2002), p. 236.

[11]On Australian national radio's "The Religion Report," 4 August 2004, Stephen Crittenden said, "Michael McKernan takes a somewhat Freudian view of Australia's role in World War I, describing a young nation, dewy-eyed and optimistic, going out into the big world in 1915, suddenly finding itself spiritually parentless, and beating a retreat to the dark and narrow decades of the 1920s and 1930s, which were also years when the churches in Australia perhaps lost their way."

[12]Fred Woods, "A Passion For Souls" *Australian Missionary Tidings*, 1 February 1913, p. 304.

Chapter 2: Australian Adolescence

[1]For four years during WWII Porter doubled as both a headmaster and principal of the Sydney Missionary and Bible College at Croyden, New South Wales. See Stuart Braga, *A Century Preaching Christ: Katoomba Christian Convention 1903-2003* (Sydney: Katoomba Convention, 2003), p. 69.

[2]Central Hurstville Assembly rejoined South Hurstville in 1970 when the property was requisitioned for a shopping complex.

[3]Garry Warren of St. George Christian Church, Hurstville, personal e-mail, 27 September 2006.

[4]Related by Stacey Woods in "The Christian's Hope A – Colossians 1:1-14," sermon no. 10049 (October 1981). Cassette recording in possession of Yvonne Woods and used by kind permission.

[5]Kenneth John Newton, *A History of the Brethren in Australia: With Particular Reference to the Open Brethren* (Ph.D. diss., Fuller Theological Seminary, 1990), pp. 82-83.

[6]"Cinema Admissions 1901-1932," in "What Australians Are Watching," Australian Film Commission <www.afc.gov.au/GTP/wchist190132.html>.

[7]Fred Woods, quoted in *Change Witness Triumph* (Chicago: InterVarsity Press, 1965), p. 212.

[8]I am grateful to Stuart Braga for these insights and photocopies of Stacey Woods's essays, received via e-mail 23 October 2006.

[9]See John Prince and Moyra Prince, *Tuned in to Change* (Sydney: Scripture Union, 1979), pp. 58-62.

[10]John Prince, personal conversation with me, 1 September 2006.

[11]Margaret Lamb, "James Beath Nicholson," *The Australian Dictionary of Evangelical Biography* (Sydney: Evangelical History Association, 1994), pp. 283-84.

[12]Pom is an Australian term of endearment or derision (depending on the context) for English immigrants. At the time it was an advantage to be so described.

[13]Sir Marcus Loane was brought to faith at St Paul's Anglican Church, Chatswood.

[14]Stacey Woods, "Some Who Have Helped Me Go with God," a typewritten manuscript in the possession of Yvonne Woods, pp. 3-5.

[15]Stacey's reference is to the thirty-three year Scripture Union ministry in England of Eric John Hewitson Nash (1898-1982). Over 7,000 boys, generally from public (i.e., private) schools, at-

tended Iwerne Minster camps under his leadership, many of whom, such as John Stott, went on to significant positions of leadership in the evangelical world. They were sometimes referred to as "bash campers" after his nickname "Bash."

[16]Transcript of an interview between Keith Hunt and Charles Troutman, Billy Graham Center archives 300.380.24.

[17]Stuart Piggin, *Evangelical Christianity in Australia* (Melbourne: Oxford University Press, 1997), p. 96.

[18]The Keswick convention, founded in 1875 for "the promotion of practical (or Scriptural) holiness" brings together British evangelicals with its motto "all one in Christ Jesus." The annual meeting, held each summer in Keswick in the English Lake District, features outstanding speakers, Bible exposition and a strong missionary appeal. The name *Keswick* has been taken for similar conferences in the United States, in Canada and around the world until 1968.

[19]Stacey Woods, letter to Oliver Barclay, 29 January 1979. (Stacey also sent a copy to me.) Stacey regarded Guinness's formation of the Crusader Union in New South Wales as a separate private schools ministry was "a tragic divisive error." John Prince, in a comment to me, disagrees and maintains that Crusaders Union has lasted and provided significant leadership both to AFES and the wider evangelical community in New South Wales.

[20]*Believer's Magazine*, February 1924, p. xxiv.

[21]*Believer's Magazine*, January 1926, p. 421.

[22]*Believer's Magazine*, May 1929, p. iii.

[23]Horace Lockett (1890-1979) was a longtime board member of IVCF Canada. For eighteen years he served Stacey as a loyal board member.

[24]Fred Woods, *Australian Missionary Tidings*, 1 October 1929, pp. 196-97.

[25]Stacey Woods, *Some Ways of God* (Downers Grove, Ill.: InterVarsity Press, 1975), p. 43. Stacey misspells Guille's name, which renders his account slightly uncertain.

[26]George E. Guille (1873-1931) pastored Presbyterian churches in the south and was a Bible teacher at Moody Bible Institute, Chicago. "Many churches have been blessed through his vitalizing ministry" (1930 DTS catalog). An anti-evolutionist, Guille was also the first president (1930) of Bryan College, Dayton, Tenn. (This information is from Lolana Thompson, archivist, Dallas Theological Seminary.)

Chapter 3: Dallas Dynamic

[1]Stacey Woods, audiotape of Stacey's Lausanne funeral 11 April and Knox Toronto memorial service 14 May, 1983, courtesy of Yvonne Woods.

[2]One of those boarding was New Zealand Prime Minister George Forbes, described by Michael King as "the wrong man in the wrong place at the wrong time" (*The Penguin History of New Zealand* [Auckland: Penguin Books, 2003], p. 346). With Forbes was the New Zealand Attorney General, Sir Thomas Sidey, both of them heading to an imperial conference in London.

[3]Rowland Hill archive, 26 August 1930, p. 171, University of Western Ontario, London, Ontario.

[4]Paul Guinness (1907-1986) ordained as a Church of England curate in 1936, served with Gordon Guinness, Howard's older brother, in Hove, Sussex. He was a military chaplain and WWII prisoner of war. In 1946, he edited the YMCA magazine in Geneva and met up with Stacey. Paul returned to inner-city Manchester in 1957. Paul continued his family's interest in Jewish outreach and wrote *Hear Oh Israel*. He died in Spain.

[5]Rowland Hill archive, 29 August, 1930, p. 173, University of Western Ontario, London, Ontario.

[6]The school was originally named Evangelical Theological College, in keeping with Canadian and English usage, under the influence of Griffith Thomas and A. B. Winchester. Because "college" proved to be confusing in the United States in 1936, the school was renamed Dallas Theological Seminary and Graduate School of Theology. It was shortened in 1969 to Dallas Theological Seminary (DTS). Information courtesy of Lolana Thompson, DTS archivist.

[7]Stacey Woods, "Some Who Have Helped Me Go with God" (unpublished manuscript in possession of Yvonne Woods and used by kind permission), p. 6.

[8]Quoted by John Hannah, "The Early Years of Lewis Sperry Chafer," *Bibliotheca Sacra* 144, no. 573 (1987): 18.

[9]John A. Witmer, "What Hath God Wrought, Part I," *Bibliotheca Sacra* 130, no. 570 (October 1973): 296.

[10]John A. Witmer, "Fifty Years of Dallas Theological Seminary, Part I: God's Man and His Dream," *Bibliotheca Sacra* 130, no. 520 (1973): 296; Lewis Sperry Chafer, *Major Bible Themes* (Chicago: Moody Press, 1944), pp. 96-97.

[11]Woods, "Some Who Have Helped Me Go with God," p. 7.

[12]Lewis Sperry Chafer, "Salient Facts Regarding Evangelism," *Bibliotheca Sacra* 101, no. 404 (1944): 386.

[13]Canon Rev. Dr. Fred Glover (1888-1980) was born Ormskirk, Lancashire. He was a 1920 graduate of Wycliffe College, University of Toronto, and in 1931 he received a Th.D. from Evangelical Theological College. From 1922-1967 he was rector of St. Margaret's Church, Winnipeg. (This information was provided by his daughter Ruth Lilly, Winnipeg, 2 September 2006.)

[14]Ruth Rich Oliver Cummings, interview with with me, 8 April 2006, Vancouver.

[15]Clipping from the local paper, undated, found in Stacey's photograph album, now in the possession of Ruth Rich Oliver Cummings, Vancouver, and used by permission.

[16]Robert Kenneth Strachan (1910-1965), like Stacey, combined studies, graduating from Wheaton College in 1935 and Dallas Theological Seminary in 1936. He returned to Costa Rica to work at Biblical Seminary of the Latin America Mission, succeeding his mother as general director of LAM in 1951.

[17]Willard M Aldrich (1910-) was president of Multnomah School of the Bible (now Multnomah Bible College and Biblical Seminary) from 1943 to 1978.

[18]Clipping from the local paper, undated, found in Stacey's photograph album, courtesy of Yvonne Woods, Thorofare, New Jersey.

[19]Lewis Sperry Chafer, letter to Fred Woods, 31 March 1933, in response to Woods's of 10 March 1933, Dallas Theological Seminary archives.

[20]Woods, "Some Who Have Helped Go With God," p. 7.

[21]Ibid, p. 10.

[22]Lewis Sperry Chafer, letter to Enoch Dyrness (registrar of Wheaton College), 27 April 1933, Dallas Theological Seminary archives.

[23]Stacey was confirmed by the Bishop George C Stewart of Chicago. Information courtesy of Trinity Church, Wheaton, Illinois.

Chapter 4: Canadian Challenge

[1]Arthur Hill, remarks at fortieth anniversary, IVCF Canada.

[2]Howard Guinness, general letter of 16 May 1933, Canadian IVCF archives.

[3]Stacey Woods, letter to Oliver Barclay, 29 December 1979, in my possession.

[4]Stacey Woods, letter to Horace Lockett, 10 May 1934, Billy Graham Center archives 300.384.4.

[5]Stacey Woods, *Some Ways of God* (Downers Grove, Ill.: InterVarsity Press, 1975), p. 44.

[6]See *Journeying Among Students* (Sydney: Anglican Information Office, 1979), pp. 90-94. Howard Guinness came out for the Sialcot Convention in August of 1934. He left Bombay on the SS *Moldavia*, 16 March 1935, very much according to plan, it would appear.

[7]Stacey Wood, October 1934 field report, Canadian IVCF archives.

[8]See David B. Vincent's "Catherine (Cathie) Anderson Nicoll" in *Gifts and Graces*, ed. John S. Moir (Toronto: Committee on History, PCC, 2002), 28-1.

[9]Africa Inland Mission, China Inland Mission, India and Ceylon General Mission, South Africa General Mission, Sudan Interior Mission and the Zenana Mission.

[10]Muriel Clark Boutwel (1913-1995) was born in Baoning, Sichuan, the daughter of CIM'ers Dr. Walter Clark and Winnie Naylor Clark. She became full-time in the Inter-Varsity office in 1936 and moved to the United States to set up the InterVarsity office in 1940. There she met research Dr. Joseph Boutel, who taught at Temple University, Philadelphia, and later worked at the Disease Control Center in Atlanta.

[11]Margaret Fish Stinton (1924-) was born in Anshunfu, Guizhou, the daughter of Dr. Ed and N. W. Fish. On graduating from the University of Toronto in 1944, she joined IVCF staff, serving on the prairies and then in the east at "the big five" universities. She married Dr. Arthur Stinton in 1949 and went to Angola as a missionary doctor under Christian Missions in Many Lands, returning in 1963.

[12]Ruth Nyquist's parents, John and Edith Bell, served with CIM in Gansu as did Marie Huttenlock Little (1918-), who came in 1947. Marie returned to the United States in 1951 to become IV staff member in New York City and married Paul Little (1928-1975) in 1953.

[13]Doris Leonard (1920-) worked in the Inter-Varsity Toronto office and went to China in 1947. She married Cyril Weller in Kunming, Yunnan, 14 January 1949. She ministered in the Philippines (1953 onward), Sarawak (1975-1977) and then had a role as home staff in Canada, finishing up with a two-year term at the international headquarters in Singapore (1980).

[14]E. A. Brownlee (1875-1955) of Hespeler, graduated from Woodstock College and McMaster University in arts and theology. He was sent to Kiangsi in 1909 by CIM and returned on furlough 1917. He was co-opted by Henry Frost to be secretary and then secretary treasurer in Toronto until retirement in 1947. He married Edith Henderson Brownlee (1885-1968) of Windsor in 1904. Information courtesy of Rose Carleton of the OMF Office, Mississauga, Ontario.

[15]Stacey Woods, "Some Who Have Helped Me Go with God" (unpublished manuscript in possession of Yvonne Woods), p. 12.

[16]Frank McCarthy influenced two generations of students, among them the writer Thornton Wilder and magazine mogul Henry Robinson Luce. I have in my possession my father's Bible, with Frank's unmistakable Chefoo copperplate, giving the date he graduated (26 July 1918) after ten years at Chefoo. Bibles were given all boys as they left with his constant prayers.

[17]Margaret Clarkson interview by Charles Tipp in 1983, copy in Canadian IVCF archives.

[18]Other than studies at Neuchatel, Switzerland, after she graduated from Chefoo. She had no academic degrees.

[19]At graduation the following year, Principal John McNichol stated: "Miss McCarthy has given herself with untiring devotion to the interests of students, not only to the men and women in her immediate classes, but also in a special way to the whole body of women students."

[20]This information is from Stacey's conversation with Muriel Stewart Beattie, as relayed by her sister Pat McCarthy, married to Eva's nephew Patrick, and repeated to me in a conversation, 12 August 2006.

[21]William McDougall (1822-1903) attended all three confederation conferences. As minister of public works in John A Macdonald's first cabinet, he negotiated the purchase of Rupert's Land.

[22]Bulletin for Baker's memorial service, 12 February 1961, in the position of Mrs Gina Baker Lamb and used by permission. Stacey came to the service specially from Philadelphia to bring a tribute.

[23]Woods, "Some Who Have Helped Me Go with God," p. 13.

[24]Victor Smith. letter, 11 March 1936. IVCF Canada archives.

[25]John R. Howitt (1892-1985) was a 1913 medical graduate of the University of Toronto who was disgraced, according to Stacey, while at the 999 Queen Street institution when he refused to allow a politician to campaign for votes among his mental patients. He was exiled to Thunder Bay as a result, becoming superintendent of the Port Arthur hospital.

[26]Whitfield Willis Naylor (1877-1963) worked as an executive for the Kayser company and was on the board of the Scott Mission in Toronto as well as his work at Knox Church.

[27]Transcribed from the tape of Donald Fleming's speech at a memorial service for Stacey Woods, 14 May 1983, at Knox Church, Toronto.

[28]Donald Methuen Fleming (1905-1987) was elected to Parliament in 1945, ran for leadership of the Conservative Party three times (1948, 1956, 1967). Stacey called him "a person of unquestionable honesty . . . only to be disgraced and vilified by the unspeakable Prime Minister Diefenbaker who viciously sacrifice a loyal supporter, throwing him to the lions." Woods, "Some Who Have Helped Me Go with God," p. 12.

[29]Lawrence Neale Jones, *The InterVarsity Christian Fellowship in the United States* (Ph.D. diss., Yale University, 1962), p. 138.

[30]1936 IVCF of Canada Constitution enclosure, Stacey Woods to Donald Fleming, 17 January 1936, IVCF Canada archives.

[31]Murphy, Ted Simmonds (later of Toronto Bible College) and Rex Symons who married Yvonne Woods's sister Jocelyn on 28 May 1941, were known as "The Holy Three" because of their evangelistic zeal.

[32]"General Secretary's Report, September 1-December 31, 1936," p. 5. IVCF Canada archives.

[33]John Clifford Harstone (1899-1988) taught chemistry and physics at Vaughan Road Collegiate Institute, Toronto, from 1927 to 1960. He served in both World Wars: in the artillery in 1917-1918 and in the early 1940s in the Air Force as a training officer at Manning Depot. A lifelong member of Knox Church, Toronto, he was ordained as an elder in 1947. He was assistant director to Howard Guinness at the first Ontario Pioneer Camp (1929). (Information courtesy of son Jack Harstone, St. Albert, Alberta.)

[34]Cyrus Dolph (1865-1937), a native of Breslau, Ontario, was the president of the Eastern Steel Co., Preston, Ontario, a radio pioneer (CKBC, 1923), and a cofounder and first president of the (Anglican) Church Army of Canada. Information courtesy of son James A. Dolph, Calgary.

[35]Quoted in William Guest and Skip Gillham, *On the Shores: A History of Ontario Pioneer Camps* (Vine-

land, Ont.: Glenaden Press, 2002), p. 30.

[36]Following a sermon by the rector at Church of the Redeemer on Revelation 3:20. "Is the Lord Jesus really standing outside the door of my heart?" she asked her mother. Receiving an affirmative answer, she and her sister "did invite the Lord Jesus into our hearts." Yvonne Woods's response to a request of her granddaughter Alicia for a school project, who informed me of this response by e-mail, 18 July 2006.

[37]From an IVCF Canada newsletter, "Your Fellowship," 2, no. 1 (1934): 1, IVCF Canada archives.

[38]Although the International Fellowship of Evangelical Students (IFES) was formally constituted in Cambridge, Massachusetts in 1947, the embryonic prewar IFES took that name for its four meetings in the 1930s.

[39]Rowland Hill, diary entry for 30 April 1938, University of Western Ontario archives.

[40]E-mail, 2 June 2006, from Stuart Braga of Sydney, married to Roger's cousin.

[41]Stacey Woods, from an interview with Ruth Oliver Cumming of Vancouver, 8 April 2006.

Chapter 5: A League Beleaguered

[1]General letter (undated, *circa* 1940) of General Secretary Robert E. Nicholas, Billy Graham Center archives 111.17.10.

[2]Buswell wrote a letter to Machen just before Machen's death. Machen never had the opportunity to respond to these points (see Ned Stonehouse, *J. Gresham Machen* [Grand Rapids: Eerdmans, 1954], pp. 504-5).

[3]Charles Troutman, in an interview with Bruce Hunt and Gladys Hunt, 14 February 1987, Billy Graham Center archives, 300.380.24.

[4]Stacey Woods, letter to J. Gresham Machen, 14 May 1936, in the Westminster Theological Seminary archives.

[5]Stacey Woods, letter to Machen, 1 June 1936, in the Westminster Theological Seminary archives.

[6]Lewis Sperry Chafer, letter to Stacey Woods, 9 January 1940, Dallas Theological Seminary archives.

[7]Stacey Woods, letter to Lewis Sperry Chafer, 18 January 1938, Dallas Theological Seminary archives.

[8]Stacey Woods, letter to Lewis Sperry Chafer, 3 February, 1938, Dallas Theological Seminary archives.

[9]Lawrence Neale Jones, *The InterVarsity Christian Fellowship in the United States* (Ph.D. diss., Yale University, 1962), p. 153 (quoting an unnamed source).

[10]Howard Atwood Kelly (1858-1943) was professor of obstetrics at the University of Pennsylvania in 1888. The next year he moved to the new Johns Hopkins Hospital in Baltimore and founded one that bore his name three years later. He was a pioneer in the use of radium to treat cancer.

[11]Michael Bliss, *William Osler: A Life in Medicine* (Toronto: University of Toronto Press, 1999), p. 216.

[12]Ibid., p. 215.

[13]Margaret Haines (1896-1983) went in 1919 to Allahabad, India, under the Women's Union Missionary Society. She returned home in 1935 due to health concerns and to be with her mother, Mary, following the death of her father, Robert Bowne Haines II, in 1932.

[14]Jones, *InterVarsity Christian Fellowship*, p. 154 (quoting from a 23 October 1960 conversation with Miss Haines).

[15]Herbert S. Mekeel (1904-1986) was a graduate of Andover-Newton Theological School, Boston,

and served as associate at First Church, Edmonton (1935-1937), interim at St. Andrew's Church, Ottawa (1937) and from 1937-1979 in Schenectady. He was dean and professor of practical theology, Fuller Seminary, Pasadena, Calif., for a year until being turned down by the Los Angeles presbytery in 1950.

[16]Stacey Woods to Lewis Sperry Chafer, 9 March 1938, Dallas Theological Seminary archives.

[17]Lewis Sperry Chafer, letter to Stacey Woods, 15 March 1938, Dallas Theological Seminar archives.

[18]C. Stacey Woods, *The Growth of a Work of God* (Downers Grove, Ill.: InterVarsity Press, 1978), p. 19.

[19]Jones, *InterVarsity Christian Fellowship*, p. 157 (quoting a letter of Johnson's he dates September 1927; *sic*, probably a typo for 1960).

[20]Minutes of International Fellowship of Evangelical Students, 1934-1939, pp. 56-57, IFES archives, Wheaton College Special Collections, SC-49.I.B.

[21]Calvin Knox Cummings, quoted in a letter to Charles Troutman, 17 January 1952, IVCF archives, Billy Graham Center, 3.17.10.

[22]Paul Woolley to Charles Troutman, 15 September 1951, IVCF archive, Billy Graham Center, 3.17.10.

[23]Charles Troutman, interview by Keith Hunt, 14 February, IVCF archive, Billy Graham Center, 300.380.24.

Chapter 6: Expansion South

[1]Charles Troutman diary entries for 2, 3, and 4 May 1939; Centre for the History of Christian Thought and Experience, Macquarie University, held at the Bible Society of New South Wales.

[2]*Australia Missionary Tidings,* 1 June 1939, p. 116.

[3]IFES minutes, 1934-1939, p. 68, IFES papers, Wheaton College Special Collections, SC-49.I.B.

[4]Stacey Woods, "Confidential memorandum to all secretaries," n.d. (September 1941), Centre for the History of Christian Thought and Experience, Macquarie University, held at the Bible Society of New South Wales.

[5]"Anti-Pacifist of Quebec," (i.e., Charles Troutman) to Stacey Woods, 18 September 1939, IVCF Canada archives.

[6]Charles Troutman, diary entry for 18 September 1939, p. 19, Centre for the History of Christian Thought and Experience, Macquarie University, held at the Bible Society of New South Wales.

[7]Stacey Woods, letter to Donald Fleming, 18 January 1940, Billy Graham Center archives, 300.380.34.

[8]John Frederick Strombeck (1881-1959) founded in 1911 the Strombeck-Becker Manufacturing Co., Moline, Illinois, specializing in wooden products, particularly toys. Described as "a self-taught Bible scholar who could make deep truths plain and down to earth for the laity," he published widely, particularly on prophetic themes. He supported generously Moody Bible Institute and Dallas Theological Seminary.

[9]Charles Troutman, diary entry for 11 September 1940, p. 26. Centre for the History of Christian Thought and Experience, Macquarie University, held at the Bible Society of New South Wales.

[10]Robert Walker (1912-), "the pioneer of Christian journalism," went on to achieve distinction as editor of *Christian Life.* He founded the *Christian Bookseller,* the Christian Writers' Institute, Creation House, was also at Scripture Press Foundation (1945-1956) and taught journalism (1941-1951) at Wheaton College.

[11]C. Davis Weyerhaeuser (1909-1999) was grandson of Frederick, the founder of the lumber and paper products company. On graduation from Yale in 1933 he joined the family firm, retiring in 1958 as Vice President of Forestry, Land and Timber. In 1962 he founded the Stewardship Foundation, which currently funds 185 charities. A member of some 60 boards, he chaired the board of Fuller Theological Seminary during a period of theological change, which he actively supported. As a Presbyterian Church (USA) layman, a particular interest was Whitworth College, Spokane, Wash.

[12]The staff present were Stacey Woods, Paul Beckwith, Ted Benson, Marshall Bier, Herb and Olive Butt, Anne Carroll, Muriel Clark, Grace Koch, Pat Lister, Mel Donald, Monica Mingie, Cathie Nicoll, Jim Rayburn, Stan Steinman, Ken and Margaret Taylor, Charles Troutman, Lola Turnbull, Bob Walker.

[13]Charles Troutman, diary entry, 26-31 May 1941; Centre for the History of Christian Thought and Experience, Macquarie University, held at the Bible Society of New South Wales, pp. 147-55.

[14]Stacey Woods, "Ave Atque Vale," *HIS* 4, no. 2 (1944): 2.

[15]Stacey Woods, letter to Mel Donald, 6 October 1941, IVCF Canada archives.

[16]Woods, "Ave Atque Vale," p. 2.

[17]Charles Troutman, quoted in Keith Hunt and Gladys Hunt, *For Christ and the University* (Downers Grove, Ill.: InterVarsity Press, 1991), p. 95.

[18]Stacey Woods, letter to Mel Donald, 15 December 1941, IVCF Canada archives.

[19]Stacey Woods, letter to Mel Donald, 20 April 1942, IVCF Canada archives.

[20]"General Secretary's Report to the Board of Directors of the Inter-Varsity Christian Fellowship, from Nov. 1 to Dec 15, 1942," IVCF Canada archives.

[21]Information courtesy of Stuart Braga in an e-mail, 29 November 2006.

[22]Stacey Woods, form letter, 29 August 1942, Billy Graham Center archives, 20.60.35.

[23]Jane Hollingsworth Haile (1919-1993) was an IVCF staff member from 1943 to 1954, originally in Northwest United States, then in New York City. She married staffer Peter Haile in 1954 and moved to Boston.

[24]Stacey Woods, letter to Joe Bayly, 17 April 1947, IVCF Canada archives.

[25]Ken Taylor (1917-2005) left Canada in 1940 to marry Margaret West and to study at Dallas Theological Seminary. He moved 1943 to Wheaton to edit *HIS*. For sixteen years he was editor at Moody Bible Institute. He started his paraphrase of the Bible with *Living Letters* in 1962 and eventually completed the whole Bible. He founded Tyndale House Publishers, initially to publish the bestselling *Living Bible*.

[26]Stacey Woods, *HIS* 7, no. 1 (1947): 2.

[27]Stacey Woods, letter to Joe Bayly, 27 April 1947, IVCF Canada archives.

[28]Joe Bayly, letter to Stacey Woods, 30 March 1947, IVCF Canada archives.

[29]Stacey Woods, letter to Wilber Sutherland, 2 June 1958, IVCF Canada archives.

[30]Grace Palmer Johnston (1883-1969), always known as Mrs. F. Cliffe, heiress to the Palmer New York City real estate fortune, was an IVCF board member from 1953 -1963. Originally with the Christian Brethren assemblies, she was active in Fifth Avenue Presbyterian Church. Connie, Constance Hammond (1920-2001), was the third of her five daughters: Grace, Jean, Connie, Pat and Ann. Ann's son Cliff Knectle has had an evangelistic ministry in IVCF.

[31]Charles Troutman, diary entry, 14 April 1941, Centre for the History of Christian Thought and Experience, Macquarie University, held at the Bible Society of New South Wales, p. 127.

[32]Charles Stilwell, "Should I Go to a Christian College This Fall?" *HIS* 3, no. 8 (1944): 9-12.

[33]Stacey Woods, letter to Harold John Ockenga, 3 June 1943, Ockenga papers 13, Gordon-Conwell Theological Seminary.

[34]Stacey Woods, "Youth Column," *United Evangelical Action* 3, no. 4 (1943): 3, 7.

[35]Stacey Woods, "Youth Column," *United Evangelical Action* 3, no. 5 (1943): 7.

[36]Stacey Woods, "Youth Column," *United Evangelical Action* 3, no. 6 (1943): 4.

[37]Stacey Woods, "Youth Column," *United Evangelical Action* 3, no 7 (1943): 4, 6.

[38]Stacey Woods, "Youth Column," *United Evangelical Action* 3, no. 9 (1944): 4.

[39]Stacey Woods, "Youth Column," *United Evangelical Action* 3, no. 11 (1944): 4.

[40]See introduction, pp. 17-21.

[41]Stacey Woods, quoted in Keith Hunt and Gladys Hunt, *For Christ and the University* (Downers Grove, Ill.: InterVarsity Press, 1991), p. 104.

[42]Stacey Woods, letter to Charles Troutman, 27 August 1945, Billy Graham Center archives, 111.12.19.

Chapter 7: To the Whole World

[1]Minutes of the U.S. board of IVCF, 29 January 1944, cited in *Growth of a Work of God* (Downers Grove, Ill.: InterVarsity Press, 1974), pp. 32-33.

[2]Keith Hunt and Gladys Hunt, *For Christ and the University* (Downers Grove, Ill.: InterVarsity Press, 1991), p. 102.

[3]Stacey Woods, "Report: Latin American Campuses," *HIS* 3, no. 12 (1944): 7.

[4]Ibid.

[5]Douglas Johnson, *Contending for the Faith* (London: Inter-Varity Press, 1979), p. 190.

[6]Carolyn Armitage, *Reaching the Goal: The Life Story of David Adeney* (Wheaton, Ill.: OMF/Harold Shaw, 1993), p. 39.

[7]Stacey Woods, letter to Mel Donald, 24 December 1941, IVCF Canada archives.

[8]J. Christy Wilson (1921-1999), born to missionary parents in Tabriz, Persia, studied at Princeton University and Princeton Seminary. He received a Ph.D. from the University of Edinburgh. Wilson served from 1951 to 1973 in Afghanistan, then eighteen years at Gordon-Conwell Theological Seminary, South Hamilton, Mass.

[9]Stacey Woods, *Growth of a Work of God* (Downers Grove, Ill.: InterVarsity Press, 1978), pp. 128-29.

[10]Woods, *Growth of a Work of God*, p. 129.

[11]Stacey Woods to staff, speakers and supporters on 19 February 1947. Ockenga archives, Gordon-Conwell Theological Seminary.

[12]Hilda Benson, report to Missionary Personnel Committee, Foreign Missions Conference, addendum to "A Report to the Student Christian Movement of the USA and Canada, Home Missions Council and the Foreign Missions Conference of the Conference for Missionary Advance, Students Foreign Missions Fellowship of the I.V.C.F. University of Toronto. December 27, 1946 to January 2, 1947." Attachment to Stacey Woods, letter to IVCF-USA and Canada boards and staff, 19 February 1947. IVCF Canada archives.

[13]Stacey Woods, letter to Sidney Smith, 11 January 1947, IVCF Canada archives.

[14]Douglas Johnson, letter, 25 August 1944. The names were omitted in the original but added later. This one with name of Mel Donald was penciled in by Douglas Johnson with notation "letter sent

to Mr Stacey Woods," IVCF Canada archives.

[15]The five potential chairmen were Rendle Short, D. M. Blair, Hugh Gough, Kenneth Hooker and Oliver Barclay.

[16]Douglas Johnson, letter, 25 August 1944.

[17]See Douglas Johnson, *Contending for the Faith* (Leicester, U.K.: Inter-Varsity Press, 1979), pp. 269-71.

[18]As a student Ole Kristian Hallesby (1879-1961) reacted against the liberalism of his professors at Oslo University and converted in 1902. He was professor of dogmatics at the Free Faculty of Theology, Oslo, 1909-1952. Outspoken against Nazi occupation of Norway, he spent 1943-1945 in prison. His books *Prayer* and *Conscience* were IVP classics.

[19]Stacey Woods, "Report of the General Secretary 18 May 1946," p. 11, IVCF Canada archives.

[20]Douglas Johnson, letter to Stacey Woods, 18 May 1946, IVCF Canada archives.

[21]Douglas Johnson, letter Stacey Woods, 27 May 1946, IVCF Canada archives.

[22]Martyn Lloyd-Jones, letter to Stacey Woods, 18 June 1946, IVCF Canada archives.

[23]Martyn Lloyd-Jones, letter to Stacey Woods, 2 December 1946, IVCF Canada archives.

[24]Stacey Woods, letter to Dr. Muntz, 18 February 1947, IVCF Canada archives.

[25]Charles Troutman, diary entry, 21 January 1940, Centre for the History of Christian Thought and Experience, Macquarie University, held at the Bible Society of New South Wales.

[26]Stacey Woods, review of John Owen's *The Glory of Christ, HIS* 10, no 6 (1950): 14.

[27]Stacey Woods, letter to Jim Nyquist, 12 May 1979, InterVarsity Press archives, Westmont, Illinois.

[28]Stacey Woods, quoted in Iain Murray, *David Martyn Lloyd-Jones* (Edinburgh: Banner of Truth Trust, 1990), 2:152-54

[29]Judge John J. Read (1888-1973) was brother of IVCF Canada board vice-chair Edith Read, founder and dean of Dalhousie University law faculty (1914-1929), legal adviser to the embryonic Canadian Department of External Affairs, and at the time (1946-1958) at the International Court of Justice at the Hague. A Baptist lay leader his support of InterVarsity in the early days was vital.

Chapter 8: Unprecedented Growth

[1]Stacey Woods, "Report of General Secretary—May 18, 1946," p. 1, IVCF Canada archives.

[2]Charles Troutman, letter to Peter Hammond, 24 December 1982, Billy Graham Center archives, 300.386.1.

[3]Ibid.

[4]Charles Troutman, letter to Stacey Woods, 6 May 1948, Billy Graham Center archives, 300.4.18.

[5]Charles Troutman, letter to Stacey Woods, 29 April 1948, Billy Graham Center archives, 300.4.18.

[6]Stacey Woods, quoted in Keith Hunt and Gladys Hunt, *For Christ and the University* (Downers Grove, Ill.: InterVarsity Press, 1991), p. 109.

[7]Five young men (Elliot, Fleming, McCully, Saint, Youderian) were martyred 8 January 1956 while attempting to reach the Stone Age Auca tribe. Their story, written up in *Reader's Digest* in August 1956, became the bestselling *Through Gates of Splendor*, authored by one of the widows, Elisabeth Howard Elliot. No event better characterized and motivated the evangelical community at the time, stirring deep feelings. *Hymns* was the book they sang from as they were about to go to their deaths, leaving wives and children soon to be widows and orphans.

[8]Mary Anne Klein, quoted in Keith Hunt and Gladys Hunt, *For Christ and the University* (Downers Grove, Ill.: InterVarsity Press, 1991), p. 115.

[9]Douglas Johnson, quoted in Andrew T. Le Peau and Linda Doll, *Heart. Soul. Mind. Strength.* (Downers Grove, Ill.: InterVarsity Press, 2006), p. 22.

[10]Stacey Woods, "Report of General Secretary—May 18, 1946," p. 10, IVCF Canada archives.

[11]Thomas Maxwell (1911-1997) graduated University of Toronto (1941); Knox College (1943); PTS (1944-1945); IVCF (1946-1948); PCC missionary, British Guiana (1948-1951); assistant pastor, Knox Church, Toronto (1951-1954); Toronto Bible College (1954-1961); pastor in W. Lorne, Ontario (1961-1964); sociology professor at Wilfred Laurier University (1966-1977).

[12]Stacey Woods, "Report to the General Secretary to the Board of Directors IVCF May 19, 1947," p. 9. Inter-Varsity Canada archives.

[13]Stacey Woods, letter to H. J. Taylor, 29 October 1947, Billy Graham Center archives, 20.62.2.

[14]Carolyn Whitney-Brown and Geoffrey Whitney-Brown, "Lives Lived: Herbert (Wilber) Sutherland," *Globe and Mail* [Toronto], 3 December 1997, A20.

[15]Wilber Sutherland, to all *Imago* supporters, 1 June 1983, courtesy of David Stewart, Ottawa. In mentioning 1934, Wilber must be mistaken, because Stacey's first ministry visit to Vancouver was in 1937.

[16]Charles Troutman, letter to Stacey Woods, n.d., probably around 15 May 1948, Billy Graham Center archives, 300.4.18.

[17]Stacey Woods, "Report of the General Secretary to the Corporation IVCF Canada," Billy Graham Center archives, 20.6.5.

[18]René Pache (1904-1979) obtained a doctorate in law at Lausanne and joined CIBA in Basle. Converted at twenty-four, he had only one year at Bible school, taking instruction from the Scofield Bible, which he had translated into French. From 1947 to 1971 he was director of the Emmaus Bible and Missionary Institute in Lausanne. He was described as a "midweek pretribulationist" dispensationalist.

[19]Stacey Woods, "Report to the General Secretary to the Corporation IVCF Canada," Billy Graham Center archives, 20.6.5.

[20]Eric Sauer (1898-1959) was director of the Bible school in Wiedenest, Germany, and was known for his mildly dispensational books *The Dawn of World Redemption* and *The Triumph of the Crucified.*

[21]Iain Murray, *David Martyn Lloyd-Jones Volume Two* (Edinburgh: Banner of Truth, 1991), p. 158.

[22]Ibid.

[23]Peter Haile, telephone interview with me, 4 October 2006.

[24]Charles Troutman, undated memo, Billy Graham Center archives, 300.18.18.

[25]Kenneth Taylor, "Why Don't Fundamentalists Preach ALL the Gospel?" *HIS* 9, no. 7 (1948): 6-9, 29-32.

[26]James E. Bennet, letter to Robert Van Kampen, 24 November 1948, Billy Graham Center archives, 20.62.2.

[27]Stacey Woods, "Annual Report of the General Secretary, C Stacey Woods, to the members of the corporation of the Inter-Varsity Christian Fellowship of Canada," 23 October 1948, Billy Graham Center archive, 20.60.5.

[28]Minutes, IVCF Board, 29 January 1949. Billy Graham Center archives, 20.62.30.

[29]Ibid.

[30]Stacey Woods, letter to the IVCF corporation and staff, 22 June 1949, Billy Graham Center archives, 20.62.2.

[31]Frank Horton, e-mail to me, 23 July 2006.

[32]Stacey Woods, untitled call to prayer, 5 November 1949, Billy Graham Center archives, 20.62.2.

[33]Stacey Woods, letter to Canadian supporters, May 1950, IVCF Canada archives.

Chapter 9: Articulate Author

[1]Scholars' Conference, Harold John Ockenga papers 20.8, Gordon-Conwell Theological Seminary.

[2]Stacey Woods, "For Your Information and Prayer," 1 November 1949, IVCF Canada archives.

[3]Stacey Woods, letter to R. L. Decker, n.d., c. 1948, Billy Graham Center archives, 20.62.2.

[4]Robert C Mackie, "Relationships with the International Fellowship of Evangelical Students," Memorandum No. 3, rev. ed., October 1948, p. 2, Harold John Ockenga papers 64, Gordon-Conwell Theological Seminary.

[5]Mary Anne Klein, quoted in Keith Hunt and Gladys Hunt, *For Christ and the University* (Downers Grove, Ill.: InterVarsity Press, 1991), p. 115.

[6]Joel Carpenter, *Revive Us Again* (New York: Oxford University Press, 1997), p. 208.

[7]Stacey Woods, "Purpose," *HIS* 12, no. 1 (1951): back page.

[8]Lawrence Neale Jones, *The Inter-Varsity Christian Fellowship in the United States: A Study of Its History, Theology and Relations with Other Groups* (Ph.D. diss., Yale University, 1961), p. 349.

[9]Stacey Woods, mimeographed sheet with copy of press article, pp. 4-7., n.d., Bouma collection, Calvin Theological Seminary archives 18.

[10]Stacey Woods, letter to Clarence Bouma, pp. 4-7, 1 October 1947, Bouma collection, Calvin Theological Seminary archives 18.

[11]Robert Van Kampen, letter to Stacey Woods, 19 February 1945, Billy Graham Center archives, 130.62.29.

[12]Clarence Bouma, letter to Virginia Lowell, 24 April 1948, Bouma collection, Calvin Theological Seminary archives 18, pp. 4-7.

[13]Henry Clarence Thiessen (1883-1947), of a Mennonite background, graduated in 1909 from Fort Wayne Bible School and taught there from 1916 to 1923. He went on to a doctorate at Southern Baptist Theological Seminary. Came to Dallas Theological Seminary in 1931-1935 and taught at Wheaton Graduate School from 1938 to 1947.

[14]Henry Thiessen, letter to Harold John Ockenga, 19 December 1944, Harold John Ockenga papers 13, Gordon-Conwell Theological Seminary.

[15]Bob Fryling, conversation with me, 15 August 2006.

[16]Stacey Woods, "Taboo?" *HIS* 5, no. 7 (1945): 31-34.

[17]Stacey Woods, "The Ten Commandments and the Campus," *HIS* 9, no. 4 (1949): 6-7.

[18]Stacey Woods, "Add to Your Faith Moral Character," *HIS* 13, no. 5 (1953): 5-6.

[19]Stacey Woods, "Caesar and Christ," *HIS* 10, no.4 (1950), back page.

[20]Edgar Metzler, letter to Stacey Woods, n.d. (received 23 February 1950), Billy Graham Center archives, 300.3.5.

[21]Jones, *Inter-Varsity Christian Fellowship*, p. 231.

[22]Stacey Woods, "The Principles of Christian Modesty," *HIS* 9, no. 5 (1948): 4.

[23]Stacey Woods, "Purpose," *HIS* 12, no. 1 (1951), back page.

[24]Stacey Woods, "This I Believe," *HIS* 5, no. 12 (1945): 28-29.

[25]Stacey Woods, "What Is Biblical Christianity?" *HIS* 9, no. 4 (1949), front page.

[26]Stacey Woods, "What Does IVCF Stand For?" *HIS* 21, no. 9 (1950): 192.

[27]Stacey Woods and John Bolten, "The Importance of the Communion Service" *HIS* 4, no. 5 (1946): 24.

[28]Jones, *Inter-Varsity Christian Fellowship*, p. 249.

[29]Stacey Woods, "A Total Christian Witness in Our Universities," *HIS* 15, no. 1 (1954): 1.

[30]Stacey Woods, "The Christian Attitude Toward Science," *HIS* 17, no.3 (1956): 17-18, 23-24.

Chapter 10: A Dark Space

[1]Senior staff conference minutes, 19-26 January, 1950, Billy Graham Center archives, 300.13 4.

[2]Charles Troutman, letter to Stacey Woods, 19 August 1949, Billy Graham Center archives, 111.2.3.

[3]Ibid.

[4]Stacey Woods, letter to the staff, 5 November 1949, Billy Graham Center archives, 20.62.2.

[5]Douglas Johnson, letter to Charles Troutman, 30 August 1951, Billy Graham Center archives, 111.2.3.

[6]Jim Nyquist, e-mail to me, 16 October 2006.

[7]George Ensworth (1922-2001), joined IVCF as a student at Michigan State, from which he got a Ph.D. in clinical psychology. He studied at Fuller and married Kathy, daughter of homiletics professor Clarence Roddy in 1951, the same year he came to Fuller. George left IVCF in 1963, taught one year at Westminster Seminary, twenty-five years at Gordon-Conwell as well as having a private practice. He retired in 1991.

[8]Charles Hummel (1923-2004) was active in InterVarsity at University of Michigan. While in the military after WWII, he helped found KGK (InterVarsity in Japan). Charles went to MIT for a master's in chemical engineering. After a year in industry, he joined the InterVarsity staff in 1949, holding many different positions. Charles married southeast staffer Anne Childs in 1951. He left IV staff in 1965 to become president of Barrington College, returning ten years later to head IVCF's faculty ministry. Charles retired in 1991.

[9]Paul E. Little (1928-1975) was born into a Philadelphia Christian Brethren family. He graduated in 1950 from Wharton School, University of Pennsylvania and joined IVCF staff immediately after. He was posted to Illinois for one year, then to New York City, where he worked with Marie Huttenlock (see endnote 12, p. 249). He married Marie in 1953 while also doing a year of graduate study at Wheaton. When he returned to New York City, he worked with the Billy Graham crusade but was then assigned to Texas in 1958 before being appointed IVCF Evangelism Director in the Chicago office in 1961. As a guest lecturer for one week at Wheaton, he gave a series of talks that became the bestselling *How to Give Away Your Faith*. He also taught at Trinity Evangelical Divinity School in Deerfield, Illinois, and in 1973 was appointed program director of the Lausanne Congress on World Evangelization. Paul was killed in 1975 when he was traveling from OPC to Toronto for a midweek service. For more information see <www.ivpress.com/paullittle>.

[10]Barbara Boyd, quoted in Keith Hunt and Gladys Hunt, *For Christ and the University* (Downers Grove, Ill.: InterVarsity Press, 1993), p. 98.

[11]Dorothy Farmer, Marilyn Kunz, Peter Northrup, Ruth Stewart, Rosalind Rinker, Anna Mary Williams, and Gwen Wong are among the Biblical Seminary graduates.

[12]Stacey Woods, minutes of the Canadian IVCF board, 4 February 1950, Billy Graham Center archives, 20.60.5.

[13] Stacey Woods, letter to Harold John Ockenga, 21 February 1950, Ockenga archives, 64.

[14] Leith Samuel, letter to Stacey Woods, 10 April 1951, Billy Graham Center archives, 300.5.8.

[15] Wilber Sutherland, "Annual Report IVCF August 31, 1951," Billy Graham Center archives, 20.60.8.

[16] Ibid.

[17] "Brief on Karlis Leyasmeyer," Billy Graham Center archives, 300.10.21. Cf. Peck to Haines, 16 July 1951, same file: "The Senior Staff, after much prayer and discussion, have the opinion that Dr. Leyasmeyer's ministry with the Fellowship, while most helpful, has been of a temporary not a permanent nature. You and I as Board members should hesitate long before overruling their opinion."

[18] Charles Troutman, letter to Stacey Woods, 27 April 1951, Billy Graham Center archives, 111.2.3.

[19] Stacey Woods, letter to Canadian IVCF board members, 25 August 1951, Billy Graham Center archives, 20.60.5.

[20] Charles Troutman, two filofax sheets and three pages, 24 June 1951, Billy Graham Center archives, 111.2.3.

[21] Carolyn Armitage, *Reaching for the Goal* (Wheaton, Ill.: OMF/Harold Shaw, 1993), p. 145.

[22] Stacey Woods, letter to Herbert Taylor, 21 August 1951; and Herbert Taylor, letter to Stacey Woods, 27 August 1951, Billy Graham Center archives, 20.60.3.

[23] Keith and Gladys Hunt, personal interview with me, 16-17 August 2006.

[24] See Gladys Hunt's *A Place to Meet God: The History of Cedar Campus, 1954-2004* (Cedarville, Mich.: Cedar Campus, 2004).

[25] Robert van Eaton Finley, letters to Charles Troutman, 14 September and 21 November, 1951, Billy Graham Center archives, 111.2.3.

[26] Senior staff council minutes, 7-11 January 1952, p. 3, IVCF Canada archives.

[27] Charles Troutman, letter to Bill Bright, summer 1952, quoted in Keith Hunt and Gladys Hunt, *For Christ and the University* (Downers Grove, Ill.: InterVarsity Press, 1993), p. 171, but the citation "ibid." is wrong. The letter is Troutman to Bright, not Woods to Troutman.

[28] Stacey Woods, "Annual Report of the General Secretary, 1951-1952," Billy Graham Center archives, 20 62, 31.

[29] Interview with Jonathan Woods, St. Nom la Bretèche (suburban Paris), 8 July 2006.

[30] Stacey Woods and Charles Troutman, letter to all IVCF staff, 14 September 1951, IVCF Canada archives.

[31] Lois Troutman, letter to Charles Troutman, dated "Sunday a.m." (16 September 1951), Billy Graham Center archives, 111.2.3. It is astonishing that Troutman not only kept all this correspondence but, thirty years later, delivered it to the Billy Graham Center archives in a file marked "Confidential" but open to researchers.

[32] Charles Troutman, letter to members of senior staff council, 4 February 1952, IVCF Canada archives.

[33] Stacey Woods, letter to Wilber Sutherland, 10 April 1957, IVCF Canada archives.

[34] Stacey Woods, letter to Charles Troutman, 12 February 1952, Billy Graham Center archives, 111.2.3.

[35] D. Miller Alloway (1920-1999) was president of General Printers in Oshawa, which later became Consolidated Graphics of Toronto. He graduated from the University of Toronto in 1945, the year after his wife, Norma, both of whom were activity in IVCF Canada. Alloway was Stacey's choice to be chair of the board in 1962. He resigned in January 1967.

[36]Stacey Woods, letter to W. E. C. Petersen and Charles Troutman, 24 April 1952, Billy Graham Center archives, 20.6.13.

[37]Charles Troutman, letter to Stacey Woods, 22 May 1952, Billy Graham Center archives, 20.1.13.

[38]David Adeney, letter to Charles Troutman, 21 May 1952, Billy Graham Center archives, 111.2.3.

[39]Charles Troutman, letter to senior staff, 9 August 1952, Billy Graham Center archives, 111.2.3.

[40]David Adeney, letter to Charles Troutman, 21 May 1952, Billy Graham Center archives, 111.2.3.

[41]Charles Troutman, unaddressed sheet with his signature, 7 November 1952, Billy Graham Center archives, 20.1.13.

[42]Herbert Taylor, letter to board member J. F. Strombeck, 22 January 1953, Billy Graham Center archives 20.61.4.

[43]Paul Westburg, letter to Herbert Taylor, 12 February 1953, Billy Graham Center archives, 20.61.4.

[44]Stacey Woods, letter to Charles Troutman, 15 August 1964, Stacey Woods, 111.6.26.

[45]Charles Troutman, letter to Mel Donald, 16 September 1986, IVCF Canada archives.

Chapter 11: International Inspiration

[1]"Minutes of the Fourth Meeting of the Third General Committee of the IFES, August 6, 1953," p. 56, Wheaton College Special Collections, 49.2.AB.1.

[2]Stacey Woods, "Report of the General Secretary to the General Committee of IFES August 1 to 10 1953," p. 7. Wheaton College Special Collections, 49.2.AB.1.

[3]"Minutes of the Fourth Meeting," p. 56.

[4]Stacey Woods, "Annual Report of the General Secretary, 1952-1953," p. 8. Billy Graham Center archives, 20.61.5.

[5]Barbara Boyd, interview with me, 23 May 2006.

[6]IVCF executive committee minutes, 23 May 1952, Billy Graham Center archives, 20.61.3.

[7]Eugene Thomas, letter to Stacey Woods, 12 February 1954, Billy Graham Center archives, 20.60.3.

[8]Stacey Woods, letter to Maurice Murphy, 12 July 1955, Billy Graham Center archives, 30.11.13. A month later Stacey wrote Murphy: "I disagree with you and would argue the right of any group of Christians so led by the Lord to have a celebration of the Lord's supper apart from a formally organized church, providing it is done decently and in order. But in practice I believe great care and caution should be used . . . it is on a very, very rare occasion that I myself have ever taken the responsibility of the consecration of the elements and dispensing of the same" (Stacey Woods, letter to Maurice Murphy, 16 August 1955, Billy Graham Center archives, 300.11.13).

[9]"The Late Rev M Murphy," *Australian Church Record,* 27 September, 1956.

[10]Stacey Woods, letter to Belva Murphy, 18 September 1956, Billy Graham Center archives, 300.11.14.

[11]Keith Hunt and Gladys Hunt, *For Christ and the University* (Downers Grove, Ill.: InterVarsity Press, 1991), p. 180.

[12]Stacey Woods, "Annual Report of the General Secretary, 1953-54," p. 2, Billy Graham Center archives, 20.62.32.

[13]Ibid.

[14]"Minutes of the Executive Session of the Board of Directors, January 8, 1955," vol. 3, no. 5, pp. 22-B. Billy Graham Center archives, 300.368.3.

[15]Stacey Woods, letter to Roy Horsey, 6 January 1955, attachment to IVCF board minutes, 8 January

1955, vol. 3, no. 5, p. 21. Billy Graham Center archives, 300.368.3.

[16]Stacey Woods, "Minutes of the Meetings of the Fourth General Committee of the IFES, September 4-7, 1956," p. 6, Billy Graham Center archives, 49.2.A1.

[17]Stacey Woods, letter to Wilber Sutherland, 24 February and 11 May 1956, IVCF Canada archives.

[18]Stacey Woods, letter to me, 25 September 1954, IVCF Canada archives.

[19]Local IVCF chapters in Canada are often known as "Varsity Christian Fellowship."

[20]Martyn Lloyd-Jones, *Authority* (London: Inter-Varsity Press, 1958), p. 1. (The 1957 date of the Glen Orchard conference, given on the inside title page, is wrong.)

[21]Ibid., p. 8.

[22]Ibid., p. 71.

[23]Stacey Woods, "Minutes of the Meetings," p. 11.

[24]Elizabeth Catherwood, telephone conversation with me, 21 October 2006.

[25]Stacey Woods, letter to Billy Graham, 13 June 1956, Billy Graham Center archives, 20.61.7.

Chapter 12: Mid-Decade Malaise

[1]John Stott, facsimile to me, 6 June 2006.

[2]Wilber Sutherland, letter to John Stott, 5 January, 1955, IVCF Canada archives.

[3]Stacey Woods, letter to Wilber Sutherland, 3 March 1955, IVCF Canada archives.

[4]Stacey Woods, letter to John Stott, 29 May 1956, IVCF Canada archives.

[5]Stacey Woods, letter to John Stott, 20 November 1956, IVCF Canada archives.

[6]Tony Tyndale, letter to supporters, 1 May 1957, IVCF Canada archives.

[7]*Yale Daily News,* quoted in William Martin, *A Prophet with Honor* (New York: William Morrow, 1991), p. 215.

[8]Timothy Dudley-Smith, *John Stott: The Making of a Leader* (Downers Grove, Ill.: InterVarsity Press, 1999), p. 396, 398.

[9]William Kiesewetter was a pediatrician at Children's Hospital, Pittsburgh, and later at Children's Hospital, Philadelphia.

[10]William Kiesewetter, letter to "Fellow Members of IVF," 1 October 1957, Billy Graham Center archives, 20.60.15.

[11]Keith Hunt and Gladys Hunt, *For Christ and the University* (Downers Grove, Ill.: InterVarsity Press, 1991), p. 182.

[12]Stacey Woods, "Are Bible Schools and Seminaries Doing the Job?" *Eternity* 7, no. 7 (1956): 14-15, 42-44.

[13]"Bible School Heads Reply to Stacey Woods," *Eternity* 7, no. 8 (1956): 24, 45-48.

[14]Keith Hunt and Gladys Hunt, *For Christ and the University* (Downers Grove, Ill.: InterVarsity Press, 1991), p. 184.

[15]Stacey Woods, to Wilber Sutherland, 10 April 1957, IVCF Canada archives.

[16]Carl McIntire, *Christian Beacon* 22, no. 43 (1957): 1.

[17]Carl McIntire, *Christian Beacon* 22, no. 45 (1957): 1.

[18]Stacey Woods, "Confidential Memo to Corporation and Staff," 12 December 1957, Billy Graham Center archives, 300.201.14.

[19]Carl McIntire, *Christian Beacon* 23. no. 3 (1958): 1, 5.

[20]Ibid.

[21]Mary Lou Bayly, e-mail to me via Tim (Joe and Mary Lou's son), 1 November 2006.

[22]Stacey Woods, letter to Bill Bright, 14 February 1957, Billy Graham Center archives, 300.8.3.

[23]Bill Bright, letter to Stacey Woods, 14 March 1957, Billy Graham Center archives, 300.8.3.

[24]Jim Nyquist, letter to Charles Hummel and Paul Little, 2 December 1960, Billy Graham Center archives, 300.8.3.

[25]"1957 IFES Executive Committee Minutes," p. 18. Wheaton College Special Collections, SC49.II.A1.

[26]Gabriel Hebert, *Fundamentalism and the Church of God* (London: SCM Press, 1957), pp. 27, 125-26.

[27]Stacey Woods, letter to Wilber Sutherland, 15 December 1958, IVCF Canada archives.

[28]Wilber Sutherland, "The Character and Philosophy of an Evangelical Student Movement," and "Summary of What Followed," p. 3, IVCF Canada archives.

[29]Stacey Woods, letter to Wilber Sutherland, 15 December 1958, IVCF Canada archives.

[30]Alister McGrath, *J. I. Packer: A Biography* (Grand Rapids: Baker, 1997), p. 82.

[31]Stacey Woods, *Growth of a Work of God* (Downers Grove, Ill.: InterVarsity Press, 1978), pp. 154-55. Stacey once used the expression "easy believism" at a KGK rally, and Mike Griffiths had an impossible time trying to translate it into Japanese (Michael Griffiths, e-mail to me, 8 November 2006).

[32]Stacey Woods, letter to Charles Hummel, 9 August 1960, Billy Graham Center archives, 300.18.18.

[33]Keith Hunt, interviewing Charles Troutman, 7 February 1990, Billy Graham Center archives, 300.380.24.

[34]Anne Hummel, interview with me, 22 May 2006. See also Hunt and Hunt, *For Christ and the University*, 433, n. 10.

[35]"Minutes of Meetings of the Executive Committee of IFES, August 26-29, 1958," p. 4, Wheaton College Special Collections, SC49.II.A1.

[36]See J. C. Pollock, *The Good Seed* (London: Hodder & Stoughton, 1959), pp. 118-19.

[37]Stacey Woods, "Fifth General Committee Minutes, Appendix A", 1. Wheaton College Special Collections, SC49.II.A1.

[38]Stacey Woods, *Growth of a Work of God* (Downers Grove, Ill.: InterVarsity Press, 1974), p. 153.

Chapter 13: American Farewell

[1]Stacey had strong reservations about Wycliffe Bible Translators because of its cosiness with various Latin American dictators.

[2]Samuel Escobar, interview with me, 30 August 2006.

[3]Luis Perfitti later joined Campus Crusade for Christ after they recruited him from IFES, much to Stacey's dismay.

[4]Stacey Woods, letter to Wilber Sutherland, 29 May 1958, InterVarsity Canada archives.

[5]Samuel Escobar, interview with me, 30 August 2006.

[6]For instance, in a 2 May 1969 letter to Samuel Escobar, Stacey says, "I have just heard through American Express that I can get you a free ticket on Swissair from Buenos Aires to Innsbruck and return. The only hitch or difficulty is that you will have to return to Geneva from Mittersill by train, in order to take an inaugural flight of Swissair from Geneva to Hamburg and return. Then you will be able to travel on to Singapore, though we will have to pay your fare there. But your return from Geneva to Buenos Aires will be free. . . . [T]his will be a great saving for us." Letter loaned to me by Samuel Escobar, from his files, and used by permission.

[7]Samuel Escobar, interview with me, 30 August 2006.

[8]"Report of the General Secretary," appendix to "Fifth General Committee Minutes," p. 20. Wheaton College Special Collections, SC49.II.A1.

[9]Samuel Escobar, interview with me, 30 August 2006.

[10]David Adeney, quoted in Carolyn Armitage, *Reaching for the Goal* (Wheaton: OMF/Harold Shaw, 1993), p. 182.

[11]Stacey Woods, report to members of the IFES executive committee, 14 January 1959, IVCF Canada archives.

[12]Gwen Wong and Mary Beaton, quoted by Pete Lowman, *Day of His Power* (Leicester: Inter-Varsity Press, 1953), p. 155.

[13]Stacey Woods, *Growth of a Work of God* (Downers Grove, Ill.: InterVarsity Press, 1974), p. 155.

[14]"Report of the General Secretary," appendix to "Fifth General Committee Minutes," p. 22. Wheaton College Special Collections, SC49.II.A1.

[15]Ibid.

[16]Ibid.

[17]Ibid.

[18]Stacey Woods, letter to Charles Hummel, 9 August 1960, Billy Graham Center archives, 300.18.18.

[19]Stacey Woods, *Change Witness Triumph* (Downers Grove, Ill.: InterVarsity Press, 1965), p. 203.

[20]Ruth Siemens, conversation with Stacey Woods, 16 August 1960, Wheaton College Special Collections, 49.6.8.

[21]Mark Hutchinson, "Charles Troutman," in *Australian Dictionary of Evangelical Biography*, ed. Brian Dickey (Sydney: Evangelical History Association, 1994).

[22]Charles Hummel, letter to Charles Troutman, 11 July 1961, Billy Graham Center archives, 36.8.9.

[23]Stacey Woods, letter to Charles Troutman, 12 December 1961, Billy Graham Center archives, 111.6.26.

[24]A dustup in March 1962 in which Troutman said that Stacey was "upset and accusing the IVCF of unethical action," or again in April 1963, "I am deeply disturbed that a senior member of the IFES [Martyn Lloyd-Jones] is visiting a member country for two months without any reference to the member movement. . . . [Y]ou have acted quite unilaterally in keeping us in the dark," Billy Graham Center archives, 111.6.28.

[25]Stacey Woods, letter to Charles Troutman, 25 January 1961, box 39, Centre for the History of Christian Thought and Experience, Macquarie University, held at the Bible Society of New South Wales.

[26]Betty Moir, letter to Stacey Woods, 21 November 1960, Centre for the History of Christian Thought and Experience, Macquarie University, held at the Bible Society of New South Wales.

[27]Ibid.

[28]John Bolten, letter to Fred Feriss of the World Evangelical Fellowship, 20 September 1961, Ockenga archives, 13.

[29]Stacey Woods, "Confidential Memorandum," 13 September 1961, Billy Graham Center archives, 111.6.26.

[30]On the merger of the free churches with the state church in 1967, the assembly bought a redundant building and is now called Chapelle de Villard, Chemin des Fleurettes 35. It was here that Stacey's funeral was held 11 April 1983, though he no longer worshiped there.

[31]Philippina Van Seters (1931-1980) was a 1952 graduate of Toronto Bible College. She studied at the University of Toronto and worked in the IVCF Canada office. Returning to Canada in 1966, she took a B.A. at Dalhousie University, Halifax, Nova Scotia. On graduating she was secretary to its president. She died of cancer in August 1980. Characteristically, Wilber Sutherland was prepared to take the funeral as the family were deeply traumatized by her passing. Her brother Arthur however rose to the occasion.

[32]Phil Van Seters, letter to Arthur Van Seters, 18 August 1963, courtesy of Arthur Van Seters.

[33]Phil Van Seters, letter to Arthur Van Seters, 5 March 1964, courtesy of Arthur Van Seters.

[34]Phil Van Seters, letter to Arthur Van Seters, 18 August 1963, courtesy of Arthur Van Seters.

[35]Phil Van Seters, letter to Arthur Van Seters, 22 February 1966, courtesy of Arthur Van Seters.

[36]Ibid.

[37]Norma Alloway, Join Us for Coffee (Toronto: Windward Press, 1978), p. 209.

Chapter 14: Global Challenges

[1]Samuel Cheng, letter to R. O. Hall, 22 July 1963, IVCF Canada archives.

[2]John Stott briefly stopped by Hong Kong and visited Hall. "We had an hour's fairly deep theological debate. We had to agree to disagree, but I hope I was able a little bit to show him that evangelicals are not as black as he has painted us." On Stott's second visit, Hall's successor was patron of the mission, and at the third time, Stott actually stayed as a guest at Bishop's House and addressed the clergy of the diocese (Timothy Dudley-Smith, John Stott: A Global Ministry (Downers Grove, Ill.: InterVarsity Press, 2001), pp. 113, 469.

[3]"Sixth General Committee Minutes," p. 34. Wheaton College Special Collections, SC49.II.AI.

[4]Stacey Woods, letter to Wilber Sutherland, 29 May 1958, IVCF Canada archives.

[5]Samuel Escobar, interview with me, 30 August 2006.

[6]"Minutes of the Sixth General Committee," p. 34, Billy Graham Center archives, 30 2 AI.

[7]"Minutes of the Sixth General Committee," p. 36, Billy Graham Center archives, 30 2 AI.

[8]Ibid.

[9]Stacey Woods, quoted in Peter Lineham, Students Reaching Students: A History of the International Fellowship of Evangelical Students (not published, n.d.), p. 166.

[10]Stacey Woods, letter to Wilber Sutherland, 10 January 1964, IVCF Canada archives.

[11]Stacey Woods, Hans Bürki, Douwe Wolters of the Netherlands, and Bodo Volkmann of Germany.

[12]Stacey Woods, report to IFES executive committee, 9 March 1964, IVCF Canada archives.

[13]Quoted in Lineham, Students Reaching Students, pp. 139-40.

[14]Lebanon, Egypt, Greece, Spain, Uruguay, Argentina, Brazil, Peru, Vietnam, Finland and South Africa.

[15]Minutes of the meeting of the Executive Committee of IFES, 25-30 September 1964, pp. 3-4.

[16]Stacey Woods, "To Members of the Corporation IVCF of Canada," 16 November 1964, IVCF Canada archives.

[17]Keith and Gladys Hunt, For Christ and the University (Downers Grove, Ill.: InterVarsity Press, 1991), p. 229.

[18]Quoted in ibid., p. 230.

[19]Ibid.

[20]Stacey Woods, letter to Wilber Sutherland, 16 November 1964, IVCF Canada archives.

[21] *Change Witness Triumph* (Downers Grove, Ill.: InterVarsity Press, 1965), p. 195.

[22] Arjunan, *"You Really Loved Us": India's Memorial to Norton and Eloise Sterrett* (Chennai: UESI Publication Trust, 1999), p. 74.

[23] Stacey Woods, unpublished 1977 manuscript found at Schloss Mittersill.

Chapter 15: Mittersill Momentum

[1] Stacey Woods, *Growth of a Work of God* (Downers Grove, Ill.: InterVarsity Press, 1974), p. 140.

[2] John Bolten Jr., "Schloss Mittersill and the IFES," 30 April 1996, Schloss Mittersill files.

[3] Alex Williams, *Holy Spy: Student Ministry in Eastern Europe* (Fearn and Budapest: Harmat and Christian Focus, 2003), pp. 59-60.

[4] Stacey Woods, letter to Harold John Ockenga, 19 March 1965. Harold John Ockenga papers 3.13, Gordon-Conwell Theological Seminary.

[5] "Minutes of the Meeting of the Corporate Board of IFES Inc in the Commonwealth of Massachusetts, 4 December 1965, Harold John Ockenga papers 3.13, Gordon-Conwell Theological Seminary.

[6] The two other IFES Inc. board members were Daniel Hogan, Andover, Mass. (absent) and Martha Lange, Methuen, Mass.

[7] Daniel Hogan left the corporation and Stanley Block of Illinois Institute of Technology, Chicago; Mrs. Antoinette (Toni) Johnson of West Palm Beach; and Jack Oliver of Vancouver were added.

[8] Harold John Ockenga to Stacey Woods, 5 May 1966, Harold John Ockenga papers 3.9, Gordon-Conwell Theological Seminary.

[9] Stacey Woods to IFES Executive and Finance Committee, 22 December 1965, IVCF Canada archives.

[10] Ian Burnard (1933-2000), from Adelaide, was a scientist, IVF Australia staffer in Melbourne and Sydney, general secretary of IVF from 1962 to 1976. Following his time in AFES he went into adult education and police recruitment. For his obituary see <www.iscast.org.au/pdf/bulletin/Bulletin0401.pdf>.

[11] Sir Harold Murray Knight (1919-) KBE, DSC, deputy governor of the Reserve Bank of Australia (1968-1975), governor of the Reserve Bank of Australia (1975-1982).

[12] "Schloss Mittersill 1966," unsigned and undated three-page statement with subsequent letter on 22 March 1966 from Ian Burnard to Stacey Woods, altering wording. Schloss Mittersill files.

[13] Stacey Woods to John Bolten Sr. and Harold John Ockenga, 25 April 1966, Harold John Ockenga papers 3.13, Gordon-Conwell Theological Seminary.

[14] Stacey Woods, letter to IFES Inc., 26 May 1966, Harold John Ockenga papers 3.13. Gordon-Conwell Theological Seminary.

[15] "Schloss Mittersill Conference Centre: A Possible Project of IFES," Schloss Mittersill files, undated (early 1966?), p. 2.

[16] "Minutes of the Executive Committee of IFES, 28-31 August, 1966," p. 12. Wheaton College Special Collections, SC49.II.A1, Billy Graham Center archives, 49.II.A1.

[17] Stacey Woods to IFES Inc. directors, 21 December 1966, Harold John Ockenga papers 3.9, Gordon-Conwell Theological Seminary.

[18] Stacey Woods to Samuel Escobar, 14 March 1967, courtesy of Samuel Escobar.

[19] James Brink to Harold John Ockenga, 10 March 1967, Harold John Ockenga papers 3.9, Gordon-Conwell Theological Seminary.

[20]Mariano DiGangi, in a telephone conversation with me, 4 November 2006.

[21]Stacey Woods to John Howitt, 19 June 1967, Schloss Mittersill files.

[22]Stacey Woods to John Nordquist, 21 June 1967, Schloss Mittersill files.

[23]Dr. Guy Fatzer, Lausanne, undated, but after 27 July 1967, Billy Graham Center archives. 300, 10.

[24]Stacey Woods to Samuel Escobar, 14 March 1967. Letter in possession of Samuel Escobar and made available to me by kind permission.

[25]"1967 IFES Executive Committee Minutes," p. 28. Wheaton College Special Collections, SC49.II.A1.

[26]"Report of the General Secretary," appendix to "Seventh General Committee Minutes," p. 4. Wheaton College Special Collections, SC49.II.A1.

[27]Ibid.

[28]Stacey Woods to Charles and Evelyn MacKechnie, 11 September 1967, Schloss Mittersill files.

[29]John Bolten Jr., "Schloss Mittersill and the IFES," 30 April 1996, Schloss Mittersill files.

[30]Anneliese Oberndorfer, letter to Stacey Woods, 6 February 1967[8], Schloss Mittersill files.

[31]Stacey Woods to John Bolter Sr., 27 June 1968, Schloss Mittersill files.

[32]Erna Kull, quoted in Alex Williams, *Holy Spy: Student Ministry in Eastern Europe* (Fearn and Budapest: Harmat and Christian Focus, 2003), p. 65.

[33]Stacey Woods, letter to Billy Graham, with enclosure "Project for Utilising Schloss Mittersill to Reach Students and Pastors in Eastern Europe," 17 July 1968, Schloss Mittersill files.

[34]Yvonne Woods, quoted in Alex Williams, *Holy Spy*, pp. 65-66.

Chapter 16: Canadian Crisis

[1]Ian Rennie, quoted in Stacey Woods, letter to Wilber Sutherland, 14 November 1966, IVCF Canada archives.

[2]Ian S. Rennie (1931-) grew up in Winnipeg where his family worshiped at Elim Chapel. On graduation from United College, Winnipeg (now University of Winnipeg), he joined IVCF Canada staff (1951-1953). While at Fuller Seminary he served part-time with IVCF-USA (1954-1956). In 1961, he received a Ph.D. from the University of Toronto, completed while at Knox Church, Toronto, as a minister to students. Ordained that year in the PCC, he served in Ontario and Fairview Church, Vancouver (1964-1972). He taught at Regent College and subsequently was dean at Ontario Theological Seminary (1980-1996), now Tyndale.

[3]Wilber Sutherland, "The Character and Philosophy of an Evangelical Student Movement," IVCF Canada archives.

[4]Stacey Woods to Wilber Sutherland, 14 November 1966, IVCF Canada archives.

[5]The quote continues, "in the days when you and the President of Columbia Seminary (sic) used to have your arguments about IVCF staff being missionary minded or FMF minded." Stacey replied: "Thanks for your dig about myself and Dr McQuilkin [the president of Columbia Bible College]. I deserve this." McQuilkin was concerned about Stacey's institutional concerns for Foreign Mission Fellowship over a personal consecrated response and commitment to the missionary call. Stacey Woods to Wilber Sutherland, 14 November 1966, IVCF Canada archives.

[6]See note 59 in John Stackhouse's *Canadian Evangelicalism in the Twentieth Century* (Toronto: University of Toronto Press, 1993), p. 258.

[7]Stacey Woods, letter to Wilber Sutherland, 15 August 1966, IVCF Canada archives.

[8]Yvonne Woods, letter to Wilber Sutherland, 26 December 1966, IVCF Canada archives.

[9]Stacey Woods to Wilber Sutherland, 1 March 1967, IVCF Canada archives.

[10]Ibid.

[11]Ibid.

[12]Geoffrey Still, "The Sixties IVCF," n.d., IVCF Canada archives.

[13]Stacey Woods to Wilber Sutherland, 30 November, 1964, IVCF Canada archives.

[14]Wilber served as patron and advocate.

[15]The director of Creation Two was the larger-than-life figure Louis Capson (1944-1996), who captivated Wilbur Sutherland and was a leading influence on him in midlife. Capson joined the Salvation Army in his rough youth in Fredericton, New Brunswick, did his undergraduate work there and got a master's degree in drama from Yale. He was described as "one of Canada's most unusual and promising young playwrights" (*Ubyssey* [University of British Columbia student paper], November 14, 1969). Existing mostly on government grants, his troupe lived in the home of Terry Martens of the Nurses Christian Fellowship at 105 Bernard Avenue in Toronto's Annex. Capson and his partner retreated to upscale Rosedale, creating resentment for other members of the committee. Barbara Sutherland was actively involved, and Wilber formed *Imago* in 1972, partly to fund the project. Creation 3 and 4 followed, but Capson's career sputtered and faded. He died of liver disease at fifty-two with Wilber at his deathbed. See Douglad Todd, "Under the Spell of a Cult," *Vancouver Sun*, March 24, 2004 <http://artsandfaith.com/index.php?show-topic=1974>.

[16]Wilber Sutherland, "Personal—from the General Director," *Intercessor*, July-August 1970.

[17]David Bentley-Taylor, "Report on a Visit to Canada, Oct. 10 to Dec. 3, 1968," p. 6. IFES Oxford files.

[18]Mr Woods' journey, Nov.-Dec. 1969-Spain, Portugal, USA, Canada," p. 13. Wheaton College Special Collections, SC49.III.B:2:22.

[19]Stacey Woods, minutes of the 1967 IFES General Committee, p. 8, Billy Graham Center archives, 30 II A I.

[20]Holy Trinity Church should not be confused with "Little Trinity" Anglican Church, where Wilber initially worshiped when he left Knox Church, Toronto, in 1963.

[21]"Lives Lived: Herbert (Wilber) Sutherland," Toronto *Globe and Mail*, 3 December 1997, A20.

[22]Stacey Woods, private conversation with me en route to London, Ontario, 20 October 1979.

Chapter 17: Final Farewells

[1]David Bentley-Taylor, *Adventures of a Christian Envoy* (Harrow: IFES, 1992), pp. I, II, 104.

[2]Ibid.

[3]Ibid.

[4]Stacey Woods, letter to Harold John Ockenga, 7 September 1966, Harold John Ockenga papers 3.9, Gordon-Conwell Theological Seminary.

[5]Stacey Woods, "Report of the General Secretary to Seventh General Committee IFES," appendix E, p. 2.

[6]David Bentley-Taylor, "Report on Visit to the Mediterranean area, 17 Nov-8 Dec 1967," p. 3. IFES Oxford files.

[7]Bob Young, quoted in David Bentley-Taylor, *Adventures of a Christian Envoy* (Harrow: IFES, 1992), p. 104.

[8]Stacey Woods, "Report on a Journey Round the World October 1968," Wheaton College Special Collections, SC49III.B:2.22.

[9]"Orient Report, 1969," p. 5. Wheaton College Special Cololections, SC49.III.B:2.22.

[10]David Penman (1936-1989) was from New Zealand. He was in Pakistan from 1966-1972, Lebanon from 1972-1975, St. Andrews Hall, Melbourne, and Palmerston, North New Zealand from 1975-1982. He served as assistant bishop in Melbourne from 1982-1984 and archbishop from 1984-1989. David came back from speaking at Lausanne II, Manila, and died suddenly.

[11]David Penman, quoted in Alan Nichols, *David Penman* (Sutherland, NWS: Albatross, 1991), pp. 37-38.

[12]David Bentley-Taylor, "Report on a Visit to West Pakistan 6-13 March 1968," p. 3, IFES files, Oxford.

[13]Mr Woods' Journey, Nov.-Dec. 1969-Spain, Portugal, USA, Canada," p. 11. Wheaton College Special Collections, SC49.III.B:2.22.

[14]Stacey Woods, "Report on Trip to Belgium and Holland, January-February 1970," p. 14. Billy Graham Center archives, SC-49, III.B.2.

[15]From a paper headed "Denmark" [7-20 November 1970], and a manuscript "Reflections on a Visit to Scandinavia, Some Thoughts Concerning a Current Biblical Problem," Wheaton College Special Collections, SC49.III.B.

[16]Ibid.

[17]Stacey Woods, "Urbana '70," p. 4. Wheaton College Special Collections, SC49.III.B:2.22.

[18]Sterrett's minister at the Blue Church, Swarthmore, Pennsylvania, Bob Cressy (who was a longtime friend of IVCF going back to the 1930s) was the one who alerted him to this (see p. 75).

[19]Samuel Escobar, e-mail to me, 29 October 2006.

[20]Stacey Woods, letter to members of IFES Inc., May 1969. See also "Report on the Proposed Condominium at Schloss Mittersill," August 1969, and "Memorandum to Members of IFES Inc., 2 March 1970, Schloss Mittersill files.

[21]Stacey Woods, letter to Keith Hunt, 9 April 1975, Schloss Mittersill files.

[22]Hand Honegger to John Bolten Sr., 26 January 1972, Schloss Mittersill files.

[23]Stacey Woods, letter to Hans Jörg Töbler, 3 August 1972, Schloss Mittersill files.

[24]Mittersill had been used by the Nazis as a center for their eugenics experiementation. The Neidhäusl, the other house on the property, had an unsavory reputation in the area. Eva McCarthy was called in to exorcise the place with days of waiting upon God in the best CIM tradition, calling on the Most High for deliverance and mercy throughout the premises.

[25]Stacey Woods, "Schloss Mittersill-M" unpublished manuscript, Schloss Mittersill files.

[26]Ibid.

[27]Ibid.

[28]Stacey Woods, "Growing in God-James 4:4-12," sermon no. 10035 (4 January 1981). Tape in possession of Yvonne Woods and used by kind permission.

[29]"1968 IFES Executive Committee Minutes," p. 15. Wheaton College Special Collections, SC49.II.A1.

[30]"1969 IFES Executive Committee Minutes," p. 17. Wheaton College Special Collections, SC49.II.A1.

[31]"1971 Retiring Executive Committee Minutes," p. 11. Wheaton College Special Collections, SC49.II.A1.

[32]"Report of the General Secretary," appendix to "Eight General Committee Minutes," p. 1. Wheaton College Special Collections, SC49.II.A1.

[33]D. M. Lloyd-Jones, *What Is an Evangelical?* (Edinburgh: Banner of Truth Press, 1992), p. 18.

[34]"1972 IFES Executive Committee Minutes," p. 20. Wheaton College Special Collections, SC49.II.A1.

[35]Stacey Woods, letter to supporters of IFES, December 1972. Letter in my possession. Anecdote contributed by Ms. Pippert, 11 November 2006.

[36]Ibid.

Chapter 18: Retirement Rites

[1]Stacey Woods, letter to "IFES Friends," December 1972. Letter in my possession.

[2]Eva McCarthy, untitled pamphlet in possession of the archives of Tyndale University College, Toronto, p. 3.

[3]Interview with Bruce Kaye, Sydney, 17 March 2006.

[4]David Bentley-Taylor, *Adventures of a Christian Envoy* (Harrow: IFES, 1992), p. II.

[5]Stacey Woods, letter to Keith Hunt, 9 April 1975, Schloss Mittersill files.

[6]John Bolten Jr., "Schloss Mittersill and the IFES," 1966, Schloss Mittersill files.

[7]James Nyquist to Stacey Woods, 22 August 1974, InterVarsity Press files, Westmont, Illinois.

[8]Melvin Friesen, letter to Keith Hunt, 22 October 1974, Schloss Mittersill files.

[9]Chua Wee Hian, letter to Stacey Woods, 17 September 1976, Schloss Mittersill files.

[10]Stacey Woods, letter to Chua Wee Hian, 7 September 1976, Schloss Mittersill files.

[11]Stacey Woods, letter to Chua Wee Hian, 5 February 1976, Schloss Mittersill files.

[12]"1972 IFES Executive Committee Minutes," Item XII ©, p. 18. Wheaton College Special Collections, SC49.II.A1.

[13]Stacey Woods, letter to Chua Wee Hian, 5 February 1976, Schloss Mittersill files.

[14]Chua Wee Hian, letter to Stacey Woods, 11 March 1976, Wheaton College Special Collections, SC49.III.B:4.1.

[15]Stacey Woods, letter to Samuel Escobar, 29 March 1969, courtesy of Samuel Escobar.

[16]Stacey Woods, letter to Brede Kristensen, 22 June 1976, Billy Graham Center archives, 30, IIIB 2:4, 4.

[17]When Hans Bürki arrived in Canada in April 1975, the IVCF interim general director Samuel Escobar was completing his three-year term. Bürki met with forty IVCF staff workers from east and west Canada. He returned the next summer to speak for three weeks at a summer school of biblical studies in Lindsay, Ontario, sponsored by Wilber's friends. I (and others) had already taken issue with Bürki before the general committee at Mittersill in 1975, citing what I regarded as Bürki's lack of solid biblical exegesis. Wee Hian, as the one to whom he reported, was asked to intervene about Bürki's appointment to Waymeet but the IFES executive committee declined to take responsibility, referring the matter back to IVCF Canada, which put the general director in an unenviable position.

[18]Stacey Woods, letter to me, 14 May 1980, in my possession.

[19]Stacey Woods, letter to Chua Wee Hian, 22 January 1976, Billy Graham Center archives, 30, IIIB 2:4, 4.

[20]Stacey Woods, letter to René Padilla, 19 February 1976, Billy Graham Center archives, 30, IIIB 2:4, 4.

[21]Chua Wee Hian, letter to Stacey Woods, 11 February 1976, Wheaton College Special Collections, SC49.III.B.2:4, 4.

[22]John Alexander, preface to Stacey Woods, *Some Ways of God* (Downers Grove, Ill.: InterVarsity Press, 1975), pp. 8-9.

[23]Stacey Woods, letter to Jim Nyquist, 15 August 1975, InterVarsity Press files, Westmont, Ill.

[24]Jim Nyquist, letter to Stacey Woods, 3 April 1978, InterVarsity Press files, Westmont, Ill.

[25]Jim Nyquist, introduction to Stacey Woods, *The Growth of a Work of God* (Downers Grove, Ill.: Inter-Varsity Press, 1978), p. 10.

[26]Stacey Woods, letter to Samuel Escobar, 18 June 1973, courtesy of Samuel Escobar.

[27]Biblical Theological Institute is now known as the Evangelical Theological Faculty, Osijek, Croatia.

[28]Yvonne Woods, letter to me, 24 November 1977, in my possession.

[29]Alex Williams, *Holy Spy* (Fearn and Budapest: Christian Focus & Harmat, 2003), pp. 176, 179.

[30]Yvonne and Stacey Woods, general letter, November 1981, in my possession.

[31]Stacey Woods, letter to me, 1 December 1979, in my possession.

[32]"Man Alive . . . A Preview of the 1979-80 Season," Canadian Broadcasting Corporation, summer 1980.

[33]Wilber Sutherland, letter to me, 2 October 1979, in my possession.

[34]Yvonne and Stacey Woods, general letter, November 1978, in my possession.

[35]Stacey Woods, letter to me, 9 June 1978, in my possession.

[36]Yvonne Woods, general letter, April 1983, in my possession.

[37]Stacey Woods, "The Christian's Hope B," cassette recording, sermon 10049, October 1981.

[38]Stacey Woods, "The Christian's Hope A," Sermon 10049, October 1981, cassette recording in possession of Yvonne Woods and used by kind permission.

Epilogue

[1]David Adeney, July 1983, statement at the IFES general committee meeting.

[2]Wilber Sutherland to *Imago* friends, 1 June 1983, courtesy of David Stewart, Ottawa.

[3]Ibid.

[4]Stacey Woods, letter to Maurice Murphy, 2 February 1955, Billy Graham Center archives, 300.11.13.

[5]Stacey Woods, letter to Wilber Sutherland, 2 November 1956, IVCF Canada archives.

[6]Samuel Escobar, *La chispa y la llama* (Buenos Aires: Ed. Certeza, 1978), pp. 57-58. Translation courtesy of Samuel Escobar.

[7]Keith Hunt and Gladys Hunt, *For Christ and the University* (Downers Grove, Ill.: InterVarsity Press, 1991), p. 158.

[8]Stacey Woods, letter to Charles Troutman, 31 January, 1964, Billy Graham Center archives, 111.6.26.

[9]Stacey Woods, letter to Mel Donald, 27 August 1942, IVCF Canada archives.

[10]Hunt and Hunt, *For Christ and the University*, p. 202.

[11]Yvonne Woods, e-mail to me, 9 September 2006.

[12]Telephone interview with Rebecca Manley Pippert, 23 October 2006.

[13]Stacey Woods, taped sermon, Colossians 1:21-3, 1 November 1981, in possession of Yvonne Woods.

Bibliography

Alloway, Norma. *Join Us For Coffee*. Toronto: Windward Press, 1978.

Arjunan. *"You Really Loved Us . . .": India's Memorial to Norton and Eloise Sterrett*. Chennai: UESI Publication Trust, 1999.

Armitage, Carolyn. *Reaching for the Goal: The Life Story of David Adeney*. Wheaton, Ill.: OMF/ Harold Shaw, 1993.

The Australian Dictionary of Evangelical Biography. Edited by Brian Dickey. Sydney: Evangelical History Association, 1994.

Australian Missionary Tidings. 1 February 1913; 1 October 1929; 1 June 1939.

Believer's Magazine. November 1921; February 1924; January 1926; May 1929.

Bentley-Taylor, David. *Adventures of a Christian Envoy*. Harrow: IFES, 1992.

Braga, Stuart. *A Century Preaching Christ: Katoomba Christian Convention 1903-2003*. Sydney: Katoomba Convention, 1903.

Carpenter, Joel. *Revive Us Again*. New York: Oxford University Press, 1997.

Cole, Keith. *A History of St Paul's Cathedral Church, Bendigo, 1868-1993*. Bendigo, Australia: Anglican Diocesan Historical Society, 1993.

Cusack, Frank. *Bendigo: A History*. Rev. ed. Bendigo: Lerk and McClure, 2002.

Davis, Audrey. *Dr. Kelly of Hopkins: Surgeon, Scientist, Christian*. Baltimore: Johns Hopkins Press, 1959.

Donald, Melvin V. *A Spreading Tree: A History of Inter-Varsity Christian Fellowship of Canada, 1928-1989*. Toronto: n.p., 1991.

Escobar, Samuel. *La chispa y la llama*. Buenos Aires: Certeza, 1978.

Guest, William, and Skip Gillham. *On the Shores: A History of Ontario Pioneer Camps*. Vineland, Ont.: Glenaden Press, 2002.

Guinness, Howard. *Journey Among Students*. Sydney: Anglican Information Office, n.d..

Hannah, John. "The Early Years of Lewis Sperry Chafer." *Bibliotheca Sacra* 144, no. 573 (1987).

Heidebrecht, Paul H. *God's Man in the Marketplace: The Story of Herbert J Taylor.* Downers Grove, Ill.: InterVarsity Press, 1990.

Hunt, Gladys. *A Place to Meet God, The History of Cedar Campus, 1954-2004.* Cedarville, Mich.: Cedar Campus, 2004.

Hunt, Keith, and Gladys Hunt. *For Christ and the University: The Story of InterVarsity Christian Fellowship, 1940-1990.* Downers Grove, Ill.: InterVarsity Press, 1991.

Johnson, Douglas, ed. *A Brief History of the International Fellowship of Evangelical Students.* Lausanne: IFES, 1964.

Lloyd-Jones, David Martyn. *Authority.* London: Inter-Varsity Press, 1957.

———. *What Is an Evangelical?* Edinburgh: Banner of Truth Trust, 1991.

McIntire, Carl. "His," and "Ferenc Kiss." *Christian Beacon,* 5 December 1957.

———. "Communist Line." *Christian Beacon,* 9 December 1957.

———. "IVCF." *Christian Beacon,* 16 January 1958.

Martin, William. *A Prophet with Honor.* New York: William Morrow, 1991.

McGrath, Alister. *J. I. Packer: A Biography.* Grand Rapids: Baker, 1997.

MacLeod, A. Donald. "Harold John Ockenga." In *Biographical Dictionary of Evangelicals,* edited by Timothy Larsen. Downers Grove, Ill.: InterVarsity Press, 2002

———. *W. Stanford Reid.* Montreal: McGill-Queens University Press, 2004.

Murray, Iain. *David Martyn Lloyd-Jones,* vol. 2. Edinburgh: Banner of Truth Trust, 1990.

Newton, Kenneth John. *A History of the Brethren in Australia: With Particular Reference to the Open Brethren.* Ph.D. diss., Fuller Theological Seminary, 1990.

Nichols, Alan. *David Penman.* Sutherland, NWS: Albatross, 1991.

Piggin, Stuart. *Evangelical Christianity in Australia.* Melbourne: Oxford University Press, 1997.

Pollock, J. C. *The Good Seed.* London: Hodder & Stoughton, 1959.

Prince, John, and Moyra Prince. *Tuned in to Change.* Sydney: Scripture Union, 1979.

Samuel, Leith. *A Man Under Authority—Leith Samuel: The Autobiography.* Fearn: Christian Focus Press, 1993.

Stackhouse, John. *Canadian Evangelicalism in the Twentieth Century.* Toronto: University of Toronto Press, 1993.

Sutherland, H. Wilber. "The Character and Philosophy of an Evangelical Student Movement," and "Summary of What Followed." Unpublished paper: Yale University, 1958.

Taylor, Herbert. *The Herbert J. Taylor Story.* Downers Grove, Ill.: InterVarsity Press, 1968.

Williams, Alex. *Holy Spy: Student Ministry in Eastern Europe.* Tain, Scotland: Christian Focus, 2003.

Witmer, John A. "Fifty Years of Dallas Theological Seminary, Part I, God's Man and His Dream." *Bibliotheca Sacra* 130, no. 520 (1973).

ARTICLES AND BOOKS BY C. STACEY WOODS

"A Sense of Direction." *HIS* 12, no. 2 (1951).

"Add to Your Faith Moral Character." *HIS* 13, no. 5 (1953).

"Affluence and a Christian Life-Style." *HIS* 31, no. 8 (1971).

"After Graduation." *HIS* 9, no. 6 (1948).

"Are Bible Schools and Seminaries Doing the Job?" *Eternity* 7, no. 7 (1956).

"Are You A Practicing Heretic?" *HIS* 31 No. 3 (1970).

"As Now So Then." *HIS* 10, no. 2 (1949).

"Ave Atque Vale." *HIS* 7, no. 2 (1944).

"The Christian Attitude toward Science." *HIS* 17, no. 3 (1956).

"Christian Frats?" *HIS* 5, no. 11 (1945).

"Christian Principle or Personality?" *HIS* 12, no. 6 (1952).

"Christmas." *HIS* 12, no.3 (1951).

"Christian Youth, 1952, Victorious or Defeated?" *HIS* 12, no. 4 (1952).

"Discipline For Spiritual Growth." *HIS* 18, no. 1 (1957).

"Do Ye Spend . . . For That Which Is Not Bread?" *HIS* 12, no. 9 (1952).

"Faith—In the Bible or Christ." *HIS* 1, no. 1 (1941).

"Faithful Men . . . Competent to Teach Others." *HIS* 10, no. 5 (1950).

The Growth of a Work of God: The Story of the Early Days of Inter-Varsity Christian Fellowship. Downers Grove, Ill.: InterVarsity Press, 1978.

"Him There." *HIS* 10, no. 7 (1950).

"HIS, 1948." *HIS* 8, no. 1 (1948).

"How to Launch a Campus Witness." *HIS* 2, no. 2 (1942).

"How to Live with the Holy Spirit." *HIS* 20 no. 7 (1960).

"I Saw Europe." *HIS* 9, no. 2 (1948).

"I Was a Stranger." *HIS* 9, no. 5 (1948).

"Inter-Varsity Overseas Advance." *HIS* 12, no. 8 (1952).

"John Owen: *The Glory of Christ.*" *HIS* 10, no. 5 (1950).

"Latin American Campuses." *HIS* 3, no. 12 (1944).

"The Living Christ." *HIS* 12, no. 7 (1952).

"Mid-century Summer." *HIS* 10, no. 9 (1950).

"My Beloved Son . . . Hear Him" *HIS* 12, no. 8 (1952).

"News of World Campuses." *HIS* 9, no. 6 (1948).

"Nobody Cares . . ." *HIS* 9, no. 5 (1949).

"Pie in the Sky." *HIS* 10, no. 6 (1950).

"Proud Thanksgiving." *HIS* 15, no. 2 (1954).

"Purpose." *HIS* 12, no. 1 (1951).

"Religious Liberty in Latin America: A Book Review by CSW." *HIS* 5, no. 4 (1945).

"Report of the General Secretary on Europe." *HIS* 10, no. 3 (1949).

"Reprobate Silver." *HIS* 9, no. 4 (1948).

"Sin—Confession and Restitution." *HIS* 10, no. 8 (1950).

Some Ways of God. Downers Grove, Ill.: InterVarsity Press, 1974.

"Taboo?" *HIS* 5, no. 7 (1945). Reprinted as an IVP booklet.

"This Business of Being Converted." *HIS* 6, no. 2 (1946).

"Throw a Party—Win Your Friends to Christ." *HIS* 2, no. 3 (1942).

"The Ten Commandments and the Campus." *HIS* 9, no. 4 (1949).

"This I Believe." *HIS* 5, no. 12 (1945).

"To Be One of God's Closest Friends." *HIS* 11, no. 5 (1951).

"A Total Christian Ministry in Our Universities." *HIS* 15, no.1 (1954). (Previously published April 1954 in *Our Hope*)

"Warning: Your Thought Life Is Dangerous." *HIS* 4, no. 2 (1944).

"What Does God Want from You?" *HIS* 31, no. 7 (1971).

"What Is Biblical Christianity?" *HIS* 9, no. 4 (1949).

"What's in a Name?" *HIS* 9, no. 1 (1947).

"What in the World Is God Doing?" *Urbana 64: Change Witness Triumph.* Downers Grove, Ill.: InterVarsity Press, 1965.

"What's Wrong with Self-Sufficiency?" *HIS* 37, no. 4 (1977).

"When It Comes to Indifference to Foreign Missions Disobedience Is Sin." *HIS* 17, no. 6 (1957).

"You May Enter Boldly." *HIS* 5, no. 1 (1945).

Youth Columns, *United Evangelical Action* 15 August 1943—September 1944.

Under the Pseudonym Charles Stilwell

"Don't Try to Get Married." *HIS* 3, no. 8 (1943).

"The Problem of Necking." *HIS* 5, no. 9 (1945).

"Should I Go to a Christian College This Fall?" 3, no. 10 (1944).

With John Bolten Sr.

"The Importance of the Communion Service." 6, no. 5 (1946).

Woods, Fred W. "A Passion For Souls." *Australian Missionary Tidings* (1 February 1913).

Woods, Fred W. *"Ye Are Brethren."* Melbourne: Jenkin Buxton, n.d (1920?).

Index

Biographical entries in the notes are in boldface.